・なぜ大切なのか
を英語でせつめい
する。

Political
Ideologies

A Comparative
Approach

Political Ideologies

A Comparative Approach

Nationalism

Fascism and Nazism

Marxism

Leninism

Guerrilla Communism

Democracy

Feminism

Environmentalism

Second Edition

Mostafa Rejai

M.E. Sharpe
Armonk, New York
London, England

Library of Congress Cataloging-in-Publication Data

Rejai, M. (Mostafa)
Political ideologies : a comparative approach / by Mostafa Rejai. —
2nd ed.

p. cm.
Includes bibliographical references and index.
ISBN 1-56324-142-0 (pbk.)
1. Political science—History. 2. Ideology—History. I. Title.
JA83.R466 1994
320.5'09—dc20
94-29696
CIP

Printed in the United States of America

The paper used in this publication meets the minimum
requirements of American National Standard for
Information Sciences—Permanence of Paper for
Printed Library Materials, ANSI Z 39.48-1984.

MV(p)   10   9   8   7   6   5

To the Memory of

THOMAS P. JENKIN

Master Teacher and Consummate Scholar

Contents

Part III. Recapitulation

Appendixes

Preface to the Second Edition

This book has three interrelated objectives. First, it sets out to develop a framework for the comparative analysis of political ideologics. Second, it examines some of the most prominent political ideologies of our time. Finally, it applies the framework to the ideologies discussed.

The first task is undertaken in Part I (chapter 1), wherein five interrelated dimensions, or components, of ideologies are identified and elaborated. These are the cognitive, the affective, the evaluative, the programmatic, and the social-base dimensions. Chapter 1 also briefly discusses Marx's influential conception of ideology, the rise of ideologies, and the functions they perform.

The second task is the subject of Part II (chapters 2 through 9). There, I present and discuss the eight most enduring political ideologies of the nineteenth, twentieth, and (most likely) twenty-first centuries: nationalism, fascism/nazism, Marxism, Leninism, guerrilla communism (in China, Vietnam, and Cuba), democracy, feminism, and environmentalism. The latter two chapters are new to this edition. (The ideologies of democratic socialism, democratic capitalism, liberalism, and conservatism are briefly discussed in the chapters on Marxism and democracy.) In all instances, I should make explicit, I am interested in analyzing and understanding political ideologies *as ideologies* and not in the politics or governments of the countries in which these political doctrines may be found. Each of the ideology chapters closes with an analysis of the particular ideology in terms of the analytical framework presented in chapter 1.

I return to this matter, the third objective, in Part III (chapter 10), where the entire discussion is recapitulated through a comparison of the eight ideologies in the light of the analytical framework. The central objective is to sharpen our focus and improve our understanding of political ideologies in general. The reader may wish to apply the framework to other ideologies as well; I have found the effort quite feasible and fruitful.

An analytical framework has no intrinsic value. It is valuable only to the extent to which it provides a useful tool for the analysis of a particular phenomenon and, in so doing, helps sharpen our understanding of that phenomenon. It is in this light that the reader should judge the framework proposed in chapter 1 and carried through the balance of the book. I return to this topic in the concluding chapter.

No chapter, I should stress, claims to be definitive or comprehensive. Rather, each chapter represents *my* particular approach to or treatment of the subject matter. The reader may find alternative approaches and orientations among the listings in the selected bibliography included at the end of each chapter.

The book concludes with two appendixes. Appendix A deals with some important distinctions between political ideology and its two brethren, political theory and political philosophy. Appendix B presents a brief discussion of the topic of "decline (or end) of ideology." These appendix topics are important in their own right and provide materials for further study and class discussion. But since they are somewhat technical and abstract, I have placed them at the end of the book so as not to risk discouraging the uninitiated reader.

This book assumes no prior knowledge of ideologies and should be readily accessible to all undergraduate students. The treatment is straightforward and relatively brief, covering the most essential points and excluding much detail. Consequently, instructors will have room to draw on their expertise to augment the ideologies discussed, as well as to introduce others, while students will be able to explore the topics further on their own. I have deliberately avoided formal footnotes throughout in the hope of improving the text's flow and readability.

Political Ideologies: A Comparative Approach may be used in a variety of courses. It can serve as a primary text in political ideologies, political thought, and political theory, and as a supplementary text in American politics and comparative politics.

A word of clarification may be in order concerning the eight ideologies selected for consideration in this book. Nationalism hardly needs justification: it has been the single most explosive ideology of the nineteenth and twentieth centuries, and it promises to remain so in the twenty-first century. Everywhere around the globe people are struggling on behalf of their identity, their ethnicity, their race, their tribe, their nationality. Close at home in the United States, African Americans, Hispanic Americans, Mexican Americans, and Asian Americans are struggling for recognition and identity; Native Americans are demanding homelands of their own; and Native Hawaiians are openly seeking independence.

A similar situation surrounds fascism/nazism. Throughout Western Europe and North America, Neo-Nazis, Skinheads, and Ku Klux Klan members are asserting a new militancy in their opposition to minority and immigrant groups. This condition is particularly grave in Britain, France, Germany, Italy, and the United States. Also ominous are expressions of racism and expansionism emanating from Russia with disconcerting regularity.

Marxism, Leninism, and guerrilla communism raise more serious issues. In particular, the reader may ask, why study these political ideologies in the face of the collapse of communism in Eastern Europe and the former Soviet Union? Let me say a few words about the relevance of each of the three chapters concerned.

To begin with, the section on the significance of Marx in chapter 4 speaks for itself, and it remains entirely unchanged from earlier versions of this book. But the reader may still insist, why study Marx? For the same reason, I respond, that one studies Plato, Aristotle, Machiavelli, Hobbes, Locke, Rousseau, Hegel, and other major figures in the history of political thought. Each philosopher has a significant sociopolitical vision to convey, even though that vision may be flawed. In other words, one acquires certain ideas from each philosopher, not a total, ideal answer.

More particularly, by no means can one argue that Marx has been a failure as a philosopher, for no society along Marx's vision has ever been established. Marx says very little about the ideal future society because, consistent with Marxist epistemology (stressing the unity of knowing and doing), he has no experience of such a society. So, in all of his writings (some fifty volumes by the latest count), only in a few places and only in very general terms does he speak of the ideal society in terms of the end of private property, the end of exploitation and alienation, the emergence of producers' and consumers' cooperatives, and the like.

In other words, the Communist societies established in the former Soviet Union, Eastern Europe, and elsewhere were created only *in the name of Marx*; and most were the products of the demented, pathological personality of a single individual: Joseph Stalin. We know little of the Leninist vision of a Communist society, for he died in 1924, shortly after the Russian Revolution and the ensuing civil war. It was Stalin who dominated and dictated the Communist movement for three decades (1924–1953), after whom things gradually began to unravel, culminating in the collapse of communism in the late 1980s and the early 1990s.

Finally, as far as Marx is concerned, a recent study of sixty-one developed, semideveloped, and undeveloped countries finds empirical evidence concerning the validity of the general thrust of Marxist propositions relating to capitalist development, economic exploitation, and violent revolts. (See Terry Boswell and William J. Dixon, "Marx's Theory of Rebellion: A Cross-National Analysis of Class Exploitation, Economic Development, and Violent Revolt," *American Sociological Review* 58, October 1993, pp. 681–702.) In a few words, it is no exaggeration to say that without Marx the contemporary world would be incomprehensible.

What about Lenin and Leninism? The section on the significance of Lenin in chapter 5 remains entirely valid and entirely unchanged. Nothing about the collapse of communism in Eastern Europe and the former Soviet Union diminishes the genius of Lenin and his unique ideology and strategy that culminated in the overthrow of the 303-year-old rule of the Romanovs in 1917. Moreover, one should recall that while communism has collapsed in some countries, it is not altogether dead. One need only think of China, Vietnam, North Korea, Cuba, Mongolia, Tibet, among others. Finally, even in Eastern Europe and the former Soviet Union, communism continues to be a force to reckon with, as the noncommunist leaders' daily trials and tribulations well document. Indeed, running as the Socialist party, "recycled Communists" captured a majority in the Hungarian parliament in May 1994, though they disclaimed any intention to reinstate the old Communist system (see *New York Times,* June 5 and June 26, 1994).

Similar observations may be made about guerrilla communism. Guerrilla, partisan, insurgency, ethnic, national, racial, and tribal warfare continue to dominate much of the contemporary world, including *Western Europe and North America* (Canada/Quebec, Mexico, Northern Ireland, Spain); *the former Soviet republics* (particularly Russia, Ukraine, Georgia, Tajikistan, Armenia, Azerbaijan); *the former Yugoslavia* (especially the Croats, the Muslims, and the Serbs in Bosnia-Herzegovina); *the Middle East* (the Arab factions, the Israeli factions, the Palestinian factions); *Asia* (Afghanistan, Cambodia, East Timor, India, Laos, Myanmar, Philippines, Sri Lanka, Thailand); *Africa* (Algeria, Angola, Burundi, Egypt, Ethiopia, Liberia, Mozambique, Nigeria Rwanda, Somalia, South Africa, Sudan, Western Sahara, Zaire, Zimbabwe); and *Latin America* (Argentina, Brazil, Colombia, El Salvador, Guatemala, Haiti, Nicaragua, Peru). Although they all have historical and indigenous roots, most of these conflicts are impacted by the legacies of Karl Marx, Vladimir Lenin, Mao Tse-tung, Ho Chi Minh, and Fidel Castro.

On the other hand, the democratic ideology will continue to remain the happy privilege of relatively few countries. Although in recent times much has been made of a new wave of democracy around the globe, culminating in the "end of history," in the 1980s genuine democratic government bore fruit in only three Western European countries: Greece, Spain, and Portugal. As the evening news routinely and persistently reminds us, the mere existence of an "elected" president or the mere establishment of an "elected" parliament does not mean democratic government as practiced in Western Europe and North America. One need only think of the pretenses of "democracy" in communist and formerly communist countries and in various parts of Africa, Asia, and Latin America. Accordingly, my conclusions concerning the future of democracy continue to remain guarded. (For a comparable position, see Seymour Martin Lipset, "The Social Requisites of Democracy Revisited," *American Sociological Review* 59, February 1994, pp. 1–22.)

Feminism and environmentalism are new to this volume. Although each has a lengthy history, as we shall see, in their present forms both ideologies are the children of the social and political upheavals of the 1960s; they have significantly gained momentum in the last three decades; and they will continue to do so in the foreseeable future.

In short, while fascism, nazism, Marxism, Leninism, guerrilla communism, and democracy will continue to hold their own, nationalism will remain the most significant political ideology of the twenty-first century, followed closely by feminism and environmentalism.

My deep gratitude goes to a generation of Miami students for continuing intellectual nourishment and stimulation. My Miami colleagues have provided a variety of comments and criticisms on this book. In particular, Sheila L. Croucher of the Department of Political Science and Vincent C. Hand of the Institute of Environmental Sciences read the chapters on feminism and environmentalism, respectively, and offered perceptive and constructive critiques. Michael Weber of M. E. Sharpe continues to be a source of inspiration and sound counsel. Betty Marak "processed" the manuscript with exemplary expertise and good humor. Susanna Sharpe did a most sensitive job of copyediting. Eileen M. Gaffney and Aud Thiessen skillfully steered the manuscript through production.

I alone remain responsible for any errors of fact or interpretation in this book.

Mostafa Rejai
Oxford, Ohio

Part I

Comparative Framework

1

Comparative Analysis of Political Ideologies

Any effort at adequate analysis of political ideologies* is contingent upon a clear understanding of (1) what ideologies are, (2) when and how they arose historically, and (3) what functions they perform for individuals, societies, and governments. These three interrelated issues constitute the subject of this chapter. A clarification of the first issue, as we shall see, is particularly helpful for developing a framework for comparative analysis of political ideologies.

The Nature of Ideologies

Definitions of ideology are legion. Some writers emphasize the socio-logical components of ideology, others its psychological characteristics, and still others its psychocultural features. No one definition is intrinsically better than any other. The acid test is utility in scholarly discourse. The superiority of one definition over another lies in the extent to which it provides a more adequate, more searching, more powerful explanation of the phenomenon at hand.

Any adequate conception of ideology must meet certain explicit criteria. It must be neutral rather than pejorative. It must be reasonably precise without being unduly restrictive. And it must be, at least in principle, operational—that is, applicable to the "real world." Rather than merely setting down a definition of ideology, I will try to identify

---

*The terms "ideologies," "doctrines," and "belief systems" are used inter-changeably throughout this book.

and disentangle its major dimensions or components. This done, perhaps we will be in a better position to pull the loose ends together into a coherent framework for analyzing—and comparing—political ideologies.

The concept of ideology embraces five important dimensions:

1. Cognition: knowledge and belief
2. Affect: feelings and emotions
3. Valuation: norms and judgments
4. Program: plans and actions
5. Social base: supporting groups and collectivities

Three clarifications are in order before we proceed to consider each dimension in turn. First, the first three dimensions are adapted from the sociologist Talcott Parsons's conception of culture. Moreover, the five components are not mutually exclusive—that is, although analytically distinct, they overlap to some extent. Finally, all ideologies share these five components to a lesser or greater extent—that is, not all ideologies are equally strong in all dimensions.

The Cognitive Dimension

"Cognitive dimension" refers to an ideology's "world view"—its outlook on society and politics, its perception of social and political reality. An understanding of this dimension, which is the most comprehensive, will put the other four components into perspective.

The world view of an ideology contains certain elements of *knowledge* and certain elements of *belief*. Knowledge is subject to the rules of logic; it is internally consistent, for example. And knowledge is subject to the tests of science—replicability and verifiability, for instance. By contrast, beliefs are not necessarily either logically coherent or scientifically established. Beliefs are accepted or adhered to on the basis of socialization, or habit, or repetition. In other words, there is no necessary consistency between beliefs and reality.

Taking this argument one step further, we can see that all ideologies have certain elements of distortion, illusion, or myth. An ideology may have a big myth or a small myth, but a myth nonetheless there shall be. So that the communists, for example, have the myths of a classless society and of the unity of the working class. The Nazis had the myths of the super race and of the superhuman leader. And in American society in the last three decades, we have had President Kennedy's "New Frontier," President Johnson's "Great Society," President Nixon's "Generation of Peace," President Carter's "Human Rights," President Reagan's "Counterterrorism," President Bush's "Thousand Points of Light," and President Clinton's "New Covenant."

The idea is not to cast a negative light on myth or to be pejorative about it. The reality, if I may put it this way, is that every society is founded upon myth and is saturated in myth. We all need myth and we cannot function without myth. We cannot deal exclusively with reality on a day-to-day or week-to-week basis. Myth cushions reality for us and makes us feel good about ourselves and our society.

Consider some examples from classical mythology. Consider the myth of Oedipus or the myth of Sisyphus. The idea of myth does not say that a story is true or that it is false—only that it is accepted. And the reason it is accepted is that it teaches us a moral lesson and helps guide our thoughts and actions. Therein lies the importance of myth.

Myth also simplifies. Any system of thought depends on simplification and interpretation of reality. Any exercise in communication is also an exercise in simplification. We do not internalize—or express—reality wholesale; we do so only in partial or segmental fashion. To use an ancient illustration from Plato, when we look upon the natural landscape, we see trees—many different kinds of trees—but we do not see all the trees, nor do we see the essence of tree or "treeness." Similarly, we may have seen many horses in our lives, but not all horses and not "horseness." Our perception of trees or of horses is a partial and simplified one; so is our communication of what we have perceived. In short, reality is far more complex than thinking about reality or communicating the results to others. Another function of myth is to simplify reality for us and to communicate it in an instantaneous fashion.

Simplification takes place, to a large extent, through the use of symbols. All political ideologies—all systems of thought—engage in symbolic perception and symbolic communication.

Symbols take two forms, linguistic and nonlinguistic. By linguistic symbols I mean that we frequently rely on words and speech in order to convey a message in a quick and efficient manner. When we appeal to "law and order," for example, this may well be a shorthand for saying that we do not tolerate any challenge to the status quo, or to our convenience, security, and possessions. As another illustration, consider the national organization whose acronym is FLAG. "F" stands for family; "L," for life; "A," for America; "G," for God. FLAG: Family, Life, America, God. So what we have here is a double symbol: each letter stands for an idea or a symbol; the acronym in entirety stands for a symbol.

Now, to appreciate the full burden of this symbol, one should know that FLAG is a "pro-life," or anti-abortion, organization. So, FLAG issues an emotional appeal to family, life, America, and God as it issues an appeal to the flag. FLAG drapes itself in some of the great values of American society. At the same time, it is an attempt at preemptive symbolism: it claims total legitimacy for itself, while denying the "pro-choice" group any justifiability. Indeed, "pro-life" is itself an exercise in preemptive legitimacy in that it carries the clear implication that the opposition is, by definition, "anti-life" or "pro-death." (This illustration teaches us that we should always be very sensitive to the ways in which people use or manipulate language. Sometimes we are not mindful of how critically important language is. We hear—or use—words and expressions in such a way as to evoke certain memories or sentiments or emotions, to identify ourselves in desirable ways, and to locate the opposition in an unfavorable light.)

Among nonlinguistic symbols, we should note national monuments, national holidays, and the like. What does the Washington Monument mean? And the Statue of Liberty? And the Fourth of July? Certainly, these are profound expressions of a nation's history embodying national values and evoking intense emotions. Whether linguistic or nonlinguistic, then, symbols capture vast expanses of meaning and convey that meaning in an instantaneous way.

The Affective Dimension

The discussion of myth and symbol brings into focus the second dimension of ideology: its emotive (that is, emotion-laden) content. This component is rather self-explanatory and does not require extended elaboration.

If they are to be viable and enduring, political ideologies must appeal to people's emotions. Accordingly, all ideologies are to some extent emotive in content, approach, and function. In any ideology there are elements of emotionality alongside elements of rationality. It is the balance between the two that varies from ideology to ideology. The ideology of fascism/nazism is an intensely emotional ideology; the ideology of communism is a rational, calculated ideology; the ideology of democracy is supposedly the most rational.

But even very rational ideologies remain rational only in normal times and conditions. A national crisis may quickly set an ideology off on an emotional course. American experience with hostage taking and other acts of international terrorism (as we perceive them) amply bear this out. Recent American encounters with Iraq, Iran, and Libya have been particularly telling in this regard.

The central issue, then, is: Under normal circumstances, how rigid—or how flexible—are we about our belief systems? How intensely do we feel? In this context, some scholars have found it useful to distinguish between open and closed belief systems. An open ideology is one that admits new evidence and information, undergoing modification and change in the process. A closed ideology does not accommodate new evidence and information; its attitude is, to use a cliché, "My mind's made up. Don't confuse me with the facts." Regardless of the relative openness or closedness, a most distinctive feature of all ideologies is an appeal to human passion, an eliciting of emotive response.

It is important to realize that ideologies cannot force themselves upon the people—or at least that they cannot rely on coercion and force alone. To one degree or another people must voluntarily identify with an ideology and extend support for it. And one's sense of identity is enhanced if "cold, hard" reasons for identification (for instance, prospects of personal gain) are combined with emotional ones (for example, prospects of national greatness).

The Evaluative Dimension

Ideologies embody normative elements. Specifically, ideologies make value judgments in two ways: negatively, by denouncing an existing system of social and political relationships; positively, by putting forth a set of norms according to which social and political reconstruction is to take place.

At least in the beginning, as they start to emerge, ideologies denounce the existing society as corrupt, immoral, and beyond reform— and they do so by appealing to high-sounding moral principles. Moral outrage and indignation are indispensable to any ideology. The attack against existing society is presented, rationalized, justified, and dignified in the light of an appeal to "higher" principles.

For illustration, consider the Declaration of Independence. Jefferson opens the Declaration by announcing the necessity to sever long-established ties with Britain, proceeds to a lengthy catalog of all the evil things the British have done in the thirteen colonies, and defends the need for independence by appealing to "the Laws of Nature and of Nature's God." The bulk of the Declaration is a negative statement of the practices and institutions of the colonial society we reject. The British, says Jefferson, have subverted our legislative and judicial systems; they have kept standing armies in times of peace; they have quartered troops among us, etc. This is what I mean by the negative value judgment of ideologies.

The positive values of an ideology revolve around such central norms as liberty, equality, fraternity, humanity, and the like. The normative propositions are characteristically presented as factual statements.

To return to the example of the Declaration of Independence, Jefferson specifies some of the positive goals we seek in the following manner:

> We hold these truths to be self-evident, that all men are created equal, that they are endowed by their Creator with certain unalienable rights, that among these are Life, Liberty, and the pursuit of Happiness. That to secure these rights, Governments are instituted among Men, deriving their just powers from the consent of the governed. That whenever any Form of Government becomes destructive of these ends, it is the Right of the People to alter or to abolish it, and to institute new Government, laying its foundation on such principles and organizing its powers in such form, as to them shall seem most likely to effect their Safety and Happiness.

All ideologies propose to move toward a "good society," however defined. Some ideologies posit an ultimate value, a final good, autopia. Marx's idea of a classless society is an apt illustration.

Ideologies, as we can see, contain statements concerning the allocation of scarce societal resources (for example, power and wealth). Such allocation naturally involves adjustments and compromises among conflicting interests and demands. It also entails questions of rulership, authority, and legitimacy.

In this context, political ideologies are systems of beliefs and values focused primarily on such questions as: By what criteria are conflicting values and interests to be adjusted? Who (what person, group, or institution) has the authority to play a role in such adjustments, and under what conditions? Under what circumstances is the legitimacy, or popular acceptability, of a regime called into question? Under what conditions should one regime be replaced by another?

The Programmatic Dimension

The values, goals, and objectives of an ideology are embodied in a more or less comprehensive program of activities. Ideologies, as many have pointed out, are action-related systems of beliefs, norms, and ideas. Not only do they posit a set of values, they also seek to relate specific patterns of action to the realization of those values. This demand for consistency between principle and behavior also serves as the basis for the imposition of ideological discipline and control.

The action or program of an ideology may be directed toward the maintenance and perpetuation of the status quo or, more characteristically, toward changing the existing social order. The needed change, in turn, may be either reformist or radical in nature. Reformist, peaceful, or gradual change is the way of democratic ideologies: we must persuade and educate the people to help us reach our limited objectives.

Radical, violent, and rapid change is the way of totalitarian ideologies—of nazism and communism, for example. Stressing national greatness, racial supremacy, and the infallible leader, the Nazis abrogated the Treaty of Versailles and launched a policy of conquest across Europe. Promising "land, peace, and bread," the communists set out, quite consciously, to put an absolute end to three centuries of Romanov rule in Russia. The communist ideology, in fact, included a statement of priorities specifying immediate, intermediate, and ultimate goals. The immediate goal was the overthrow of the bourgeois regime; the intermediate goal, social and economic reconstruction; the ultimate goal, a classless society.

The Social-base Dimension

Ideologies are necessarily associated with social groups, classes, collectivities, or nations. Ideology, to be ideology, must have a mass base.

It must be presented to the populace in such a way as to be readily understandable and, in this understanding, to elicit a commitment to action toward the realization of goals and objectives. As many have pointed out, ideologies are mobilized belief systems. In this context, one may wish to make a distinction between personal ideology and political ideology.

Let me illustrate this distinction by drawing on two pivotal figures in Western philosophy, Plato and Marx. Imposing as it is, Plato's political philosophy remains in the private realm: it is studied by a relatively small number of philosophers and intellectuals; it has found no mass appeal; it is not the object of social movements; "Platonism" has no particular ideological connotation.

When we contrast Plato to Marx, the distinction between private ideology and political ideology becomes immediately apparent. Marxism is a philosophical system, to be sure, but it is also a potent ideology. It has helped mobilize the masses throughout the world; it has become the basis of ideological movements; and it is a mainspring of collective action.

The mobilization function of ideology is impossible without organization. Indeed, organization is the link between belief and action. But organization does not evolve spontaneously. Nor is it put together by the masses. Organization is an elite concept and an elite function.

It is necessary to draw a distinction between ideology of the elites and ideology of the masses. Briefly, the belief system of the elites will tend to be comprehensive, articulate, and coherent; that of the masses, partial, inarticulate, and incoherent. Stated differently, elites are always in a position to give a comprehensive statement of what they believe and why they believe as they do. The masses typically lack this capacity.

The elite–mass distinction gives rise to some intriguing questions. To what extent do elites use ideologies to move their peoples toward higher goals and objectives? To what extent do ideologies serve as covers for the elites' personal ambitions and motives? To what extent do elites use ideologies in order to manipulate and control the masses?

Although it is impossible to attempt blanket, categorical answers to these and related questions, the possibilities of manipulation and control are, of course, quite real and frequently present in all ideologies. The form and degree of manipulation, needless to say, will vary from ideology to ideology. Both would be more intense in extremist ideologies and less intense in moderate ones.

Summary

I have identified five principal dimensions of ideological belief systems and have discussed each in some detail. In so doing, I have proposed a framework for the analysis of political ideologies, either as individual phenomena or, more importantly, in a comparative context. The framework is applied specifically at the end of each chapter as well as in the concluding one.

At this point, a summary definition of political ideology will necessarily sacrifice the intricacies of the concept, and I would prefer to avoid one. Since this is not a realistic option, however, I offer the following conception of ideology as consistent with the foregoing analysis.

Political ideology is an emotion-laden, myth-saturated, action-related system of beliefs and values about people and society, legitimacy and authority, that is acquired to a large extent as a matter of faith and habit. The myths and values of ideology are communicated through symbols in a simplified, economical, and efficient manner. Ideological beliefs are more or less coherent, more or less articulate, more or less open to new evidence and information. Ideologies have a high potential for mass mobilization, manipulation, and control; in that sense, they are mobilized belief systems.

Before turning to an analysis of some specific political ideologies, I must address three related matters: clarification of a very influential conception of ideology developed by Karl Marx, discussion of the rise of ideologies, and elaboration of the functions ideologies perform.

Marx's Conception of Ideology

A watershed in the study of the concept of ideology was reached in the work of Karl Marx. First stated in 1845–1846, in *The German Ideology*—a book coauthored with his lifelong friend and collaborator, Friedrich Engels—Marx's conception of ideology has had a profound and lasting effect on all subsequent discussion of the subject. For this reason, it deserves special attention.

To begin with, for the time being we are interested in Marx's analysis of the ideology concept, not in Marx's own ideology (Marxism is the subject of chapter 4). The analysis of ideology as a generic concept (for example, its nature and function) is an intellectual activity of a quite different order than the analysis of ideology as a body of political beliefs (for instance, nazism or Marxism). Though interrelated, these two issues are analytically quite distinct. To use an obvious illustration, in this chapter I have presented my analysis of the concept of ideology without saying anything about what my own ideology is: whether I am a Democrat or a Republican, a liberal or a conservative.

Marx agrees that ideology is an idea system, but one, he insists, that is derivative, secondary, and false. "Derivative," the reader wonders, from what? "Secondary," to what? "False," how? In order to understand Marx's meaning here, we must grasp a basic distinction that runs through all of Marx's thinking.

According to Marx, social reality has two basic dimensions: the *substructure* and the *superstructure*. The substructure consists of the material, economic foundation of society. The substructure, according to Marx, is the most important aspect of a society, and, in turn, it gives rise to superstructure. The superstructure consists of all other elements of society: art, culture, religion, social and political institutions, ideology, and the like.

Now, taking a closer look at the substructure, Marx understands the material, economic foundation of society to consist of social classes. Specifically, using the criterion of ownership, Marx identifies an owning class, which is at the same time the ruling class, and a nonowning class, which is at the same time the ruled class. The ruling class is also the oppressor and the exploiting class; the ruled class is the oppressed and the exploited class. For Marx, the paramount form of ownership is the ownership of property that is used as the arena of oppression and exploitation—the (feudal) land, the factory, and the assembly line being prime examples.

Now, with this Marxist conceptualization of substructure and superstructure, one begins to understand what Marx means by the proposition that ideology is an idea system that is derivative, secondary, and false. He does not say that ideology is unimportant. Rather, as we shall see momentarily, it is very important. What he does mean is that ideology is a reflection of a far more important reality, the economic foundation of society. The superstructure has no *independent* reality, mirroring as it does a much more elemental force.

How, then, *is* ideology (or more generally, the superstructure) important? In order to answer this question, Marx raises and answers two subsidiary questions. Question 1: Ideology by whom? Who formulates and propagates ideology? Answer: Ideology by the ruling class. Question 2: Ideology for whom? For whom is ideology intended? Answer: Ideology for the ruled class, for the masses. So, ideologies, politics—all aspects of the superstructure—are deliberate creations of myths, falsehoods, and lies by the ruling class in order to maintain and perpetuate itself, and to keep the underclass in its place.

Stated differently, ideology is a statement of class position and a justification for class rule. It is a means for manipulating the underclass and keeping it under control. Wrote Marx and Engels: "The ideas of the ruling class are in every epoch the ruling ideas: i.e., the class which is the ruling material force of society is at the same time its ruling intellectual force."

Marx attached a derogatory connotation to ideology, since he viewed all ideological thought as the dishonest use of reasoning, the conscious distortion of facts in order to justify the position of the ruling class. Ideology represents, in Engels's memorable phrase, "false consciousness."

The proposition that false consciousness may provide a basis for action suggests that ideas and ideologies enjoy a measure of autonomy, a realization that runs counter to Marx's earlier assertion about the dependence of ideas on the economic system. Engels was to explain, after Marx's death, that Marx had indeed overemphasized the economic factor, and for a good reason. He wrote:

> Marx and I are ourselves partly to blame for the fact that younger writers sometimes lay more stress on the economic side than is due it. We had to emphasize this main principle in opposition to our adversaries, who denied it, and we had not always the time, the place, or the opportunity to allow the other elements involved in the interaction to come into their own right.

However, Engels maintained, although there is no inflexible one-way relationship between idea systems and economic systems, sooner or later the two will coincide.

Such is Marx's formulation of the concept of ideology. One need not be a Marxist in order to perceive the power of this analysis and its impact on the history of modern political thought. Today, a century and a half later, every writer on ideology must come to terms with Marx's analysis: ideology as a system of falsehoods deliberately promulgated by the ruling class as a means of self-perpetuation.

The Rise of Ideologies

Ideologies as we have defined them—systems of beliefs, values, and emotions that are collectively acted upon—have existed only in the last two centuries. In fact, the French Revolution of 1789 is generally considered to have coincided with the rise of ideologies. (The coincidence of the French Revolution with nationalism is also important to the emergence of mass ideologies, a topic we will cover in the next chapter.) A host of changes, events, and developments coalesced to produce an environment highly conducive to the rise of political doctrines. This environment simply did not exist in the agrarian, absolutist, tradition-dominated context of the pre–nineteenth-century world.

To begin with, the French Revolution shattered the foundations of the old politics and introduced the age of new politics. The old politics were the politics of kings, princes, the nobility, and the clergy; the new politics are the politics of the people, the masses.

Before the French Revolution, all the major decisions were made by the king and his close personal advisers, sometimes in association with the Estates General. The Estates General consisted effectively of two orders or estates of people: high aristocracy and high clergy. The Estates General was a consultative body and a sounding board, not a representative assembly, and it met at the wishes of the monarch. It had last met in 1614.

In 1789, under pressure from revolutionary masses, the Estates General was expanded to incorporate representatives from the ordinary, middle-class commoners, called the Third Estate. Having scored this victory, the Third Estate pushed for—and accomplished—the abolition of the Estates General and its replacement with the French National Assembly, a representative body.

"Liberty, Equality, Fraternity" was not an accidental slogan of the French Revolution. The growing middle class was demanding new rights and a new identity—an experience that was repeated in other European countries as well.

The principal document of the French Revolution, the French counterpart of the Declaration of Independence, is the Declaration of the Rights of Man and Citizen (1789). This document is remarkable in many ways, some of which we shall return to in other contexts. For now, let me mention two things. First, note the insistence in the very title that from now on, human beings should be treated as "Man and

Citizen."* Up to this point, human beings have been considered as a somewhat lower order of beings, the *subjects* of the monarch. A subject has only duties, no rights; a citizen has rights as well as duties. Second, the document declares that from now on, sovereignty shall reside with the people—that is to say, the people, not the king, shall be the final source of power and authority.

A democratic revolution, indeed. The monarchy is overthrown, Louis XVI and Marie Antoinette are put to the guillotine, the aristocracy is disbanded, the church is dispossessed. All traditional institutions have been weakened; in their place people have risen to claim liberty, equality, fraternity, and citizenship. Now, what do I mean by repeated references to "popular" or "mass"? I mean, of course, the middle class. Going back to the fourteenth century, a middle class had gradually emerged as a consequence of the development of towns and cities, the rise of commerce and industry, and urbanization and industrialization. At first, the middle class wanted a larger share of the economic pie. As it attained economic security, it began a strong push for political rights as well. Hence, the English Revolution of the 1640s, the American Revolution of 1776, and the French Revolution of 1789 are regarded as the three "Great Democratic Revolutions."

As the nineteenth century progressed, the phenomenon of mass participation intensified and spread to the lower classes. Three factors played especially important parts in this process. First, the rise of trade unionism (as a concomitant of industrialization) improved the economic position of the working classes. Second, the growth of workers' (or labor) parties penetrated the parliamentary systems of European countries to incorporate political representatives from the lower classes. Third, the gradual extension of the franchise guaranteed, at least in principle, popular participation in politics in the fullest sense. In short, as the nineteenth century opened, the middle class had become involved in politics; as it drew to a close, the working class was so involved as well.

Having begun well before the nineteenth century, urbanization achieved new heights during this period. Urbanization means many

---

*Constrained by conventional usage and by stylistic convenience, but free, I hope, from sexist bias, at many points throughout this book I will allow "man" to stand for "man and woman." When Locke and Rousseau speak of the "nature of man," for example, I shall understand them to include both sexes.

things, of course. Important for our purposes is the pattern of population movement from the farms to the cities, from the hinterland to the urban centers. By concentrating populations in relatively small places, urbanization provided the mass base of ideologies and the primary ingredient of ideological movements.

When combined, the twin forces of urbanization and industrialization produced yet another significant consequence: the increasing complexity, compartmentalization, and depersonalization of human life. The ideas and ideals of community and face-to-face relationships were destroyed. In their place appeared a growing sense of human impotence, uprootedness, anonymity, and alienation. The spiritual and emotional gap thereby created called for a new source of cohesion, a new source of belonging, a new source of security, a new faith. And ideologies, of course, fulfill these fundamental human needs by making isolated men and women parts of much larger wholes.

A further series of nineteenth-century developments deserve attention: the rise of literacy, the increasing importance of education, and the emergence of great systems of public universities in Europe and North America. Now, the rise of education has many implications. For our present purposes, the point is that illiteracy is conducive to the acceptance of one's perceived lot and to political acquiescence. Once this condition of ignorance is broken, one begins to challenge one's subservient status. One's inclination is toward activism, not submission. In short, illiteracy is conducive to acquiescence; literacy, to rebellion. This is as true in Eastern countries as in Western ones. Education, it may fairly be said, has been a globally revolutionary force.

Advances in science and technology—particularly transportation and communication—should also be noted. These developments made possible the rapid dissemination of ideologies. Ideologies became mobile, as it were, crossing national and international boundaries with great ease.

One final development. To have discussed economic development, urbanization and industrialization, the rise of education, science and technology, etc., is to have discussed "modernization." A major concomitant of modernization is secularization. Indeed, beginning in the nineteenth century, religion began to lose its hold on people. In other words, secularization created another kind of emotional or spiritual void. Ideology began to fill this gap also, as it offered itself as a substitute for or an alternative to the unbeliever.

Functions of Ideologies

Ideologies perform an array of important functions, whether for individuals, groups, or governments. Some of these functions, implicit in what has been said above, will be made explicit in the interest of a well-rounded treatment.

First, any ideology provides a perspective on social and political reality and calls upon the believer to behave in a way that is consistent with that perspective. Ideologies propose to "explain" political reality to us, give meaning to the ambiguities of the world around us, and give order to our lives. They set forth standards of behavior and provide rationales for our words and deeds. If we are believers in democracy or Nazism or communism, we are expected to behave in a way that is consistent with the democratic or the Nazi or the communist doctrine.

Second, ideologies provide the individual with a sense of identity and belonging. They put the individual at one with a larger whole. Ideologies counteract our anxieties and insecurities. This function, as we have seen, is particularly important in mass, urban, industrial societies.

Third, looked at from the standpoint of the collectivity, ideologies serve to achieve social solidarity and cohesion. For one thing, they bind a group together and give it a sense of unity. For another, they rationalize and justify group goals, values, and objectives. In giving a group legitimacy and respectability, ideologies improve not only the group's self-image but its external image as well.

Fourth, ideologies engender optimism. They provide hope, promise, utopia, paradise. Such optimism, needless to say, is essential to human life and to the mass appeal of ideologies. Human beings always look forward to a better life.

Fifth, ideologies serve to support and maintain a political regime or to challenge and destroy it. In this sense, we may distinguish between ideologies of status quo and ideologies of change, although ideologies may perform both functions at the same time. So, for instance, the ideology of communism seeks to destroy the existing order and replace it with an alternative one.

The German sociologist Karl Mannheim made a distinction between ideology and utopia. Ideology, he said, is an idea system that seeks to support and justify a political regime, whereas utopia is an idea system that seeks to oppose and destroy it. I am suggesting that ideologies may perform both of these functions at the same time. Ideology, in Mannheim's terms, is both "ideology" and "utopia."

Sixth, all ideologies serve as instruments for the manipulation and control of the people. A country's leaders are always in a position to dupe the masses, particularly in the light of contemporary advances in technologies of communication. The only questions are the regularity, extent, and intensity with which popular manipulation and control are exercised.

Finally, ideologies perform—or *should* perform—a self-maintenance function. A viable ideology must keep up with changing times and conditions; it must adapt its tenets and principles to the needs and requirements of the times. Ideologies that engage in this process of continuous adaptation are likely to thrive and flourish; ideologies that do not are likely to fall on hard times.

Selected Bibliography

Adorno, T. W. et al. *The Authoritarian Personality.* New York: Harper & Bros., 1950.

Apter, David E., ed. *Ideology and Discontent.* New York: Free Press, 1964.

Aron, Raymond. *The Opium of the Intellectuals.* New York: Norton, 1962.

Bell, Daniel. *The End of Ideology.* New York: Free Press, 1960.

Burns, James. "Political Ideology." In *A Guide to the Social Sciences,* ed. by Norman MacKenzie. New York: Mentor Books, 1966.

Corbett, Patrick. *Ideologies.* New York: Harcourt, Brace & World, 1965.

Cox, Richard H., ed. *Ideology, Politics, and Political Theory.* Belmont, Calif.: Wadsworth, 1969.

Hacker, Andrew. *Political Theory: Philosophy, Ideology, Science.* New York: Macmillan, 1961.

Harris, Nigel. *Beliefs in Society: The Problem of Ideology.* London: C. A. Wats, 1968.

Jenkin, Thomas P. *The Study of Political Theory.* New York: Random House, 1955.

Lane, Robert E. *Political Ideology.* New York: Free Press, 1962.

Larrain, Jorge. *The Concept of Ideology.* Athens: University of Georgia Press, 1980.

Lichtheim, George. *The Concept of Ideology and Other Essays.* New York: Vintage Books, 1967.

Lipset, Seymour M. *Political Man: The Social Bases of Politics.* New York: Doubleday, 1960.

Loye, David. *The Leadership Passion: A Psychology of Ideology.* San Francisco: Jossey-Bass, 1977.

MacIver, Robert M. *The Web of Government.* 1947. Reprint. New York: Free Press, 1965.

Mannheim, Karl. *Ideology and Utopia*. New York: Harcourt, Brace, 1936.
Parsons, Talcott. *The Social System*. New York: Free Press, 1951.
Rejai, Mostafa, ed. *Decline of Ideology*. New York: Atherton Press, 1971.
———. "Ideology." In *Dictionary of the History of Ideas*, ed. by Philip P. Wiener. 4 vols. New York: Scribner, 1972.
Rokeach, Milton. *The Open and Closed Mind*. New York: Basic Books, 1960.
Sartori, Giovanni. "Politics, Ideology, and Belief Systems." *American Political Science Review* 63 (June 1969): 398–411.
Selinger, Martin. *Ideology and Politics*. New York: Free Press, 1976.
Shklar, Judith N. *Political Theory and Ideology*. New York: Macmillan, 1966.
Waxman, Chaim I., ed. *The End of Ideology Debate*. New York: Funk & Wagnalls, 1968.

Part II

Selected Ideologies

2

Nationalism

Nationalism is the most important ideology of the nineteenth and twentieth centuries. Nationalism can be an ideology in its own right, as we shall see in this chapter, or it can be a component of other ideologies, as we shall see in the chapters on fascism/nazism, communism, and democracy.

Our treatment of nationalism in this chapter is highly selective. It would be impossible to attempt, in a single chapter, a comprehensive analysis of a phenomenon that has affected virtually all countries over a period of some two hundred years. Instead, we will concentrate on: (1) the meaning of such key terms as "nationalism," "nation," and "state"; (2) the historical development of nationalism; (3) nineteenth-century expressions of nationalism in the West, with particular attention to France, where it all began, and the United States; (4) twentieth-century expressions of nationalism in the East, with particular reference to Africa and Asia; and (5) the resurgence of nationalism in the West in the postwar period.

In examining the foregoing topics, we shall come into contact with another set of phenomena. We shall see that nationalism is closely related to imperialism. And we shall see that imperialism, in turn, is related to aggression, conquest, and war. We shall see how nationalism, imperialism, and war are interrelated—both in theory and in practice.

The Meaning of Nationalism

Like many other subjects, there is no one, universally accepted definition of nationalism. If you consult the sources listed in the bibliography for this chapter, you will find a series of definitions that have two characteristics in common. First, they will refer to nationalism as states of mind or as collective sentiments, beliefs, and emotions— all of which are consistent with our definition of ideology in the previous chapter. Second, they will define nationalism, nation, state, and nation-state in terms of one another—which tends to confuse the reader.

Let me therefore offer a definition of nationalism that is based on the extant definitions, but one, I hope, that avoids unnecessary confusion. Nationalism refers to a feeling of membership in a nation together with collective desire and action to achieve and enhance the status, power, and well-being of that nation. Since I have defined nationalism in terms of nation, it is <u>incumbent</u> upon me to indicate what I mean by nation.

Nation comes from the Latin *natio*. In its original meaning, *natio* referred to a human group characterized by the community of birth— that is, a human group in a particular geographic area. Later on the meaning of nation was expanded to include common values, common ideals, common customs, common territory, common religion, common race, common past, common future, and the like.

Now, this is much too broad a definition of nation. There has probably never been a group of people that has possessed all of these characteristics. So I will define a nation as a group of people who feel they belong together because they share any one of these features. In other words, I have modified the traditional definition in two ways. One, I say any one element is enough. Two, I say a group of people who "feel" that they share. <u>As a matter of actual fact, a people may have nothing in common;</u> what is important is the belief that they do. That is the <u>acid test</u>, and it is consistent with the definition of ideology developed in chapter 1.

Let me illustrate. In the 1920s and the 1930s, the <u>German</u> people came to believe that they were members of a super race, the <u>Aryans</u>. This belief was totally fictitious. The Aryan people are Indo-European, existing in certain parts of Asia and the Middle East. The German people are Teutonic, not Aryan. But through a constant barrage of propaganda and emotional appeals, Adolf Hitler and his propaganda chief Joseph Paul Goebbels persuaded the German people to believe that they were Aryan (we will go into this subject later).

To recapitulate, so far I have defined nationalism in terms of na-

formative — The commitment of the people to the process of building a nation where none existed prior.

tion. I have defined nation as a group of people who feel they belong together because they have something in common. Now, let me go one step further and introduce three forms or types of nationalism.

To begin with, the nationalist sentiment or ideology may be directed toward creating a nation that does not now exist—a nonexistent nation—or toward enhancing the status and power of a nation that already does exist. Let me give an example before proceeding.

Think of America in the 1760s and the 1770s. There was no United States, but a group of thirteen colonies under the domination of Britain. It is not until the Constitution (1787) that we have a reference to "We the People of the United States. . . ."

The Founding Fathers, to state the obvious, were trying to found a nation. This process of creating a nonexistent nation differs from the process of trying to improve the power and status of a nation that already exists. In the latter case, think of Britain in the 1760s and the 1770s.

Accordingly, I shall call the process of founding a nonexistent nation *formative nationalism,* and the process of augmenting the status of an existing nation *prestige nationalism.* In the one case, we are putting together the raw materials, as it were, of a new nation; in the other, we are glorifying and aggrandizing an old nation.

Now, what if in this process of aggrandizing or glorifying one nation (a group of people who feel they belong together because they have something in common), we infringe upon the rights of another nation (another group of people who share similar feelings)? What if one nation engages in a process of conquering or annexing another nation? If that happens, we no longer have formative nationalism or prestige nationalism, we have *expansive nationalism.* And expansive nationalism is, needless to say, imperialism: one nation penetrating and dominating another nation.

Let me introduce two footnotes before proceeding. First, these three forms of nationalism (especially the second and the third) are not fixed and final: formative nationalism may become prestige nationalism; prestige nationalism may undergo an expansive stage; and then we may go back to prestige.

Let me discuss the best illustration I know: Germany before and after 1871. Before 1871, there was no Germany, only a group of principalities that felt they shared certain qualities of "Germanness." In 1871, following a successful war with France, formative nationalism

Prestige . . . and expansive — the commitment by the people of a nation to the process of enhancing the power, position, or reputation of their nation relative to others.

bore fruit and the nation of Germany was founded. From 1871 to 1914, German nationalism was in a prestige phase, as German leaders developed the economic, political, military, and diplomatic might of Germany. From 1914 to 1918, Germany was in the third stage, expansive nationalism. From 1918 to 1939, Germany was back in the prestige business: a defeated Germany had to get back on its feet, economically, politically, militarily. From 1939 to 1945, again expansive nationalism. And from 1945 until today, again prestige.

So you can see how these three forms of nationalism can fluctuate or alternate, especially forms two and three. Technically, if a country is completely wiped out, nationalism can be thrown back to phase one. But I do not know of any country that, having been annihilated, went back to formative nationalism. Palestine is the closest approximation.

For our second footnote, as you can see, nationalism is closely related to imperialism. In fact, imperialism is a form of nationalism, another variety. Imperialism, the policy of conquering and annexing other people, cannot be implemented except through conflict, aggression, and war. Nationalism and imperialism are brethren. So far, we have seen how conceptually—or in theory—this is the case. In the pages that follow we shall see how historically—or in reality—this has been the case.

Let me introduce two other, related concepts: *state* and *nation-state*. A state is an independent political entity occupying a well-defined and specific territory, with a legal system and a concentration of power to maintain internal and external security.

As you can see, nation and state are two very different things: nation is a cultural and psychological concept; state, a political and legal one. Accordingly, nation and state do not always go together: we may have nation without state, or state without nation. When the two do coincide, we shall have either a nation-state or a state-nation, depending on which came first.

Let me illustrate. For thousands of years, the "nation of Israel" consisted of a group of people who felt a sense of unity but were not territorialized in a state. The state of Israel came into being only in 1948, making Israel a classic example of a nation-state.

By contrast, consider the American situation. Each of the thirteen colonies was a state: each was a territorial entity with a recognized legal and political system. The idea of nationhood began to emerge in the mid-eighteenth century, culminating in the adopting of the Constitution in 1787, making the United States a classic example of a state-nation.

As a rule of thumb, colonial countries tend to be state-nations; noncolonial countries, nation-states. There are, of course, exceptions.

Two more footnotes will round out this introductory discussion. First, we have defined nation as a group of people who feel they belong together because they have something in common. Now, what must they have in common? How much commonality? How much homogeneity must there be?

The issue of homogeneity is particularly pressing in Eastern, colonial countries. Consider the map of Africa, for example. What do those territorial boundaries signify? Cultural identity? Tribal unity? Religious commonality? Topographical distinctiveness? No, they signify none of these. African boundaries mean only one thing: the administrative convenience of the imperialist powers in governing their colonies. To this topic we shall return shortly.

Meanwhile, what about the sense of homogeneity? How much unity do we expect in colonial nationalism? Directly put, very little. The Indian leader Nehru maintained that Indian nationalism is an "anti-feeling"—that is to say, a state of being against the British. In other words, anti-imperialism alone may serve as a unifying force. This is consistent with our definition of nation (and our discussion of ideology in chapter 1) as a group of people who *feel* they belong together because of some commonality.

The second footnote concerns the issue of size. How large does a group of people need to be before we can consider it a nation? Do we need one billion Chinese? One hundred fifty million Russians? Three million Cambodians? Three thousand people on a South Sea island? Just what?

Pressing as the issue may appear, we must leave the question open if we are to keep our definition of nation a neutral one. If we specify *any* number, say twenty million, then any time we find a group smaller than that number, we have to conclude that it is not a nation. Thus, for example, using the criterion of size, sometimes a distinction is drawn between a nation as something that is modern and advanced, and a tribe as something that is primitive and backward. Tribe, in other words, assumes a pejorative connotation. We cannot fall into this trap. We must keep our definition as neutral as possible, even at the risk of losing neatness. There is no reason that the people of Nigeria, say, are any less of a nation than the people of Russia.

There are, of course, many countries that accommodate several—or many—nationalities, such as the United States, the former Soviet Union, and the former Yugoslavia. Fine, let us call them multination-states. And let us contrast them with multistate-nations: that is, a group of people that spills over several countries rather than being territorialized in a single state. The Jewish people, the Palestinian people, and the Armenian people are good examples. (The Soviet and Yugoslav experiences suggest that in the absence of strong central authority, multination-states are unstable and prone to possible anarchy.)

Historical Development of Nationalism

Three periods in the rise of nationalism may be identified: (1) prior to 1789: the absence of nationalism; (2) 1789 to today: the rise and spread of Western nationalism; and (3) 1918 (and 1945) until today: the rise and spread of Eastern nationalism. Bearing in mind that, although at times arbitrary, dates are used as matters of convenience, let me proceed to discuss the three periods in turn.

Period 1

What do I mean by the absence of nationalism? I do not mean that love of country did not exist. I do not mean that people did not have warm feelings and sentiments toward the fatherland or the motherland. These sentiments have always existed, but they were qualitatively different before and after the French Revolution. Before the revolution, I suggest, we had patriotism; after the revolution, nationalism.*

Let me elaborate. We are all born to a culture and a tradition. We are all patriots in that we have a patrimony or legacy that we cherish and to which we are indebted. But we are not all nationalists bent upon expounding the superiority of our patrimony and exporting it to other countries. Patriotism is old; it came into being thousands of years before the French Revolution. Nationalism is new; it dates, conve-

---

*For a similar distinction between ''nation'' and ''nationalism,'' see Armstrong, *Nations before Nationalism*, listed in the bibliography for this chapter.

niently, to 1789. Nation has always existed; nationalism is a phenomenon of the last two centuries.

Let me use a couple of illustrations to drive the point home. For
thousands of years, the Chinese people have had a sense of cultural
distinctiveness. Ancient Chinese thinkers made a distinction between
the Great Han (main-stock Chinese) and all other people, whom they
called "Barbarians." The word "China" consists of two (Chinese) char-
acters that translate into the "Middle Kingdom": China as the mighty
center of the universe.

These qualities and claims notwithstanding, not until the late nineteenth century do we have the beginnings of Chinese nationalism. And
not until the twentieth century does nationalism combine with communism to become a most explosive force.

Similarly, the ancient Greeks were quite convinced of their cultural
uniqueness. They too made a distinction between the Hellenes and the
Barbarians. But not until the nineteenth century does Greek nationalism emerge.

Nationalism, in short, involves intense feelings concerning one's
distinctiveness, feelings that become the subject of mass movements,
and mass movements that set out to impose the presumed cultural
superiority of one people upon another people.

Period 2

The roots of modern nationalism go back to the middle of the eighteenth century and a movement called romanticism. Affecting art, literature, philosophy, music, and politics, romanticism was a mood or a
predisposition that defied rigid definition. It did signify a revolt against
rationalism and a corresponding emphasis on sentiment, feeling, and
imagination. The emotions of the heart, it was argued, however irrational, should be valued over and above the intellectualizations of the
head. So that whereas René Descartes had said, "I think, therefore I
am," Jean-Jacques Rousseau proclaimed, "A thinking man is a de-
praved animal."

Romanticism rejected the idea of the self-sufficiency of the individual and emphasized identification with an external whole, with something outside of oneself. Quite frequently, this outside whole took the
form of nature, as manifested in the works of such romanticists as
Wordsworth in England; Herder, Schiller, and Goethe in Germany;

and Hugo, Rousseau, and Madame de Staël in France. Frequently also, the focus of one's identification was the "folk," the cultural group, or nation. Nationalism, in other words, was a political expression of romanticism.

In many ways, the prime philosopher of nationalism was Rousseau, whose influence on the French Revolution has been universally recognized. Rousseau's ideal was the small, well-knit community in which each person willingly gave himself over, quite literally, to every other person. We must obey the community, Rousseau taught, because in obeying the community we obey ourselves. The identity and unity of our *wills* produce a "General Will" that is absolute, indivisible, infallible, and always for the common good. The individual's commitment and devotion to the community and the General Will are total. (For more on Rousseau, see the chapter on democracy.)

Following the French Revolution, as we shall see in the next section, nationalism spread across the continent of Europe and beyond. In a real sense, the history of nineteenth-century Europe is the history of nationalism—or at least this is one way of looking at it. The twentieth century saw the diffusion of nationalism throughout the world. No country has been spared; none is an exception.

With the exception of two brief periods, Western nationalism has continued unabated. For about a decade after each of the two world wars, Western nationalism was in a state of decline, even of ill repute. It was nationalism, after all, that had set in motion cataclysmic events, leading to unspeakable waste of human and material resources.

But the decline of Western nationalism did not last long. Its resurgence after World War I was much accelerated by the fascist and the Nazi movements of the 1920s and 1930s. After the Second World War, Western nationalism owed much of its vitality to the French Gaullist movement of the 1950s and the 1960s. More about this presently.

Period 3

The same world wars that led to the transitory decline of nationalism in the West set the stage for the rise of nationalism in the East. The "new nationalism," as it came to be called, took place, for the most part, in colonial areas; and it was in large measure a reaction against the Western policies of imperialism and conquest.

At the turn of the century, colonial nationalism (more precisely, anticolonial nationalism) was virtually an unknown phenomenon. Following World War I and the disintegration of the Ottoman and the Austro-Hungarian empires, nationalism began to emerge in a few countries, most notably in India. After the Second World War and the disintegration of the German, British, French, and other imperial designs, nationalism mushroomed in formerly colonial countries. Why this should be the case is the subject of another section of this chapter. For now, suffice it to say that the collapse of empires points to imperialist weaknesses and highlights vulnerabilities. If Germany is beatable, so in principle is France. If France is beatable, so in principle is Britain. And if Britain is beatable, so in principle is every country. In short, the two world wars shattered once and for all the myth of white invincibility.

Western Nationalism

As stated earlier, we shall examine the Western experience with nationalism in two countries: France and the United States.

France

The French Revolution was the culmination of nationalist feelings and sentiments that had been gathering for decades. The French Revolution was a revolution of nationalism; nationalism and revolution coincided. As French nationalist intellectuals claimed, overnight, as it were, France became a nation; and the nation assumed responsibility for its citizens, demanding loyalty and devotion in return.

As we said in another context in chapter 1, the French Revolution destroyed the age of aristocratic politics and introduced the era of popular politics. The middle classes expressed their newfound power to the fullest as they transformed the Estates General into the French National Assembly.

The French Revolution did not look to the monarchy, the aristocracy, or the clergy. The new idols were "People," "Nation," "Revolution," "France"—all used interchangeably. The monarch was guillotined, the aristocracy disbanded, the church dispossessed. People, the French Revolution taught, have a right of their own, an identity of their own, an integrity of their own. People or Nation are the source of all power, all authority, all sovereignty. The Declaration of the Rights of Man and Citizen (1789) boldly proclaims: "The Nation is essentially the source of all Sovereignty; nor can any individual, or any body of men, be entitled to any authority which is not expressly derived from it." The French people abandoned their status as subjects of Louis XVI to become, in quick order, not only citizens but also sovereign.

Now, consider the revolutionary nature of the concept of popular sovereignty as of 1789. Sovereignty refers to that position or status of ultimate authority in any society: Who is the final arbiter of disputes? When this concept was first developed by philosophers like Jean Bodin (1530–1596), sovereignty was associated with the person of the monarch, at first because he was the ruler of the land and later because he was perceived to have "divine rights." Because eventually the idea of monarchical sovereignty was difficult to justify, later thinkers associated sovereignty with the institution of the state. Now the French revolutionaries rejected the idea of state sovereignty in favor of popular sovereignty. Revolutionary, indeed.

As we can see, the French Revolution was a revolution of nationalism as well as of democracy. "Liberty, Equality, Fraternity" was not an accidental slogan. Having attained economic and political power, the middle classes were demanding new rights, especially the right of participation in public affairs.

National honor, national self-determination, self-government, and popular sovereignty were inescapable components of the doctrine of nationalism. A nation, it was asserted, should choose its own form of government; it should decide for itself the course of action it wishes to pursue. Authoritarianism was categorically rejected.

Equally important was the fact that the values of French nationalism and democracy were not seen as belonging to the French people alone; they were seen as belonging to all peoples and nations. People everywhere should enjoy the blessings of liberty, equality, fraternity, self-determination, and popular sovereignty.

Although nationalism would benefit every nation, the spreading and propagation of the new order was seen as the special mission of France. Stated differently, French nationalism became messianic: it claimed for itself a special role, a special mission, a special calling. The French saw themselves as deliverers of supreme values and as trustees of a new civilization.

French nationalist intellectuals saw France as the center of universal history. The French people would bring enlightenment and civilization to all nations of the world. Upon France depended the salvation of humankind. Herein lies the genesis of the French doctrine of "assimilation": people everywhere should embrace, embody, and internalize the values of France.

Let us pause and reflect for a moment. What does it mean for one nation to set out to bring its values to other nations? What does it mean for the French to expect the Germans, the Italians, the Spaniards, and the Russians to internalize the values of the French civilization? Why should the French people feel compelled to universalize their values? Manifestly, because of a perceived sense of superiority to other nations: French values must be of a higher order, else why expect others to assimilate them?

So, in the nineteenth century there are definite notions of superiority and inferiority as the European confronts the European. Later, when the European confronts the non-European, this attitude takes the form of the "White Man's Burden"—that is, the white man has a God-given responsibility to civilize and Christianize the black man and the brown man and the yellow man. But more about this later. Let us return to French nationalism and its consequences.

Inspired by the example of France, people throughout Europe should rise to overthrow monarchy and dictatorship and to claim the values of the French Revolution. If they were unwilling to do this—if they were unable to do this—then the French people would take it upon themselves to accomplish the task for them. By force of arms, if necessary. By military might, if necessary.

From early in its beginnings, then, French nationalism became associated with expansionism, militarism, and war. In the name of nationalism and democracy, Napoleonic armies launched a policy of conquest across Europe. The uniqueness of Napoleon's armies was that they were the carriers of ideology.

Soon after the French Revolution, nationalism flourished throughout the Continent. In Italy, Germany, Spain, Russia, and elsewhere, it became a consuming force. Frightened by French expansionism, the peoples of Europe rallied around their own rulers and formed their own nationalist ideologies.

The Italian nationalist movement, for example, dates back to the 1820s. Giuseppe Mazzini (1805–1872), the foremost intellectual-activist of the day, founded an organization, Young Italy, as early as 1831. Italian independence did not come until 1870, however, when the French position in Italy had weakened. Similarly, after decades of nationalist struggle under the leadership of Prussia, Germany was founded in 1871, on the heels of a victorious war with France.

In short, war and conquest by one nation heightened nationalist consciousness in other nations. Military buildup in one nation created a uniform need for large-scale military establishments in other nations. (One needs a military force for both launching imperialism and fighting imperialism.) In 1799, conscription, hitherto an emergency measure, was formally adopted as a permanent policy in France: every able-bodied young man was to serve in the armed forces for five years. The concept of a "nation in arms" became a reality.

Let us round out this discussion of French nationalism. From early in its beginnings, nationalism was associated with democratic values. But also from early on, nationalism was associated with messianism, imperialism, and war. Democracy collapsed into autocracy; nationalism subverted its own values.

Earlier in this chapter, I indicated how *in theory* nationalism, imperialism, and war are interrelated. The experience of France has shown how *in reality* the three are intertwined. A nation's intentions may be noble—as in sharing the blessings of democracy with others, for instance—but the consequences of those intentions may be altogether unfortunate, even brutalizing. This is a lesson not easily or soon forgotten.

The United States

Let us begin by addressing an issue we have touched on before. Why is it that the American people are reluctant to acknowledge their nationalist feelings and sentiments, preferring "patriotism" instead? We recognize the nationalism of the French, the British, the Russians, the Chinese, the Algerians, the Nigerians—in short, of every country save our own. Why should this be the case?

Put directly, because since its beginnings, nationalism has had many negative connotations. For one thing, as we have seen, immediately after the French Revolution, nationalism took on an aggressive meaning. According to some scholars, all the wars of the nineteenth century were due to the imperialist aftermath of French nationalism.

For another, since Lenin and the Bolsheviks, communist revolutions everywhere have been undertaken, in part, in the name of nationalism. In Russia, China, Vietnam, Cuba, and many other countries, the driving force of revolution has been a combination of nationalism and communism. And for a very good reason: Nationalism is something with which everybody can easily identify.

Nationalism has had other unhappy associations as well. What started World War I? The nationalism of Germany. What about World War II? The nationalism of Germany, Italy, and Japan. In other words, nationalism has shown its aggressive face not only on the left wing of the ideological spectrum but on the right wing as well. Finally, nationalism has been quite evident in the independence movements of almost all colonial or developing countries. For these reasons, I think, we tend to avoid association with nationalism.

Our distaste for nationalism notwithstanding, let me try to touch on the highlights of American history through this medium. There are many prisms through which one can examine a given phenomenon. Nationalism is one such prism—a different kind of spotlight on a topic.

At the outset, we should note that (in contrast to the French Revolution) the American Revolution was a revolution of individualism, not of nationalism. "Life, liberty, and the pursuit of happiness"—these are inalienable rights, God-given rights, rights no government can deny. Compare these ideals to their counterparts in the French Revolution: liberty, equality, fraternity. In the American case, all three are individualistic values; in the French illustration, two of the three are communal ideals. The chief philosopher of the American Revolution is John Locke; his focus is individualism and liberty. The main spokesman for the French Revolution is Jean-Jacques Rousseau; his concern is community and equality.

If you examine the Declaration of Independence from this perspective, you will find that the Declaration says nothing about nation, nationalism, or national unity. By contrast, the Preamble of the Constitution says explicitly:

> We the People of the United States, in order to form a more perfect union, establish Justice, insure domestic Tranquility, provide for the common defense, promote the general Welfare, and secure the Blessings of Liberty to ourselves and our Posterity, do ordain and establish this Constitution for the United States of America.

Up until this point there had been no such thing as "We the People of the United States" with a distinct identity. "We" had been former British subjects living in Rhode Island or New Hampshire or Massachusetts or Virginia or New York. But thirteen separate states were now replaced by one United States of America. For this reason, one scholar has referred to the United States as "the first new nation."*

The Constitution, then, lays the foundation, the building blocks, as it were, of nation and nationalism. And by the turn of the century, American nationalism begins to take hold. Once it emerges, American nationalism comes with considerable speed and fury—and it is tied very explicitly to notions of America's future, fate, and mission.

I am alluding to a concept with which every American is familiar—two words found in every civics text. By way of background, keep in mind the defining characteristic of the United States: a new country, a fresh experiment in democracy quite separate and apart from the corrupt, old European practices that we left behind. In other words, there is very little by way of a past to rely on. Rather, we turn our attention to our future and our mission—our Manifest Destiny—a fate that is preordained, predetermined, and obvious to any sentient creature.   定められ?,

But what, exactly, does manifest destiny mean? How is it defined? How does it find expression in the unfolding of American history? Let me first clarify the meaning and then use the illustrations of a poet, a president, and a senator to amplify it.

Remember the backdrop: thirteen states on the East Coast and the South have come together to form the new world. Manifest destiny is going to refer, among other things, to the physical direction in which the country is going to be moving. Coming from the points we do, our natural direction of movement is toward the West. So, manifest destiny means, in the first place, that the new nation is bound to expand over the entire continent—and with it, the values of life, liberty, and pursuit of happiness will spread from coast to coast. Later on, we will have such expressions as "from sea to shining sea" and "from the mountains, to the prairies, to the oceans" to capture this aspect of manifest destiny. So, the westward move-

---

*See the book of the same title by Seymour Martin Lipset listed in the bibliography for this chapter.

Manifest destiny
→ 19c中ごろ。アメリカの西部への領土拡大は神の使命であるとした。

ment is manifest destiny in action. The frontier is manifest destiny in action. The purchase of Louisiana is manifest destiny in action. The annexation of California and Texas is manifest destiny in action.

Now, manifest destiny means much more. Having expanded over the entire continent, the new nation is bound to go across the seas. It is our preordained mission to go beyond the continent. Why? Because wherever we go, life, liberty, and the pursuit of happiness go with us. We have to bring the blessings of democracy to the less fortunate peoples of the world. Accordingly, the acquisitions of Cuba, Puerto Rico, Guam, Hawaii, Alaska, and the Philippines—these are all manifest destiny in action. And as early as 1823, we promulgate the Monroe Doctrine, the central message of which is, "Hands off this hemisphere." We say this first to the European powers and eventually to all countries.

A third component of manifest destiny is that in expanding over the continent and in crossing the seas, conflict, struggle, and war may be unavoidable and necessary. How else can we expand but by taking on the Indians, the Mexicans, the Spaniards, the Filipinos—whoever stands in the way? Conflict and war may be justified in the name of a higher goal: the realization of manifest destiny.

Manifest destiny has at least one other dimension. How are things preordained and predetermined? Who gave us this mission and destiny? But, of course, God Himself. We are the children of God, His chosen people. Manifest destiny is God's will; it is divinely sanctioned. God has selected us to bring democracy to humankind, to bring civilization and Christianity to the far ends of the earth. We have no alternative but to fulfill God's will.

Let us pause and reflect on history. Remember France's civilizing mission? Remember the white man's burden? Now we have the American counterpart, manifest destiny. In the case of France, we said, there was a serious discrepancy between intention (to spread the values of French democracy) and consequence (the Napoleonic wars). Can we examine manifest destiny in the same light? The intention, to be sure, was noble. But what about the consequence? What happened to Native Americans in the westward march? Do they enjoy the blessings of life, liberty, and the pursuit of happiness? And what about the conflicts involving the Mexicans, the Spaniards, the Cubans, the Filipinos?

In any event, let me illustrate and document the points I have made by drawing on various intellectuals and politicians of the times. We turn first to a poet, Walt Whitman, best known for his *Leaves of Grass*. In 1871, Whitman wrote a book called *Democratic Vistas*, which, as the title suggests, reflected on the future of the new American nation. America of the future, says Whitman, will be made up of

> . . . some forty to fifty great states, among them Canada and Cuba. The Pacific will be ours, and the Atlantic mainly ours. What a land! Where, elsewhere, one so great? The individuality of one nation must, as always, lead the world. Can there be any doubt who the leader ought to be?

Why should forty to fifty states become part of America? Because, Whitman believes, wherever America goes, the blessings of democracy follow.

Presidents William McKinley and Theodore Roosevelt were particularly vigorous spokesmen for American nationalism. America, they maintained, has responsibilities of "international stewardship." To make such a claim is to declare oneself the guardian and protector of a certain state of affairs, one, needless to say, that is congenial to one's global objectives. For McKinley and Roosevelt this meant a state of affairs conducive to the spread of American civilization and democracy.

On a related point, here is McKinley's explanation, in 1899, of how and why he decided that the United States should take over the Philippines:

> I walked the floor of the White House night after night until midnight and I am not ashamed to tell you, gentlemen, that I went down on my knees and prayed Almighty God for light and guidance. . . . And one night late it came to me this way . . . that there was nothing left for us to do but to take them all, and to educate the Filipinos, and uplift and civilize and Christianize them, and by God's grace do the very best we could by them.

Let me suggest another illustration, an extremist one. Now, to be sure, not everyone feels this intensely, but a little intellectual shock may jolt us into reality. The year is 1899, the speaker is Senator Albert Beveridge of Indiana. He is a firm believer in the white man's burden and a strong supporter of the American acquisition of the Philippines. He rises on the floor of the Senate and addresses the presiding officer. His talk is titled "Racial Expansionism." Here is a lengthy quotation:

> Mr. President, the times call for candor. The Philippines are ours forever, "territory belonging to the United States," as the Constitution calls them. And just beyond the Philippines are China's illimitable markets. We will not retreat from either. We will not repudiate our duty in the archipelago. We will not abandon our opportunity in the Orient. We will not renounce our part in the mission of our race, trustee, under God, of the civilization of the world. And we will move forward to our work, not howling out regrets like slaves whipped to their burdens, but with gratitude for a task worthy of our strength, and thanksgiving to Almighty God that He has marked us as His chosen people, henceforth to lead in the regeneration of the world. . . .
>
> Mr. President, this question is deeper than any question of party politics; deeper than any question of the isolated policy of our country even; deeper even than any question of constitutional power. It is elemental. It is racial. God has not been preparing the English-speaking and Teutonic peoples for a thousand years for nothing but vain and idle self-contemplation and self-admiration. No! He has made us the master organizers of the world to establish system where chaos reigns. He has given us the spirit of progress to overwhelm the forces of reaction throughout the earth. He has made us adept in government that we may administer government among savage and senile peoples. Were it not for such a force as this the world would relapse into barbarism and night. And of all our race He has marked the American people as His chosen nation to finally lead in the regeneration of the world. This is the divine mission of America, and it holds for us all the profit, all the glory, all the happiness possible to man. We are trustees of the world's progress, guardians of its righteous peace.

No doubt you noted the alternation of good and evil, light and darkness, "us" and "them." You also saw the interplay of patriotism and profit, national glory and limitless markets. And, of course, you did not miss the assertion of racial superiority, or the invocation of God at every turn.

This statement is most likely extremist, as I said. But still, one cannot rise on the floor of the United States Senate and make a statement that is entirely devoid of context or that makes one appear insane or that makes one persona non grata with one's colleagues. In other words, Beveridge must have perceived a hospitable environment. 快適な

In any event, Beveridge brings us into the twentieth century. America's entry into World War I was motivated in part by a desire to universalize her superior moral values and ideals—or, to use Woodrow Wilson's phrase, "to make the world safe for democracy." In Wilson's view, the American flag was "the flag not only of America, but of humanity." In his mind, the League of Nations would represent the global institutionalization of American ideals. The popular unwillingness to participate in the League reflected a failure to understand the Wilsonian image. It was also a testimony to the intensity of nationalist feelings and sentiments. (聖書)証明

Disillusionment with the progress of democracy abroad, coupled with the Great Depression, led to the isolationism of the 1930s. For about a decade, America's mission appeared to be in eclipse as the 消滅 country turned to domestic problems of unprecedented magnitude. The fall of France to Nazi Germany in June 1940 called attention once again to America's stake in the fate of Europe and generated a new sense of international responsibility. The Japanese attack on Pearl Harbor spelled the end of American isolationism. A renewed desire to fulfill the American dream became the guiding principle of American foreign policy. Some aspects of the postwar scene will be discussed later in this chapter.

Eastern Nationalism

It is now time to turn to a discussion of Eastern nationalism, focusing on colonial or formerly colonial countries. We will also examine a landmark book—and a highly controversial one—on colonial nationalism, Frantz Fanon's *The Wretched of the Earth*.

The topic before us is sometimes called Eastern nationalism, sometimes new nationalism, sometimes colonial nationalism. Probably the most accurate name is anticolonial nationalism: people rising to protest their colonial status. Let me begin by touching on the background of the subject. 反植民地主義の

Whereas Western nationalism dates to the French Revolution, Eastern nationalism is a twentieth-century phenomenon. It is a response to or a reaction against Western imperialism. The beginnings of anticolonial nationalism are to be found in the period after World War I and the rise of nationalism in such countries as India and China. The war meant, among other things, the disintegration of certain empires; and this disintegration provided hope and encouragement to people living under imperialist control. In other words, the war taught that in principle imperialism is vulnerable. Combine World War I with the Russian Revolution of 1917 and the result is literally earth-shattering. These two developments vastly accelerated the pace of nationalism and communism in many countries, especially China and Vietnam. Lenin showed (or so he claimed) that Marxism can be integrated with the specific experience of a country to change the lives of millions, and the course of history. So if it can be done in Russia, why not in China? Why not in Vietnam?

The Second World War brought a snowballing effect to the spread of nationalism. National liberation movements (or wars of national liberation) began to pick up momentum and engulf virtually all developing countries in Africa and Asia. The reason was that the postwar period saw the disintegration not only of the German, Italian, and Japanese empires, but also the demise of the British and French imperial designs as well. Many other European countries were similarly weakened.

People who have been under colonial rule for decades begin to develop insight into the conditions under which they live. This consciousness, in turn, is coupled with a perception of alternatives to colonial subjugation. It dawns on the colonial people that they can have a different kind of life, their own government, their own country.

World War II played a key role in another respect as well. During the war, the allied powers called upon the colonial people to join the good fight to defeat Hitler. The colonial people cooperated. The war eventually ended. The situation of the English people changed, the situation of the French people changed, the situation of everybody changed—everybody, that is, except the colonial people. The colonials began to wonder: As far as the African and the Asian are concerned, what is the difference between Adolf Hitler and Winston Churchill (then British prime minister)? The nationalist leader Reverend Sithole of Zimbabwe has been most explicit on this point:

World War II . . . had a great deal to do with the awakening of the peoples of Africa. During the war the African came into contact with practically all the peoples of the earth. He met them on a life-and-death struggle basis. He saw the so-called civilized and peaceful and orderly white people mercilessly butchering one another just as his so-called savage ancestors had done in tribal wars. He saw no difference between the so-called primitive and so-called civilized man. . . .

But more than this, World War II taught the African most powerful ideas. During the war, the Allied Powers taught their subject peoples . . . that it was not right for Germany to dominate other nations. They taught the subject people to fight and die for freedom. . . .

The big lesson that the African learned during the last war was that he fought and suffered to preserve the freedom he did not have back home. . . .

The hatred against Hitler was transferred to European colonialism. . . . An Asiatic once told me, "We owe our independence to Adolf Hitler!"

Two other developments should be noted. For one thing, in the process of consciousness development, the role of education became crucial. When imperialist powers colonize a country, they occupy all the top positions themselves. But controlling the top positions does not enable you to run a country on a day-to-day basis. One needs managers, technicians, technocrats—in other words, educated people. As a means of responding to this need, the imperialist power—let us say the French—identified a number of promising Algerians and Vietnamese and sent them to France for education. For a long time the Algerians and the Vietnamese did just that: they picked up an education in France in order to return to Algeria and Vietnam and occupy the managerial and technical positions. But when you go to France to be educated, there is no telling what kind of an education you are going to get; once you learn to read, there is no telling what you will read. To be sure, one reads texts that increase one's competence as a manager or a technocrat, but one also reads works of Marxism, socialism, nationalism, anarchism, etc. As a result, a point was reached when the Algerians and the Vietnamese returned home only to say to the French, "No more!" While the economic status of these educated colonials had improved, they came to realize that they had no corresponding political power— indeed, that they were foreigners in their own land.

Religion also played an important role in the rise of anticolonial nationalism: unconsciously, inadvertently, it undermined empire. How? Whatever their denomination or sect, the missionaries go to various parts of Africa and Asia in order to convert people to Christianity. The main tool they use in this process is the Bible. And the Bible teaches, among other things, Christian brotherhood, Christian love, Christian charity, good works, concern for your fellow human beings. Given their newfound education, colonial people began to wonder: Why is it that we only *talk* about Christian brotherhood? When and where do we *practice* our religious beliefs?

Nationalism before Independence

Having developed a consciousness of their colonial status, the colonial peoples of Africa and Asia used their own resources to launch national revolutionary movements or wars of national liberation. In the interest of manageability, we focus the balance of this section on the typical or the generic nationalist movement in Africa, drawing from time to time on the experience of Asian countries as well.

Independence being the pivotal and watershed event that it is, we can direct our attention to the characteristics of the nationalist movement before and after independence is attained. Each phase has exhibited certain outstanding features.

To seek independence is to throw out the foreigner in the name of a country to call our own. It follows that initially we encounter the type of nationalism we have called "formative." Formative nationalism entails much protest and revolt, anti-imperialist outbursts, antiforeign feelings and sentiments. In other words, we are united on one issue. We know that we do *not* want: the British, the French, the Belgians, the Portuguese.

This returns us to the issue of homogeneity in anticolonial nationalism. How much unity does a people need in order to rise against imperialism? Apparently, as we concluded earlier, very little. Anti-imperialism alone has served as a unifying force.

We defined "nation" as a group of people who feel they belong together because they have something in common. In many African lands, there is no such thing as "a people"; there are several peoples. Recall that the boundaries of African colonies do not signify cultural or linguistic homogeneity. They represent the convenience of the colonizer in collecting taxes, providing police service, running jails and hospitals, and the like.

Another feature of pre-independence nationalism lies in the extremely important role played by the intellectual elite. Intellectuals have played important parts in all nationalist movements, but in the colonial world nationalism has been almost exclusively their handiwork. Given the general state of underdevelopment (e.g., lack of transportation and communication), the intellectuals literally go on foot from village to village to teach about the evils of imperialism and the glories of nationalism. In Vietnam, for instance, Ho Chi Minh and his associates trained and fielded a whole cadre of traveling speakers.

At the same time, colonial intellectuals have served as intermediaries between Western and Eastern cultures. As we know, a great many nationalists of Africa and Asia were educated at British, French, and American universities.

Being movements of negativism, protest, and revolt, colonial nationalist movements inevitably involve violence on a large scale. The philosopher of violence in the colonial context is Frantz Fanon, and his book *The Wretched of the Earth* invites close examination.

Before proceeding, it is important to ask: Who was Frantz Fanon and what qualifications did he have to write on colonial violence? A blurb inside the book's front cover informs us that Fanon was a black man, born in Martinique, a French possession; that he had a variety of personal and professional experiences living in Martinique, the Antilles, France, and Algeria; that he is a professional man with formal training in medicine and psychiatry; that he had professional field experience treating both whites and blacks in France, the Antilles, and Algeria.

Fanon's specific focus is Algeria, to be sure, but his argument is supposed to be of general applicability to all colonial countries. In fact, the publisher's blurb on the jacket describes the book as "The handbook of the Black revolution that is changing the shape of the world." The blurb is an exaggeration, but the book's claim to fame is twofold: first, it offers an unrelenting focus on the role of violence in society; second, it draws a sharp distinction between physical and psychological violence.

Our working definition of violence is very simple: any act *intended* to damage or destroy persons or property. Psychological violence is any act that generates mental anxiety and anguish, in addition to its physical effects. Perhaps the most total act of violence is rape. Rape is a power act that has to do with domination and subordination: one person demeaning and humiliating another person. Most of the physical repercussions of rape will in time disappear; the psychological impact may always remain.

To begin with, the French used violence of both a physical and a psychological nature in order to subdue Algeria and maintain their rule. One cannot control another people except through the use of the military and the police. Moreover, the French destroyed much of the native society and culture, replacing them with French practices and institutions. Indeed, the French doctrine of assimilation required the Algerians to renounce their own values and replace them with French norms.

Now, certain aspects of native society and culture are encouraged. Religious practices may be retained. Native rituals and dances may be retained. Other social and cultural activities may be retained. The reason is that rituals and dances may perform the function of psychological catharsis: the release of pent-up energies, hostilities, and emotions on the part of the natives. Moreover, some rituals may serve the function of pitting the natives against each other, thus diverting attention from the real enemy in their midst.

In this context, let me digress long enough to indicate what the British were doing in China in the middle of the nineteenth century. You may be familiar with the Opium War of 1839–1842. As you may know, East Asia is famous for its supply of opium and other derivatives. Being very influential in the area, the British would gather up the opium, take it to China, and trade it for such prime Chinese goods as silk and tea. In one simple act, the British accomplished two substantial objectives: first, they used opium as a medium of exchange and trade; second, they encouraged the use of opium among the Chinese—perhaps if the Chinese people were kept high on opium, they would not rebel against the British. And, as we know, the Chinese lost the Opium War, as a result of which they ceded Hong Kong to Britain and opened their ports to foreign trade. (The war was begun by Britain in response to Chinese confiscation of cargo shipments of opium.)

Getting back to Frantz Fanon, the French used psychological violence against the Algerians as well. You do this when you treat the natives as somehow less than human. Using very strong language, Fanon says:

> The colonial world is a Manichean world. It is not enough for the settler to delimit physically, that is to say with the help of the army and the police force, the place of the native. As if to show the totalitarian character of colonial exploitation the settler paints the native as a sort of quintessence of evil. Native society is not simply described as a society lacking in values. It is not enough for the colonist to affirm that those values have disappeared from, or still better never existed in, the colonial world. The native is declared insensible to ethics; he represents not only the absence of values, but also the negation of values. He is, let us dare to admit, the enemy of values, and in this sense he is the absolute evil. He is the corrosive element, destroying all that comes near him; he is the deforming element, disfiguring all that has to do with beauty or morality; he is the depository of maleficent powers, the unconscious and irretrievable instrument of blind forces. . . .
>
> At times this Manicheism goes to its logical conclusion and dehumanizes the native, or to speak plainly, it turns him into an animal. In fact, the terms the settler uses when he mentions the native are zoological terms. He speaks of the yellow man's reptilian motions, of the stink of the native quarter, of breeding swarms, of foulness, of spawn, of gesticulations. When the settler seeks to describe the native fully in exact terms he constantly refers to the bestiary.

In a few words, the colonial world is dualistic: the French are all good; the Algerians are all evil. Indeed, the Algerians are nothing but animals.

There is a section in the Fanon book titled "Colonial Wars and Mental Disorders," in which Fanon discusses how the mere presence of the French in Algeria triggered psychological problems among the natives. He reviews case study after case study to show that the Algerians he treated have psychological problems whose genesis is to be found in the simple fact of French presence in Algeria. (If you have difficulty grasping Fanon's point, try to think of a condition in which *you* live under foreign rule.)

Now for the other side of the equation: Fanon tells the Algerians that if they are to free their country and recapture their own humanness, they must do to the French precisely what the French have done to them. In fact, Fanon invokes a biblical dictum: "The last shall be first and the first last." The Algerians, says Fanon, will need physical violence in order to get rid of the outsider. But they also need to visit psychological violence as a means of regaining their own selfhood and humanity. In other words, violence becomes a means of the psychological rehabilitation of the Algerians. Fanon says:

> Violence is in action all-inclusive and national. . . . At the level of the individual, violence is a cleansing force. It frees the native from his inferiority complex and from his despair and inaction; it makes him fearless and restores his self-respect.

He also says that killing a Frenchman is killing two birds with the same stone. One is killing a colonizer; the other is recapturing one's selfhood.

That, in brief, is Fanon's argument. Note, this is neither a practical man nor a realistic one. This is not a planner or an organizer. This is not a Lenin or a Mao or a Castro. He is a prophet of violence; and he is trying to open the eyes of the colonial people, be they Algerians or Zimbabweans, to their circumstances. Once you get a Lenin, then you have to undertake a very deliberate and careful process of organizing the people, educating them, and mobilizing them toward your objectives.

Take the Algerian Revolution itself, 1954–1962. It was led by nine men, typically referred to as the Nine Brothers, including Ahmed Ben Bella, Mourad Didouche, Belkassem Krim, and others. They took the whole country of Algeria, divided it into several strategic areas, posted to each area the Brother most familiar with it, and fought the French to eventual independence.

So, Fanon was the philosopher of the Algerian Revolution in the same sense that Locke was the philosopher of the American Revolution and Rousseau was the philosopher of the French Revolution. Fanon is a man on a moral crusade against the French and against imperialism in general.

Nationalism after Independence

Let us now turn to the characteristics of the nationalist movement after independence is attained. First, following independence, almost all nationalist movements undergo a process of internal fragmentation. Any country—even the most homogeneous—has competing leaders, parties, and programs. However, the existence of a foreign enemy brings together divergent groups; the goal of independence unifies people of different political, ethnic, and linguistic identities.

Once this unifying focus, independence, is gone, competing leaders, groups, parties, and programs surge to the fore. A process of competition and rivalry occurs: political leaders of various backgrounds and orientations start fighting each other.

In Nigeria, for example, the three major groups or "tribes"—the Ibo, the Hausa, and the Fulani—united to gain independence from Britain. Once this goal was accomplished, internal divisions exploded into the Biafra War in which thousands perished.

Or take the more recent example of Zimbabwe. (Zimbabwe, by the way, is the new name: the country under black majority rule since 1980. The old name was Rhodesia: the country under white minority rule.) Zimbabwe has two major social groups: the Shona majority, led by Robert Mugabe, and the Ndebele minority, led by Joshua Nkomo. As long as the country was under white minority rule, the two groups and their leaders united in cooperation. As soon as white rule ended, the two groups started fighting each other.

Typically, what happens in these circumstances is that the person who has the numbers or the guns (or whatever it takes) declares the country a one-party state. Under this arrangement, which is found in many African countries, the party of the chief leader is recognized as the sole legal party. Other parties or groups or organizations or trade unions are either outlawed or become appendages of the sole legal party.

The formal rationale given for the one-party state is the need for national unity in the face of continued threat from the former imperialist power. In reality, the one-party state is a formula for authoritarian rule befitting the whims of the top leader. In any event, the domestic scene is one of fragmentation, conflict, and rivalry.

In time, there arises a series of rivalries at the international level as well. Having gone through similar experiences of colonization and exploitation, one is tempted to think that the postindependence stage heralds an age of friendship and cooperation among the new states. Far from it. The situation is one of intense competition and rivalry as each country seeks to enhance its position and status vis-à-vis the others. In other words, another feature of Eastern nationalism is that following independence, formative nationalism turns into prestige nationalism, the second variety of nationalism we discussed earlier in this chapter.

Whenever a new country is formed (for example, when Algeria becomes independent or when Rhodesia becomes Zimbabwe), it must be "recognized" as an independent sovereign state by the other countries of the world. This is the standard practice of recognition in international law. Now, the African countries, for instance, are not so interested in being recognized by each other; rather, they want to be recognized by the major powers: the United States, Russia, Britain, France, etc.

The new states also have an opportunity to become members of the United Nations. The U.N. Charter is based on the premise (Article 2, Section 1) that the organization rests on the sovereign equality of all member states. In other words, to interpret the charter literally, the new countries, however small, enjoy the same status as the largest and the most powerful states. This is linguistic compensation, to be sure, but one can see why new countries would compete for the prestige of becoming members of the United Nations.

United Nations membership is not exclusively symbolic; it has practical value as well. Having the requisite resources and skills, the major powers enhance their diplomatic activities by establishing embassies and consulates throughout the world. Lacking the resources and skills, the new states may create diplomatic missions in the major capitals (Washington, Moscow, Paris, London), but the burden of their diplomatic efforts centers upon the United Nations. In effect, the United Nations becomes an arena for the conduct of international relations for the newer and smaller states.

Some Eastern countries have gone beyond prestige nationalism, experiencing an expansive phase as well. The most dramatic example is found in Southeast Asia. As long as the American and French forces were in Indochina, from 1858 until 1975, the peoples of China, Vietnam, Cambodia, and Laos got together and formed a united front. As soon as the last American soldiers pulled out, the Chinese and the Vietnamese clashed on their common border. Vietnam invaded Laos and Cambodia in order to install friendly governments in those countries. In short, in the Eastern experience, too, prestige nationalism has become expansive or imperialistic but not to the same extent as Western nationalism.*

Another feature of postindependence nationalism surrounds the con-

---

*The Iraqi invasion of Kuwait in August 1990 is a more recent example of expansive nationalism.

troversy regarding neocolonialism. What is this new form of colonialism? The idea is that although the imperialist power has granted independence, it continues to maintain all kinds of ties with the former colony—military, economic, diplomatic, cultural—and that through these ties it continues its policies of oppression and exploitation. Moreover, the argument runs, new colonialism is worse than old colonialism because it is more subtle, covert, and devious, and hence not subject to any form of international supervision or control.

For instance, to the present day, some Indian intellectuals protest the cultural imperialism of Great Britain. In what sense, one wonders, are the British exercising cultural imperialism in India? Through the persistent use of the English language, comes the retort. What are the native languages of India? Hindi, Urdu, Farsi, perhaps others. In what language are many Indian newspapers, magazines, and books printed? English! English, it is said, is not the language of India; it is the language of the imperialist power. And insofar as any language denotes a system of logic and a cultural system, and insofar as human beings think with language, language becomes a means of imposing values upon others.

On the question of neocolonialism, two points of view define the position of African states. Such established and conservative countries as Liberia and Sudan argue that ties with the former imperialist power are acceptable because they are mutually beneficial. The French or the British use our raw materials and cheap labor, to be sure, but in turn they provide military aid, economic assistance, and technical expertise.

By contrast, such newer and radical African states as Guinea and Libya maintain, at least on the surface, that we must break all ties with the imperialist powers and remove all vestiges of foreign rule. Thus, the Guinean president Sekou Touré's argument is that we must get rid of the French completely if we are to re-Africanize our country. The implication is that once upon a time there was Africa—pure, simple, innocent, unspoiled. Then the French came, and they brought their own culture, politics, and institutions. They spoiled, or de-Africanized, Africa. The task now is to recapture Africa's purity: we must re-Africanize the pure Africa that the French de-Africanized.

This argument represents a good ideological position, but hardly a practical one. Like it or not, the newer states will continue to need the resources, skill, and expertise commanded by the imperialist powers.

The Resurgence of Nationalism in the West

For about a decade after World War II, nationalism was in a state of decline in the Western world; it no longer seemed either urgent or desirable. Nationalism was associated with the aggressor countries—Germany, Italy, Japan—whose ambitious schemes had generated cataclysm.

Moreover, since the European countries were left in a state of military and economic disintegration, their mutual aims and aspirations spurred a desire for common military and economic organizations. Thus, the postwar European scene was characterized by a mushrooming of international organizations in various fields. Of these, the most important were the Organization for European Economic Cooperation, the Brussels Treaty, the Council of Europe, NATO, and the European Economic Community or the Common Market—to say nothing of the United Nations. Together these organizations signaled a trend toward increasing international cooperation designed to meet common needs and solve common problems.

The decline of European nationalism did not last long. Its resurgence was sharply accelerated by Charles de Gaulle, who emerged as the personification of the French Fifth Republic in 1958. Once again, declarations of French "sovereignty" and "grandeur" echoed across the continents.

As the European countries gradually recaptured their economic and military footing, nationalism underwent a subtle shift. Today, European nationalism must be understood in a dual perspective. When confronted with an external threat—for instance, American or Japanese challenge—the European countries have been able to modulate their nationalism and put forward a united front. In the absence of such a threat, rivalry among the European countries continues to be intense, modified only by pressing economic and military considerations of mutual concern.

Turning to the two Western countries on which we have focused in this chapter, in postwar France nationalism represents a reaction against two compelling phenomena: the loss of French colonies and the predominance of American power on the European continent. Nationalist revolts in the colonies were particularly disillusioning to the French because they directly challenged the myth of "assimilation." Anticolonial nationalism became an object of French resentment because it directly challenged the universality of French values, in addition to threatening to undermine France's status among the great powers. Not prepared to come to terms with colonial nationalism, the French continued to entertain illusions in Indochina, Algeria, and elsewhere. Defeat after defeat finally drove home the point that the universal mission of France had come to an end. Disillusioned in its self-assigned mission abroad, France turned inward—to the task of revitalizing itself.

Revitalization meant, among other things, confronting U.S. military and economic dominance on the Continent. France had suffered defeat at the hands of Germany in World War II. The end of German occupation did not mean the end of French humiliation, however, for the United States quickly replaced Germany (or so it seemed to many French citizens). French nationalism, dispossessed of its universalistic mission, had now to contend with continued humiliation. The nuclear stalemate between the United States and the former Soviet Union ("the two hegemonies," de Gaulle called them) further intensified French nationalism. Only substantial economic growth, the development of nuclear power, and the end of reliance on American aid could serve to abate the intensity of French nationalism.

Since the French economy was weak in the years immediately following the war, economic strength was sought in union with other continental powers, particularly Germany. Having reinvigorated their economy, the French turned to military matters. "The two hegemonies" could only be challenged if France had its own independent nuclear force. A *force de frappe* (nuclear striking force) was to be sought at any price, for it symbolized the resurgence of France as a superpower. Having reestablished France militarily, de Gaulle could now afford to weaken NATO and force the American military establishment out of France.

Meanwhile, having emerged as a world superpower, having determined to take an active role in world affairs, having revived the idea of the American mission to spread democracy and freedom, the United States found herself in sustained conflict with a new enemy, "international communism." Concern with Soviet expansionism abroad and fear of Communist subversion at home, together with setbacks in China and Korea, set in motion a virtually pathological reaction in some segments of the American population, typified in the wave of McCarthyism that gripped the country in the 1950s. Mc-

Carthyism was many things, of course, but its core was witch-hunting and scapegoating.

In general, the cold war era was dominated, from the American point of view, by policies of "brinkmanship" and "containment." Largely an invention of John Foster Dulles, secretary of state under President Dwight Eisenhower, brinkmanship was, fundamentally, a policy of threats and confrontations: going to the brink of war in an effort to forestall war. Containment meant, essentially, throwing a ring of military bases around the Communist countries, especially the former USSR and China. But one cannot forge the kinds of military alliances that containment requires without becoming deeply involved in the internal affairs of distant lands. And this is precisely what came to pass, rationalized and justified once again as bringing freedom and democracy to other countries, as American policy toward Greece, Turkey, and Vietnam, for example, well illustrates. There is reason to believe, however, that national security and international stability are more compelling justifications, else why not set out to bring democracy and freedom to such police states as Thailand and Taiwan also?

Nowhere did American nationalism crystallize more sharply than in regard to the Vietnam conflict. As in most every war, the Vietnam adventure produced its own brand of slogan-shouting "true" Americans. Presidents Lyndon Johnson and Richard Nixon repeatedly invoked the nationalist spirit in their efforts to gain support for the war. They formally committed the nation's "honor" to the conflict, implying for good measure that criticism of their policies would be patently unpatriotic. Flag waving swept the country as the military, the police, the hard hats, and the Middle Americans castigated "the effete corps of impudent snobs" (to use then Vice President Spiro Agnew's well-publicized characterization) who dared challenge the morality or efficacy of a war in the swamps of a strange land that by some accounts ultimately cost the country nearly 60,000 lives and upwards of 200 billion dollars.

The post-Vietnam era witnessed, for a short while, another eclipse of American nationalism. The Reagan presidency, on the other hand, marked a vigorous renewal of nationalist pride and sentiment. Foreign and defense policy took center stage as a new emphasis was placed on America's international mission against the twin evils of communism and terrorism. And the Strategic Defense

Initiative (or "Star Wars") by far outshone the earlier space programs.

Being primordial, nationalist feelings and sentiments have a tendency to persist, triggered by both national crisis and national achievement. In this context, the following events deserve attention: the Iran hostage crisis of 1980–1981, the Grenada invasion of 1983, the Los Angeles Olympics of 1984, the Libya bombing of 1985, the Miss Liberty celebration of 1986, the Constitution bicentennial celebration of 1987, the Iran naval confrontation of 1988, the Gulf War of 1991. Some of these events brought frustration and others generated euphoria. In its own way, each event was a testimony to the enduring nature of nationalism.

The Framework Applied

As we have seen, the cognitive dimension of nationalism involves elements of knowledge (fact) as well as of belief (fiction). Western nationalism sees the world through the prism of "the best and the greatest," seeking to enhance a country's economic, political, military, diplomatic, and cultural status. In the East, nationalism typically begins with the experience and perception of oppression, exploitation, and humiliation under foreign regimes, which lead, in time, to demands for independence, sovereignty, and all the prestige trappings attached thereto. Both types of nationalism rest on the assumption of the relative superiority of one country and the relative inferiority of all others. The French, for example, are not the only people who believe in their cultural supremacy; many an African people have internalized and expressed similar beliefs.

The affective component of nationalism stresses the feeling of belonging to a unique—because superior—group or nation. It follows, by definition, that every individual constituting the group is unique and superior as well. These feelings of unity, distinctiveness, and superiority are captured in such emotionally charged symbols as national flags, national anthems, and national holidays.

The affective ingredient of nationalism, which in part overlaps with the evaluative, is also well illustrated in the concepts of civilizing mission, white man's burden, and manifest destiny and divine ordination.

The evaluative dimension of Western nationalism is summed up in the French Declaration of the Rights of Man and Citizen (1789): glorification of people and nation, popular sovereignty, individual rights and liberties. Other values include national pride, honor, and dignity, as well as collective welfare and security. In the Eastern experience, another aspect is added to this dimension: colonial countries not only want independence and sovereignty, they also wish to "get even" with the colonizers by seeking revenge, righting historic injustices, and releasing pent-up psychological frustrations.

Historically, the programmatic component of nationalism has found three expressions: (1) formative nationalism—educating, organizing, and mobilizing a people to assert their unity, identity, and independence; (2) prestige nationalism—mobilizing a people to improve their status, welfare, and power; (3) expansive nationalism—mobilizing a people to aggrandize themselves by infringing upon the rights of another people. Thus, having become a "nation" overnight, as it were, France set out to increase its power and prestige. In so doing, it violated the rights of the Germans, the Italians, the Spaniards, the Russians, and others in a series of wars that dominated the nineteenth century. Similarly, having attained independence from Britain, the United States, under the presumably divine ordination of manifest destiny, set out to expand over the entire continent and cross the seas to take over not only Cuba and Puerto Rico but Hawaii and the Philippines as well. That the implementation of manifest destiny entailed conflict and war was treated as a matter of course.

The social base of nationalism incorporates the entire population except, perhaps, the radical intellectuals (the internationalists), the poor, the indigent, and the uneducated. In such diverse, multiethnic societies as the United States, national unity is more difficult to achieve than in homogeneous lands. Even in the United States, however, there is an "umbrella ideology" that brings together peoples of various regions and nationalities—the Northerners and the Southerners, the Poles and the Irish—and identifies them as "Americans."

Selected Bibliography

Armstrong, John A. *Nations before Nationalism*. Chapel Hill: University of North Carolina Press, 1982.

Burns, Edward. *The American Idea of Mission*. New Brunswick, N.J.: Rutgers University Press, 1958.

Canadian Review of Studies in Nationalism 1 (1973). Journal devoted to the subject of nationalism.

Carr, E. H. *Nationalism and After*. New York: Macmillan, 1945.
Coleman, James S. "Nationalism in Tropical Africa." *American Political Science Review* 48 (1954): 404–26.
———. *Nigeria: Background to Nationalism*. Berkeley: University of California Press, 1958.
Deutsch, Karl W. "The Growth of Nations: Some Recurrent Patterns of Political and Social Integration." *World Politics* 5 (January 1953): 1968–1995.
———. "Nation and World." In *Contemporary Political Science*, ed. by Ithiel de Sola Pool. New York: McGraw-Hill, 1967.
———. *Nationalism and Its Alternatives*. New York: Knopf, 1969.
———. *Nationalism and Social Communication*. 2d ed. Cambridge, Mass.: MIT Press, 1966.
Deutsch, Karl W., and Richard L. Merritt. *Nationalism: An Interdisciplinary Bibliography*. Cambridge, Mass.: MIT Press, 1966.
Emerson, Rupert. *From Empire to National: The Rise to Self-Assertion of Asian and African Peoples*. Cambridge, Mass.: Harvard University Press, 1960.
Fanon, Frantz. *The Wretched of the Earth*. New York: Grove Press, 1968.
Gellner, Ernest. *Nations and Nationalism*. Ithaca, N.Y.: Cornell University Press, 1983.
Hartz, Louis. *The Founding of New Societies*. New York: Harcourt, Brace & World, 1964.
Hodgkin, Thomas. *Nationalism in Colonial Africa*. New York: New York University Press, 1967.
Kautsky, John H. *Political Change in the Underdeveloped Countries: Nationalism and Communism*. New York: Wiley, 1962.
Kedourie, Elie. *Nationalism*. New York: Praeger, 1960.
Kohn, Hans. *The Idea of Nationalism: A Study of Its Origins and Background*. New York: Macmillan, 1944.
———. *Nationalism: Its Meaning and History*. Princeton, N.J.: Van Nostrand, 1955.
———. *Prophets and Peoples: Studies in Nineteenth Century Nationalism*. New York: Macmillan, 1957.
———, ed. *Readings in American Nationalism*. New York: Van Nostrand Reinhold, 1970.
Lipset, Seymour Martin. *The First New Nation: The United States in Historical and Comparative Perspective*. New York: Anchor Books, 1967.
Memmi, Albert. *The Colonizer and the Colonized*. Boston: Beacon Press, 1967.
Pfaff, William. *The Wrath of Nations: Civilization and the Furies of Nationalism*. New York: Simon & Schuster, 1993.
Rejai, Mostafa, and Cynthia H. Enloe. "Nation-States and State-Nations." *International Studies Quarterly* 12 (June 1969): 140–58.
Schaar, John H. "The Case for Patriotism." In *American Review 17*, ed. by Theodore Solotaroff. New York: Bantam Books, 1973.
Shafer, Boyd C. *Faces of Nationalism*. New York: Harcourt Brace Jovanovich, 1972.
Sigmund, Paul E., Jr., ed. *The Ideologies of the Developing Nations*. New York: Praeger, 1963.

Sithole, Ndabaningi. *African Nationalism*. 2d ed. New York: Oxford University Press, 1968.

Smith, Anthony D. S. *Nationalism in the Twentieth Century*. New York: New York University Press, 1979.

———. *Theories of Nationalism*. London: Buckworth, 1971.

Snyder, Louis L. *The Meaning of Nationalism*. New Brunswick, N.J.: Rutgers University Press, 1954.

———. *The New Nationalism*. Ithaca, N.Y.: Cornell University Press, 1968.

Touré, Sekou. *Toward Full Re-Africanization*. Paris: Présence Africaine, 1959.

Ward, Barbara. *Nationalism and Ideology*. New York: Norton, 1966.

3

Fascism and Nazism

The opening decades of the twentieth century witnessed the rise of totalitarian regimes in Russia (communism), Italy (fascism), and Germany (nazism). Although these regimes differ in many ways among themselves, Western scholars labeled them "totalitarian" because they have some features or attributes in common. After a discussion of the ideological foundations of fascism and nazism, we shall examine these commonalities and differences. But first let us look at the two principal leaders of fascism and nazism and the historical and societal contexts in which they emerged.

Mussolini and His Times

Benito Mussolini was born on July 29, 1883, near a small town in central Italy, the first of three children. His father, the local blacksmith, dabbled in socialist journalism, which left a strong impression on the young child. The family lived in small and dingy quarters and led a meager existence.

Unloved at home, the young Mussolini became rebellious, violent, and aggressive. He was transferred from school to school for stabbing classmates with his penknife and attacking his teachers. At the same time, however, he was sufficiently intelligent to pass his examinations. Eventually he obtained a teaching certificate and taught school for a time.

Mussolini was not, however, to remain a teacher for long. Restless and ambitious, in 1902 he left Italy for Switzerland in search of fortune and adventure. What he found was a drab life, and he moved from menial job to menial job, and engaged in acts of violence as a means of venting his anger and frustration.

Meanwhile, Mussolini managed to read widely in philosophy and literature, particularly the works of Georg W. F. Hegel (1770–1831), Friedrich W. Nietzsche (1844–1900), Georges Sorel (1847–1922), and others. Highly eclectic in approach, he retained only those ideas that appealed to his temperament and outlook. Though he had not formed anything approaching a philosophy of his own, he impressed others with his knowledge. He began to develop a reputation as a journalist, orator, and radical activist. Advocating violence and strikes as the means of improving the condition of the workers, he was arrested and imprisoned several times. By the time he returned to Italy in 1904, he had begun to make a name for himself.

After a period of relative inactivity, Mussolini returned to journalism, trade unionism, activism, and oratory in 1909. During World War I, he experienced front-line fighting and later became one of the most popular war correspondents in Italy. Soon thereafter these experiences and his intense reading of German nationalist literature and philosophy combined to effect a sharp ideological conversion. He had witnessed the middle-class fear of communism and he believed he had felt the pulse of the Italian people: his socialist tendencies gave way to intense nationalism. He became convinced that he was called upon to lead Italy to a new age of glory and vitality—indeed, to revive the great Roman Empire. "*Viva l'Italia*" became his rallying cry.

In 1919, a small and disparate group of republicans, nationalists, socialists, anarchists, unemployed former soldiers, and other individuals came together in Milan to form what Mussolini called Fasci Italiani di Combattimento: a group of fighters united by close emotional bonds. So was born fascism in Italy—and so emerged Mussolini as Il Duce, the supreme and unchallenged leader.

A restless figure and always on stage, Mussolini launched a campaign of mass mobilization throughout Italy, traveling from place to place, holding rally after rally, drawing ever larger crowds, and mesmerizing listeners with his oratory stressing national greatness. Meanwhile, squads of his Blackshirts unleashed a campaign of violence against all opponents, particularly the Socialists and the Communists.*

---

*Fascist supporters wore black shirts as a means of identification and as a demonstration of solidarity and strength.

In the summer of 1922, at the gathering of a large group of Fascist supporters, Mussolini cried for a "March on Rome" as a means of usurping political power. Word spread, and all over the country Fascists seemed prepared to march. Sufficiently impressed and alarmed, King Victor Emmanuel II invited Mussolini to become prime minister. Assuming office in October, Mussolini remained in power for more than twenty years. In 1932, he teamed with his comrade Giovanni Gentile to write the definitive article "The Doctrine of Fascism," which glorified the state and outlined the social and political programs of the Fascist party.

Hitler and His Times

Adolf Hitler was born on April 20, 1889, in a border town in Austria. His father, a minor government official, was an autocratic drunkard who paid little attention to family matters. The young Hitler, in turn, became moody, stubborn, and rebellious. The father died in 1903 but left sufficient money in savings and pension to keep the family in relative comfort.

For lack of acceptable grades, Hitler never completed secondary school. He aspired to become an art student but was twice denied admission to the Academy of Fine Arts in Vienna. Angry and disillusioned, he lived a drifter's life in his late teens and early twenties, sustaining himself on demeaning and menial jobs.

Hitler moved to Munich in 1913 and enlisted in the German army soon after the outbreak of World War I. Decorated twice for bravery, he found military life much to his liking—particularly the camaraderie, discipline, hierarchy, and potential for heroic deeds. At the same time, he became embittered at the German defeat and considered the peace settlements unacceptable.

In 1919, Hitler joined the German Workers' party in Munich (the political heart of conservative Bavaria), which organization was renamed the following year the National Socialist German Workers' party (Nationalsozialistische Deutsche Arbeiterpartei, "Nazi" being a contraction of the first word). He found the party lacking in effective leadership, organization, discipline, a coherent ideology, and an ability to mobilize the people by capitalizing on their frustration and discontent. The Germany of the 1920s and 1930s was in the grip of acute political instability and economic problems, including unemployment and depression. The humiliation of their defeat in the war lingered, and the resentment of the people increased.

Through his commanding personality, his oratorical skills, and his unceasing propaganda, Hitler set out to address Germany's political and economic problems and to restore to the German people their sense of national pride and integrity. Like Mussolini, he was a mesmerizing performer. Having assumed the leadership of the party in 1921, Hitler continued to draw larger and larger crowds. Patterned after Mussolini's Blackshirts, the Nazi Brownshirts, or Stormtroopers, were originally organized to provide protection for party leaders and party meetings; later, they were put to other, violent purposes as well.*

In November 1923, Hitler participated in the unsuccessful Munich *putsch* (revolt or uprising), as a consequence of which he was sentenced to five years in prison. He served less than one year and he used the time to write the chief document of Nazi ideology, *Mein Kampf* (My Struggle), a rambling work in which he gave expression to the ideas of racism, expansionism, the leadership principle, the "folkish" state, and the like.

The economic crash of 1929 provided a fresh boost for the fortunes of the Nazi party. The Nazi leaders' unceasing and skillful manipulation attracted people in huge numbers. "Germany, Germany, Germany" had become Hitler's perpetual battle cry. By the election of 1930, the Nazis had become the second largest party in Germany.

In 1932, Hitler ran for the presidency of the German Republic against Paul von Hindenburg. A military hero of World War I, Field Marshal von Hindenburg had been persuaded to enter politics by some conservative parties and became president in 1925. He managed to prevail over Hitler in 1932, but the Nazis captured a staggering seventeen million votes (44 percent of the electorate) and emerged as a most significant political force. In recognition of this fact, von Hindenburg appointed Hitler chancellor in 1933.

Once in office, Hitler moved swiftly to consolidate power and remove all opposition. The Reichstag (the lower house) fire of February 1933, apparently set by a Dutch communist, became a rationalization

---

*Hitler had been an admirer of Mussolini, although at first Mussolini did not reciprocate. In fact, during their first meeting in the mid-1930s, Mussolini formed a very low opinion of Hitler. Only repeated demonstrations of German military might during World War II changed Mussolini's mind.

for a decree severely curtailing all freedoms, eliminating or nazifying the media, revamping the educational system, erecting concentration camps, and launching a campaign of violence against all opponents, especially Marxists, Communists, and Jews (whom Hitler blamed as the root cause of German problems). In March, Hitler maneuvered the Reichstag to pass an enabling act giving him full powers. After von Hindenburg's death in August 1934, Hitler moved to monopolize all power by merging the offices of the chancellorship and the presidency, the latter carrying the supreme command of the armed forces as well.

In 1936, Hitler formed an alliance with Mussolini. And the world stood on the brink of apocalypse.

Why Mussolini and Hitler Attained Power

Given the sociohistorical contexts of Italy and Germany of the 1920s and 1930s, Mussolini and Hitler gained power for several identifiable reasons. First, their political doctrines were well in tune with the cultural and philosophical climate of the times—particularly the teachings of such towering figures as Hegel and Nietzsche, which had penetrated virtually all intellectual circles. Second, Mussolini and Hitler promised economic and political stability—indeed, unprecedented progress—in the midst of national crisis, turbulence, and chaos. Third, they mobilized their respective peoples by appealing to their grievances, frustration, and discontent—in particular the acute fear of communism among the middle classes. Fourth, Mussolini and Hitler promised to replace the humiliation of defeat with a new age of national pride and glory. Fifth, they used their "charismatic" personalities and superb oratorical skills to maximum advantage. Finally, Mussolini and Hitler offered strong leadership at a time when the Italian and German peoples seemed to crave it and when national consolidation seemed the most urgent need. In short, Mussolini and Hitler were children of their circumstances, and they responded to those circumstances with uncommon effectiveness.

It follows, then, that had Mussolini and Hitler appeared on the scene twenty years earlier or twenty years later, they probably would not have had the impact that they had. In studying social movements, one must be very attentive to the interaction of a particular leader's personality and a particular social and historical context at a particular point in time. When a personality is able to translate his own inner frustration and discontent into national frustration and discontent, and when he is skillful at deploying an effective ideology and an appropriate organization, that is when a social movement is most likely to get under way. It is not enough merely to appeal to people from an emotional or ideological level. One must also use organization to tap people's energies and skills and direct them toward the realization of goals and objectives. We shall return to some of these topics later in this chapter.

Ideological Foundations of Fascism and Nazism

Irrationalism and Activism

Fascism and nazism systematically downgraded the role of reason, logic, and intelligence in human behavior, stressing instead its irrational and emotional components. Life, according to these ideologies, defies rational explanation. Truth is elusive and ordinary minds are incapable of understanding anything in depth. What is needed is intuition, instinct, and emotion as the means of mobilizing and binding the masses. What is also needed is *action*: the simple and unambiguous assertion of one's power, force, and strength against all perceived corruption and evil. In a chaotic universe only the superior *will* can prevail. Political action—particularly of a violent nature—has value in and of itself: it is an exhibition of one's strength, an imposition of one's will, a demonstration of one's superiority. Violent action, in a word, is its own justification.

The ideas of irrationalism and activism drew heavily on a school of thought known as Social Darwinism, which sought to apply the teachings of Charles Darwin (1809–1882) to human society, national and international. Darwin had argued that the ability of organisms to adapt and survive depends on the possession of certain characteristics that make them most suitable to their environments, and that this adaptation in turn leads to a process of "natural selection." Misinterpreting Darwin, the Social Darwinists (for instance, the Englishman Herbert Spencer [1820–1903]) saw the world in terms of an "open struggle" in which there is "natural selection" leading to the "survival of the fittest." Both within and between nations, they maintained, it is the struggle for survival that leads to the selection of the best. The implications of Social Darwinism for racism and expansionism are rather clear, and they will be briefly discussed in the following section.

The ideas of irrationalism and activism also drew on the work of the French thinker Georges Sorel, who had stressed the importance of developing and propagating a social myth as a means of accomplishing one's objectives. Sorel's particular concern was the myth of the general strike as a means of improving the condition of the workers. Myth, according to Sorel, has no necessary foundation in reality; it is simply a statement of determination to undertake violent action, an emotional force inspiring and mobilizing the masses. Mussolini's "March on Rome" may well have been an expression of the Sorelian myth.

Nationalism, Racism, and Expansionism

Among the most prominent myths of fascism and nazism were those of nationalism, racism, and expansionism. The word *fasciare* means to bind or unite—and Mussolini sought to unite the people of Italy in search of a transcendent goal, namely, the revival of the glory of ancient Rome. Similarly, the two words *national* and *sozialistisch* had been combined by some German intellectuals in the early part of the twentieth century in an effort to incorporate the working classes into a harmonious nationalist and democratic state, thereby overcoming the Marxist doctrine of class struggle (see chapters 4 through 6). Hitler used (or misused) "national socialism" as a means of uniting and aggrandizing Germany at the expense of all "inferior" nations and peoples.

Racism was more a characteristic of nazism than of fascism. Strongly influencing Hitler were the writings of the Frenchman Arthur de Gobineau (1816–1882) and the Germanized Englishman Houston Stewart Chamberlain (1855–1927). These writers distinguished between the white, yellow, and black races, stressing the superiority of the first. Within the white race, they distinguished between the Semites (presumably a combination of white and black races), the Slavs (presumably a combination of white and yellow races), and the Aryans (presumably the pure white race). Thus generated, Hitler quickly embraced the myth of Aryan supremacy because it justified both anti-Semitism and expansionism.

Within a nation, it follows, being superior to Slavs and Semites, the Aryan race should subjugate—even eliminate—the former in the interest of racial purity.* Similarly, *between* nations, the Aryans are superior to all others and hence justified in subduing and conquering them. Consistent with Social Darwinism, conquest and victory in war were seen as concrete manifestations of national vitality and superiority. This expansionism was formally justified in the Nazi concept of *Lebensraum*: the perceived need for more "living space."

As for fascism, Mussolini's commitment to the idea of the superiority of the Italian people may have had an underlying racial rationale, but the idea was not openly and blatantly racist. Although Mussolini at times appealed to racial themes, these themes appeared to rest on cultural (not biological) foundations.

By the mid-1930s, Mussolini did come to adopt an anti-Semitic posture, but most likely he did so in order to ensure full alliance with Germany. While introducing anti-Semitic legislation, however, he quietly deplored the brazen racism of Hitler. And he had severe misgivings about the polarization that the race issue introduced in Fascist party circles.

Party and State

The irrationalism and emotionalism of fascism and nazism found expression in their glorification of the party and the state as well. Relying heavily on Hegelian philosophy, the Fascists considered the state as the embodiment of all that is morally, spiritually, and materially valuable. In fact, Mussolini equated fascism with a theory of the state. Hence, in "The Doctrine of Fascism," we read: "Everything is the State and nothing human or spiritual exists outside the State."

Such a state, it follows, monopolizes all power and authority. It becomes a gigantic corporation swallowing and controlling all other aspects of society: economy, industry, labor, capital, family, school, church, peer group—nothing is outside its grasp. The "corporate state" is the protector of individuals, their rights, their welfare, their security: it makes individuals what they are. Hence, there can be no rights or freedoms apart from the state. Individuals find freedom and fulfillment

---

*Anti-Semitism had another root as well: according to a popular interpretation of the times, Germany lost World War I not because of the superiority of its external enemies but because of the betrayal and treachery of some internal elements—the Jews, particularly, and the Marxists.

only in total submission to the state. Individuals, groups, nation, state—all constitute one integral whole.

Relying on another German philosopher, Johann von Herder (1744–1803), the Nazis fashioned the concept of the "folkish *(völkisch)* state," stressing the peculiar, primeval, racial qualities of the German people. The folkish state is an organic whole protecting, preserving, enhancing, and glorifying the quintessential traits of the Aryans—a "higher humanity," Hitler called them. Racism, in a word, became a definitional component of the Nazi state and nation.

The principal agent making possible the realization and fulfillment of the Fascist and Nazi states is the political party. The party is the supreme—indeed, the only—organization; all other parties and groups are outlawed, the media are silenced, freedoms are revoked. The party functions as the link between (1) the leader and the cadre (middle- and lower-level officials), (2) the leader and the rank and file, and (3) the leader and the general public.

The party is the sole decision-making organism. And in order to implement its decisions, special methods may be used. Such was the rationalization for the formation of such paramilitary units as Mussolini's Blackshirts and Hitler's Sturmabteilungen (the SA, the stormtrooper division) and Schutzstaffel (the SS, an elite guard and special police force).

Leader

The supreme person presiding over and guiding the state and the party was the leader: "Der Führer" in the case of Hitler; "Il Duce," in that of Mussolini. Hitler and Mussolini were in fact depicted as the very personifications of their respective nations. They were seen as having superhuman qualities of will, drive, ambition, vision, wisdom, and moral judgment. They supposedly possessed mystical gifts that enabled them to lead their countries toward ever higher goals. Their heroic deeds and actions, in turn, called for total quiescence on the part of their peoples.

The Fascist doctrine of leadership was heavily influenced by the work of Vilfredo Pareto (1848–1923) and Gaetano Mosca (1858–1941). Known as the "elitists," these writers argued, in general terms, that human society at all times has been characterized by a minority that rules and a majority that is ruled—that is, elite and mass. They interpreted politics in terms of violent conflicts among contending elites for the ruling positions in society, which conflicts, in turn, produce a constant "circulation of elites"—that is, one group overturning another. In this historical process, ordinary human beings are simply materials to be manipulated, duped, and used for elite goals and objectives.

The Nazi concept of leadership (*Führerprinzip*) drew on the ideas of Nietzsche and Richard Wagner (1813–1883), who glorified the great deeds of superhuman and all-conquering heroes. Leadership qualities, they maintained, are always inborn, not cultivated. Only a few possess these qualities, and they alone are in a position to compete for the top leadership roles. In the process, some are destroyed, the best prevail. The ultimate arbiters are will, power, force. And hence we come full circle back to the doctrines of irrationalism and activism.

Fascist and Nazi Use of Propaganda

The Fascists and the Nazis relied on the systematic use of propaganda to appeal to the Italian and German peoples. Propaganda is any organized attempt to manipulate the people, their outlooks and beliefs, through the use of words, messages, images, and acts. Propaganda is intended to build acceptance and support for a social movement by evoking appropriate attitudes, prejudices, and preferences.

The Fascists and the Nazis relied heavily on propaganda to publicize their ideas of irrationalism, activism, nationalism, and expansionism. They did everything to glorify the party, the state, and the infallible leader.

The Fascist Decalogue is the Ten Commandants of the Italian soldier under Mussolini. In the space of about half a page, the Decalogue captures the essence of Italian fascism, calling upon the soldier to do everything in the name of leader, country, discipline, obedience, and duty. It is a good example of political ideology turned into propaganda and tenets of action. The Decalogue was reissued periodically as a means of keeping its propaganda value fresh and alive. Here is the 1938 version:

>   1. Remember that those who fell for the revolution and for the empire march at the head of your columns.
>   2. Your comrade is your brother. He lives with you, thinks with you, and is at your side in the battle.

3. Service to Italy can be rendered at all times, in all places, and by every means. It can be paid with toil and also with blood.

4. The enemy of fascism is your enemy. Give him no quarter.

5. Discipline is the sunshine of armies. It prepares and illuminates the victory.

6. He who advances to the attack with decision has victory already in his grasp.

7. Conscious and complete obedience is the virtue of the Legionary.

8. There do not exist things important and things unimportant. There is only duty.

9. The Fascist revolution has depended in the past and still depends on the bayonets of its Legionaries.

10. Mussolini is always right.

The Nazis took a big step further by making explicit what is implicit in the Decalogue (Commandment 1): they promised immortality to those who sacrificed themselves for the party. The Nazi propaganda chief Joseph Paul Goebbels, himself a master of the use of oratory, developed the machinery for the Nazi use of propaganda. A story he particularly liked to use had to do with one Horst Wessel and the myth of his resurrection and return. First, a few facts about Wessel.

Born in 1907, Horst Wessel had a maladjusted and rebellious childhood and youth. Given to intense nationalism and anticommunism, he found the Nazi party an effective outlet for his feelings and sentiments. Soon, he became a minor party leader, tireless speaker, and composer of party songs. For these activities, he was admired and loved by his comrades. He was killed by a band of communists in questionable circumstances in 1930.

Capitalizing on Wessel's popularity, Goebbels transformed Wessel's inauspicious death into a deed of heroism and immortality. Let me quote from Professor Jay Baird, an expert on the Nazi use of propaganda (his article is listed in the bibliography for this chapter):

> During the years of the "period of struggle" in Weimar Germany, Goebbels was to give new meaning to the Nazis' irrational world view with his use of myths which served to cloak a brutal reality. The most effective of these myths grew out of the conditions of the political civil war waged by the paramilitary forces of Weimar Germany's most radi-

cal parties—the Nazis and the communists. The blood myth—which featured the death of a noble warrior, his resurrection, and ultimately his spiritual return to the fighting columns of Brown Shirts—was the most compelling theme of all, and it found its apotheosis in the saga of Horst Wessel.

The development of the myth of resurrection and return must be viewed against the background of Nazi ideology and practice. The epic of the fighting, dying warrior who through his sacrifice won not only glory but eternal life, struck a responsive chord in the period. Party leaders baptised their following in the blood of the fallen, and they inspired them with irrational motifs which, taken together, formed a coherent ideological structure.

In recent years, in connection with the rise of Islamic fundamentalism, much attention has been paid to some Islamic leaders who call upon the faithful to sacrifice themselves—literally to go to their deaths—in the greater cause of God and religion. Such a death is glorious in itself, we are told, in addition to guaranteeing the believer's way to heaven. We find a similar appeal in nazism, only in a secular form. Let me quote from Professor Baird again:

> Goebbels learned through his experiences as a graveside orator that through the proper use of propaganda, defeat can be transformed into victory. The homilies he delivered in Berlin cemeteries over the bodies of slain SA men celebrated the noble dead fighter theme, and occasioned an emotional response among those present which approached religious transcendence. Utilizing rhapsodic flights from reality, Goebbels merged Nazi myths with pagan warrior motifs, and shrouded the whole in the incense of mysticism.
>
> For Goebbels, it was insufficient to intone chants over the bodies of countless SA men. He was convinced that generalities do not move the masses; only easily identifiable symbols would serve such a purpose. The agony and death of Horst Wessel, killed by communists in the winter of 1930, was exactly the theme that the Gauleiter needed to offer his propaganda the unifying symbol it lacked.
>
> The Wessel mythology and liturgy were entirely Goebbels's conception and he approached the theme with great intensity. . . .
>
> Horst Wessel became the source of myth and legend, celebrated in poetry and song, biography and film, Party ritual and indoctrination. Town squares and streets were named after him, as were units of the German and Italian armed forces. Hitler named an SA section in his

honour, and his grave remained a Nazi shrine until 1945. He was revered as the composer of the Party anthem, the "Horst Wessel Song," and hailed as an exemplar of bravery, comradeship, love of country, and self-sacrifice for Führer, Volk, and Fatherland.

Totalitarianism—Right and Left

The word "totalitarianism" is of relatively recent origin. First used to describe Fascist Italy and Nazi Germany, the term was later broadened to include all Communist countries as well. Although differing in many ways among themselves (some theoretical, some practical), these regimes are labeled totalitarian because they have some things in common. Totalitarianism, in turn, differs from such older concepts as authoritarianism, dictatorship, despotism, and tyranny. For example, the kind of regime we have in Cuba is significantly different from the regime in pre–1994 Haiti. The same may be said of the regime on the mainland of China in contrast to the political system on the island of Taiwan. Let us begin by examining the commonalities.

Commonalities

Scholars have analyzed totalitarianism in various ways, but the two central and interrelated features of totalitarianism are ideology and organization. Every totalitarian regime has an ideology to which everyone is expected to subscribe. Every totalitarian regime is compartmentalized into a fine system of organization.

Now, of course, *every* society has ideology and organization. In totalitarian regimes, however, we encounter a particular type of ideology and a particular type of organization.

A third possible feature of totalitarianism deserves mention. All totalitarian regimes are identified with a particular type of personality: a Mussolini, a Hitler, a Lenin, a Stalin, a Mao, a Ho, a Castro. What are the characteristics of this personality type? What motivates or propels this personality? What kinds of circumstances are hospitable to it? Why do people rally around it?

While these topics have been studied in great detail in connection with individual leaders, no uniform or definitive answers have been uncovered. It is, of course, true that the aforementioned leaders emerged in times of national crisis or emergency, as our biographical sketches of Mussolini, Hitler, Lenin, and Mao demonstrate. However, it seems, the particular leader personality we have in mind is crucial to the *rise* of totalitarianism, not to its continuation. The experiences of Russia, China, Vietnam, and other countries amply support this point. The leaders who have followed Stalin, Mao, and Ho, for instance, have been quite bland and pragmatic by comparison. For this reason, we do not consider leader personality a *lasting* feature or requirement of totalitarianism. Moreover, the subjects of personality and leadership are much too large for us to investigate in this book.*

So, let us return to the two principal features of totalitarianism: ideology and organization. The ideology of a totalitarian regime is typically an "official ideology." One thinks of fascism as the official ideology of Mussolini's Italy, nazism as the official ideology of the Third Reich, and communism as the official ideology of Communist countries. By "official" I mean that the totalitarian ideology is the authoritative ideology, the formal ideology, the sole ideology. Totalitarian societies do not entertain competing ideologies. There is only one ideology; and every effort is made to persuade the people actively to identify with it and support it.

The official ideology has three identifiable components. First, it begins by criticizing and rejecting the existing order as corrupt, immoral, unjust, beyond hope, and beyond repair. The existing society must be smashed. The slate must be wiped clean. We must seek a new beginning.

Second, the denunciation of the existing system takes place through appeals to "higher" norms and principles. The totalitarian ideology proposes an alternative vision of a better, superior society. The alternative typically embodies a utopian vision or a grand myth—for example, the super race, or the classless society—that becomes a rallying cry for the masses.

Third, totalitarian ideology incorporates a statement of plans and programs intended to realize the alternative order. It seeks to relate specific patterns of action—both violent and nonviolent—to the realization of values and visions.

These components, it will be recalled, are found in all ideologies.

---

*The interested reader may consult M. Rejai and K. Phillips, *Loyalists and Revolutionaries: Political Leaders Compared* (New York: Praeger Publishers, 1988).

What distinguishes totalitarian ideology is the extremism and fanaticism with which these components are stated and pursued.

Given the foregoing features, it does not come as a surprise that totalitarian ideology is all-comprehensive, all-pervasive, all-encompassing. Totalitarian ideology presumes to have an answer for any problem or contingency one may confront. Totalitarian ideology is rigid and inflexible. Claiming infallibility, totalitarian ideology becomes mystical and magical in nature. Totalitarian ideology is intolerant, demands total conformity, and seeks total control.

The demand for conformity and control is assured by the second major feature of totalitarianism: organization. Totalitarian societies are strictly hierarchical, compartmentalized, organized from top to bottom. Dominated usually by one man, *political* organization (the party) reaches out from the center and penetrates the entire country. *Social* organization is perpetuated by youth groups, professional groups, cultural groups, sports groups, and the like. Government and military bureaucracies, respectively, are emplaced in *civil* and *military* organizations. *Paramilitary* organization is pervasive in the form of the secret police. *Information* is effectively monopolized through the control of all media of communication: television, radio, the press.

Needless to say, the political party is the master organization, shaping and controlling all other organizations, particularly in Communist regimes. Accordingly, the organization of the party deserves special attention.

The basic principles of Communist party organization were laid down by Lenin in a 1902 pamphlet titled *What Is to Be Done?* These principles remain intact up to this day. How is the generic Communist party set up?

Like any organization, the Communist party is set up on the principle of the pyramid, or the hierarchy, which is notable for its rigidity. At the head of the organization stands the National Party Congress (to which we shall return momentarily). Then come, in descending order, state party organization, county party organization, and municipal party organization. Below this, at the very lowest level, are the so-called "primary party organizations," also known as communist cells. This means that in every shop, every office, every store, every restaurant, a small group of party members (as few as three, four, or five) meet on a regular basis to ensure that party policy is observed throughout the land and that violations are appropriately treated.

In this scheme of organization, as in all others, the lines of authority run downwards, the lines of responsibility run upwards. But here all relationships are rigid and absolute: every higher level has complete authority over every lower level; every lower level has complete responsibility to every higher level. So, for instance, if a policy issue is to be determined at any level, the higher level will propose Alternatives A, B, and C, and then call upon the lower level to choose among them. Now, needless to say, the three alternatives are equally acceptable to the higher level. The Communist party creates the illusion that there is "participation" and "democracy" at all levels. As a matter of fact, Lenin called this scheme "democratic centralism."

Now, let us return to the top of the pyramid. How is the National Party Congress constituted? Since members at each lower level "elect" representatives to each high level, members at the state level elect representatives to the national level, thus forming the National Party Congress, or NPC. This will be a body of, say, 1,000 members in our generic Communist party. What our organizational principle has done so far is to take a country of, say, 100 million people and reduce it to the will of 1,000.

But this is only the beginning. For one thing, the NPC typically convenes once every four years to establish broad party policy. (In fact, it may go without meeting for years.) For another, a deliberative body of 1,000 people is entirely unwieldy.

So, the NPC delegates authority for the day-to-day running of the country to a Central Committee consisting of, say, 100 regular members and 100 alternates. The Central Committee is a government within (or should we say, outside of) the government: it has its own agriculture bureau, industry bureau, housing bureau, education bureau, and the like. The most important unit is the Political Bureau, or Politburo: this is the body that establishes party policy for all other bureaus. And what is the membership of the Politburo? About two dozen people, usually all male.

Now, anyone who has been a member of any organization knows that a deliberative body of twenty-four cannot be either manageable or effective; the optimum committee size is five or seven members. Accordingly, the Politburo creates its own Standing Committee, consisting of half a dozen members and dominated by the chief leader. And there it is: the Standing Committee of the Politburo of the Central Committee of the National Congress of the Communist party—the effective decision maker for a whole country.

As we can see, then, totalitarian regimes are single-centered regimes: all power and authority radiates from a small decision-making
body at the very top of the party. Totalitarian regimes seek *total* control of all aspects of society. (They do not, however, *achieve* total
control. The family and the church have always escaped totalitarian
control, becoming "islands of separateness" in totalitarian regimes.) As
such, totalitarianism differs from such older concepts as authoritarianism, despotism, dictatorship, or tyranny. For one thing, authoritarianism seeks limited—typically political—control. Totalitarianism seeks
"total" control: political, social, economic, religious. For another, totalitarian regimes are, at least initially, mass mobilization regimes: significant portions of the population actively identify with the movements.
In contrast, authoritarianism seeks only pacified and submissive populations. Finally, totalitarian regimes seek complete *reconstruction* of
man and society. Authoritarian regimes attempt simply to rule over
man and society.

Differences

Scholars have distinguished two types of totalitarianism: that of the
right (nazism and fascism) and that of the left (communism). Although they share the ideological and organizational features discussed above, the two differ in some respects. Right totalitarianism
has been associated with relatively advanced societies (Germany,
Italy), left totalitarianism with relatively undeveloped countries
(Russia, China). This difference in turn is related to the social base
of totalitarianism. Right totalitarianism draws its popular base principally from the middle class (which seeks to maintain the status
quo and advance its own social position), whereas left totalitarianism relies primarily upon the lower class (which seeks egalitarianism). Moreover, right totalitarianism is outspokenly racist and
elitist, whereas left totalitarianism is presumably nonracist and non-
elitist. I say "presumably," because (1) ethnic minorities did in fact
suffer discrimination under communist regimes, and (2) while right
totalitarianism rests on the cult of the hero, left totalitarianism proclaims a belief in "collective leadership." In practice, however, the
cults of Stalin and Mao have been as pronounced as those of Hitler
and Mussolini.

A final difference lies in the role of terror and violence in the two types of totalitarian societies. Left totalitarianism comes to power through massive exercise of violence and terror and the elimination of all opponents—political, social, military, economic—in short order. Therefore, terror and violence tend to level off or actually decrease as left totalitarian regimes continue in power.* By contrast, rather than eliminating their opponents outright, right totalitarian regimes (particularly the Nazis) created a system of dual elites in which the old leaders continued to exist side by side with (but were subordinated to) the new leaders. In other words, the old elites continued to pose as sources of threat and vulnerability. Accordingly, the level of terror and violence stayed constant or actually increased in those regimes. Right totalitarian regimes attempted to deflect attention from their vulnerability and insecurity by scapegoating the Jews or by undertaking expansive foreign policies or both. In so doing, they paved the way for their own eventual demise, whereas until recently left totalitarian regimes continued to flourish.

Having examined the totalitarianism of the Fascist and Nazi varieties, we turn to an examination of the Communist experience in the next three chapters. Before doing so, however, we should check the fit between these two ideologies and the analytical framework proposed in chapter 1.

The Framework Applied

The cognitive dimension of fascism and nazism views the world in terms of a permanent struggle involving individuals, nations, and states. In such a world, will, power, strength, and force become indispensable for asserting oneself, one's nation, and one's state—and demonstrating superiority at all levels. Violence needs no other justification.

In some respects, the affective and evaluative components of fascism and nazism overlap to such an extent that it is difficult to separate them. Nationalism—the promised restoration of national greatness, pride, and honor—constitutes an irresistible value that is laden with equally irresistible emotional appeal.

Racism—whether biological or cultural—has quite similar charac-

---

*Stalin's "Great Purge" of the 1930s constitutes a glaring exception, and it has been attributed to his pathological personality rather than to the needs of the Soviet system.

teristics. In the 1920s and the 1930s, for example, it was apparently easy for many Germans to compensate for the humiliation of defeat by embracing the myth of Aryan supremacy and scapegoating the Jews.

Another aspect of the evaluative dimension is the glorification of the state—whether "corporate" or "folkish"—as the repository of all that is good and valuable. Similar attributes are associated with the party. And insofar as the superhuman leader-hero stands at the apex of both the party and the state—indeed, insofar as he personifies them—he assumes the highest value. Accordingly, total obedience and submission to the party/state/leader become values in themselves.

The programmatic component of fascism and nazism has two principal aspects. Internally, the party/state/leader launches a program of purifying the society of the "undesirable" elements and of improving the condition of the "desirable" ones. Externally, the party/state/leader embarks upon a policy of expansionism and imperialism in order to conquer other lands and acquire fresh "living space." The heroic deeds of the leader must find concrete expression at both the national and the international levels.

The social base of fascism and nazism is necessarily limited to the loyalists—to disciplined and slavish followers, to those of presumed cultural or racial purity, to the insecure members of the middle and lower classes. Fascism and nazism made systematic efforts to identify friends to be cultivated and enemies to be eliminated. Nothing came in between.

Selected Bibliography

Abel, Theodore. *The Nazi Movement.* New York: Atherton Press, 1965.

Adorno, T. W., et al. *The Authoritarian Personality.* New York: Harper and Brothers, 1950.

Arendt, Hannah. *The Origins of Totalitarianism.* New York: Harcourt, Brace, 1951.

Baird, Jay W. "Goebbels, Horst Wessel, and the Myth of Resurrection and Return." *Journal of Contemporary History* 17 (October 1982): 633–50.

Bracher, Karl D. *The German Dictatorship.* New York: Praeger, 1970.

Bullock, Alan. *Hitler: A Study in Tyranny.* New York: Harper & Row, 1964.

Cohen, Carl, ed. *Communism, Fascism, and Democracy.* 2d ed. New York: Random House, 1972.

De Felice, Renzo. *Fascism: An Informal Introduction to Its Theory and Practice.* New Brunswick, N.J.: Transaction Books, 1976.

Erickson, Erik H. "The Legend of Hitler's Childhood." In *Childhood and Society.* 1950. Reprint. New York: Norton, 1963.

Fest, Joachim C. *Hitler.* New York: Random House, 1975.

Finer, Herman. *Mussolini's Italy*. London: Victor Gollanez, 1935.

Friedrich, Carl J., ed. *Totalitarianism*. Cambridge, Mass.: Harvard University Press, 1954.

Friedrich, Carl J., and Zbigniew Brzezinski. *Totalitarian Dictatorship and Autocracy*. 2d ed. New York: Praeger, 1965.

Fromm, Erich. *Escape from Freedom*. New York: Holt, 1941.

Gregor, A. James. *Italian Fascism and Developmental Dictatorship*. Princeton, N.J.: Princeton University Press, 1980.

————. *Young Mussolini and the Intellectual Origins of Fascism*. Berkeley: University of California Press, 1979.

Hitler, Adolf. *Mein Kampf*. Boston: Houghton Mifflin, 1962.

Langer, Walter C. *The Mind of Adolf Hitler*. New York: New American Library, 1978.

Merkl, Peter H. *The Making of a Stormtrooper*. Princeton, N.J.: Princeton University Press, 1979.

————. *Political Violence under the Swastika*. Princeton, N.J.: Princeton University Press, 1975.

Mosse, George L. *The Crisis of German Ideology: Intellectual Origins of the Third Reich*. New York: Grosset, 1964.

Mussolini, Benito. "The Doctrine of Fascism." Reprinted in *Communism, Fascism, and Democracy*, ed. by Carl Cohen. 2d ed. New York: Random House, 1972.

Neumann, Franz. *Behemoth: The Structure and Practice of National Socialism*. New York: Octagon Books, 1963.

Nolte, Ernst. *Three Faces of Fascism*. New York: New American Library, 1969.

Payne, Robert. *The Life and Death of Adolf Hitler*. New York: Popular Library, 1974.

Schapiro, Leonard. *Totalitarianism*. New York: Praeger, 1972.

Shirer, William L. *The Rise and Fall of the Third Reich*. New York: Touchstone Books, 1981.

Smith, Denis Mack. *Mussolini*. New York: Knopf, 1982.

Sorel, Georges. *Reflections on Violence*. 1906. Reprint. New York: Collier Books, 1961.

Speer, Albert. *Inside the Third Reich*. New York: Macmillan, 1981.

Toland, John. *Adolf Hitler*. New York: Ballantine Books, 1977.

Trevor-Roper, H. R. *The Last Days of Hitler*. New York: Macmillan, 1981.

Woolf, S. J., ed. *Fascism in Europe*. Rev. ed. New York: Methuen, 1982.

4

Marxism

Socialism, Marxism, Communism, and Capitalism: An Introduction

We now turn from the right-wing totalitarianism of the Fascist and Nazi variety to the left-wing totalitarianism that is associated with Marx and the communists. Marxism is a variety of socialism. Communism is a variety of socialism. Socialism, in other words, is a generic concept of which Marxism and communism are expressions. In this and the following two chapters, we will focus on the socialism of Marx and then the changes that were introduced by Vladimir Lenin in Russia, Mao Tse-tung in China, Ho Chi Minh in Vietnam, and Fidel Castro in Cuba. Our coverage will be cumulative, each chapter building on materials covered in the previous chapter.

The world "socialism" is relatively new, first used in England in the 1820s. The word "communism" first appeared in France in the 1830s, when it referred to secret, underground societies. The pivotal figure in the evolution of socialism is Karl Marx. But socialism does not begin and end with Marx. There is socialism before Marx and there is socialism after Marx.

In the interest of precision, one should note that "Marx" is often a shorthand for Karl Marx and Friedrich Engels (1820–1895). Having met in 1844, the two men maintained a lifelong collaboration until Marx's death in 1883. They had an intellectual division of labor, Engels concentrating on the philosophical aspects of "dialectical materialism" and Marx on its practical applications.

Marx and Engels claimed to have founded "scientific" socialism by

78

focusing on the hard facts of reality, namely, the economic structure of societies and the social formations (that is, social classes) to which they give rise. Note, however, that this is only a claim, unsubstantiated in reality. As we shall see, there is, strictly speaking, very little that is scientific about Karl Marx. Instead, there is a great deal of moral outrage and moral indictment.

Before Marx, there are many kinds of socialism. There are, among others, guild socialism, trade union socialism, agrarian socialism, anarchistic socialism, Christian socialism, and Jewish socialism. Marx and Engels lumped all of these socialisms together and labeled them pre-scientific or "utopian" socialism. (Engels wrote a pamphlet called *Socialism: Utopian and Scientific.*) These socialist thinkers, Marx and Engels charged, were visionaries or daydreamers, writing about imaginary places and situations.*

Now, as it turns out, one pre-Marxist socialist did try to put socialism into actual practice. This is the Englishman Robert Owen (1771–1858). When he inherited his father's textile manufacturing business in 1800, he tried to show that one could be a capitalist and still care about one's workers, their wages, their working conditions, their education, their welfare. Stressing sharing and cooperation, Owen's experimental community, New Lanark, was a resounding success.

Then Owen got the idea that perhaps one could create a similar community in the United States as well. Having traveled to America in the 1820s, he tried to set up the New Harmony community in Southeast Indiana. But, as you might imagine, conditions in the United States, where emphasis was placed on competition and rugged individualism, were not conducive to socialism. New Harmony failed. But Owen had already established, in principle, that he was not a "utopian" in the Marx-Engels sense of the word.†

In any event, *before* Marx we have the utopian socialists. *After* Marx, the socialist movement breaks into two major schools, or streams. On the one hand, we have thinkers and activists who claim to

---

*The word *utopia* is from the Greek *ou topos*, meaning, quite literally, "no place" or, better yet, no real place. Thus, Thomas More's *Utopia* deals with ideal forms of politics and society on an imaginary island. Samuel Butler titled his utopian book *Erehwon*, which is nowhere spelled backwards.

†Other important pre-Marxist socialists include the Frenchmen Charles Fourier (1772–1837) and Pierre Joseph Proudhon (1809–1865), and the Swiss Jean Charles Sismondi (1773–1842).

be (I am choosing my words deliberately to convey a point) orthodox
Marxists, that is to say, they follow Marx's line (the teaching, the
tradition established by Marx) in an undeviating fashion. They represent revolutionary socialist movements that stress rapid, cataclysmic
change, and that culminate in totalitarian regimes and governments.
Examples include socialism in Russia, China, Vietnam, Cuba, and
other countries.

On the other hand, there are thinkers and activists who claim to be
revisionist or reformist Marxists, that is to say, they make important
changes and modifications in the teachings of Marx. They represent
evolutionary socialist movements that stress gradual change, and that
culminate in democratic regimes. Examples include socialism in Sweden, Britain, France, Greece, and almost every other Western European country.

This, then, is a quick sketch of the evolution of socialism over the
last two centuries. We have mentioned many forms of socialism: guild,
anarchistic, agrarian, Christian, Marxist, orthodox, totalitarian, reformist, democratic, and more. In other words, the one common denomina-
tor—or irreducible core—of all these movements is *socialism*. That is
what they all share. What, then, is that irreducible core or kernel? What
is socialism?

The irreducible constituents of socialism, in its pure form, are three
in number. I will list them. I will compare them to the corresponding
principles of capitalism, again as an ideal type, so as to facilitate understanding.

The primary value of socialism is equality; the primary value of
capitalism, liberty. But this is in ideal form. In practice, socialism
allows for liberty just as capitalism allows for equality. In particular,
socialism believes in relative equality in the realm of economics; not in
absolute equality and not in any and all fields. Socialism does not say
that we are all equal in appreciation of art and culture—only that we
should have equal opportunity to cultivate our artistic and cultural
sensibilities. Translated into social policy, the principle of relative economic egalitarianism means that all individuals in a society should
enjoy a minimal level of material welfare; that individuals—old and
young, man and woman—should not die of malnutrition, hunger, cold,
or disease.

Why should this be the case? Because socialism believes that every
individual has a fundamental human dignity, and that individuals in a

given society are all bound together by a system of moral reciprocity. Morality bids us help each other.

The second principle of socialism is communalism. That is to say, socialism stresses the welfare of the community as a whole and the cooperation of individual members in reaching the communal goal. This is a natural extension of the idea of moral reciprocity.

Where socialism stresses communalism, capitalism stresses individualism (or corporatism). And where socialism stresses cooperation, capitalism stresses competition. Competition, capitalism teaches, will bring out the best in individuals, in addition to allowing them to maximize their own welfare. Welfare of the individuals, moreover, coincides with or culminates in the welfare of society as a whole. So that, to recall a common cliché, "What is good for General Motors is good for the country."

The operative difference between socialism and capitalism in this regard is that socialism has an organic view of the community in which the whole is greater than the sum of the individual members. By contrast, capitalism has a mechanistic view of the society in which the whole is merely a summation of the individual parts.

Following from the first two principles, the third principle of socialism is communal ownership and control of major sources of national wealth in the interest of the community as a whole. The corresponding principle in capitalism is, needless to say, private ownership and control of either an individual or corporate nature. The socialist position in this regard has been that the interest of the community as a whole can only be guaranteed through the community's control of its own wealth.

These principles, I repeat, are ideal types. In practice, they have undergone many changes. For example, capitalism has modified its emphasis on liberty by providing a measure of equality through the so-called welfare state, even in the United States since 1936. Such welfare measures as Social Security, Medicare, Medicaid, and aid to education enhance the relative equality of people availing themselves of those services; they suggest a measure of social responsibility and moral concern.

Correspondingly, socialism has modified the principle of public ownership and control in rather drastic ways. In recent years, socialist governments everywhere have moved away from the idea of public ownership, stressing instead the importance of private ownership and control. This is in part a self-protective measure and an effort to as-

assuage popular fears of big government under socialism. In any event, as we can see, in practice capitalism has been moving toward socialism and socialism has been moving toward capitalism.

These, then, are the core, or the constituent, elements of socialism. As ideologies, Marxist socialism, democratic socialism, and totalitarian socialism (or communism) are alike only in that they have these three principles in common. Beyond this, these three ideologies differ in many ways. They differ in their interpretation of society and history. They differ in their strategy and tactics of reaching power. And they differ in the policies they would implement after coming to power.

As far as strategy and tactics are concerned, for instance, the main differences are these: Marxist socialists argue that a socialist society will come about only through a spontaneous revolutionary upheaval. Democratic socialists reject the idea of revolution, stressing instead piecemeal and peaceful social change. Totalitarian socialists retain the idea of revolution but argue that a revolution will never come about spontaneously, that without leadership and organization there can be no revolution. Organization and leadership, as we shall see, are quintessentially Leninist concepts; therefore, it is only after we add Lenin to Marx that we get communism. In any event, these are three distinct ideologies that should not be lumped together.

Before we turn to an examination of the major ideas of Karl Marx, it would be helpful to place him in the context of the times in which he lived.

Marx and His Times

Karl Marx was born in 1818 in the city of Trier to a moderately well-to-do family. His father, a lawyer by profession, was of Jewish origin but had converted to Protestantism, a religion Marx shared in his early youth.

At age seventeen, Marx went to study in Bonn and Berlin, finally receiving a doctorate in philosophy from the University of Jena in 1841 at the age of twenty-three. Having returned to Bonn in search of a teaching post, he found the doors closed because of both his Jewish name and the reputation he had developed as an atheist, radical, and subversive.

German universities at this time were hotbeds of intellectual and political activity, in which Marx had become totally immersed. Most of the intellectual ferment surrounded the ideas of the renowned philosopher G. W. F. Hegel, which drew both intense opposition and intense support.

Hegel's philosophy is too complicated to go into here. Suffice it to say, in highly oversimplified terms, that he was an idealist who (1) stressed the importance of spiritual and cultural forces and ideas in human history, (2) glorified the idea of the state as the embodiment of the highest spiritual force, which he called *Geist*, or universal spirit, and (3) generally defended and justified the status quo whether in religion, politics, or culture. (More about Hegel later in this chapter.)

Marx devoted much time and effort to mastering Hegel's philosophical system, at the end only to transform and transcend it. As an intellectual "leftist" and "radical," he set out to set Hegel "right side up" or, alternatively, to "put him on his feet."

Meanwhile, in 1842, Marx turned to journalism, first as a writer for, and subsequently as editor of, a major daily newspaper in Bonn. He used this post to expound his ideas on freedom of the press, religion, and the like, and to write exposés on the conditions of poor and exploited people in the area (for example, the vineyard workers). As might be expected, Marx's journalism did not sit well with the authorities, who suppressed his newspaper in 1843.

Marx then emigrated to Paris, where he first met Friedrich Engels, a wealthy German industrialist who worked and lived in England. During his Paris years, Marx studied the works of English economists as well as of French and Russian socialists and anarchists. He also came into direct contact with the squalid conditions of urban workers, which further intensified his radicalism, and his newly intensified radicalism found expression in his journalistic activities. In 1845, the Paris authorities, having decided that his contributions to a Franco-German journal were subversive, expelled him.

Marx moved to Brussels, where there was a fairly large German émigré group, only to face yet another expulsion within a few years. Meanwhile, he had come into contact with the leaders of the League of the Just, later renamed the Communist League, an organization heavily involved in the working-class movement. In order to provide the league with an ideological and philosophical perspective, Marx and Engels drafted the *Communist Manifesto* in 1848, calling for worldwide revolution to overthrow the ruling classes and bring about a new age of peace and brotherhood.

n 1849, Marx began his exile in London, where he lived the balance of his life. There, he gained fresh exposure to the wretched condition of the working classes and the oppression and exploitation under which they lived. This experience further documented and justified the depiction of the dismal lives of the English lower classes in Engels's *Condition of the Working Classes in England*, published in 1845.

Marx devoted the rest of his life to participating in radical activity, writing trenchant critiques of capitalism as an exploitative and inhuman economic system, and expounding the need for worldwide revolution. He did all this in the midst of either outright poverty or financial mismanagement. Three of Marx's children died for lack of food and medicine, and the whole family lived in a constant state of fear and anxiety.

Marx's wife, Jenny, to whom he was devoted from early youth, came from an aristocratic background, and in the 1870s, the family's financial situation improved when she came into a substantial inheritance. The physical condition of both Marx and his wife soon began to deteriorate, however. Jenny's death in 1881 was a blow from which Marx never recovered. He died two years later, in 1883.

The Ideas of Marx

Since Marx wrote so prodigiously (some fifty volumes), we cannot possibly do justice to all aspects of his thinking. We can, however, cover the broad outlines of his intellectual concerns by focusing on a controversy that has raged in Marxian scholarship for quite some time. This controversy surrounds the periodization of Marx's writings and the issues of continuity or discontinuity that ensue therefrom.

Briefly, one group of scholars argues that the beginning of Marx's collaboration with Engels in 1845 marked a sharp departure from his earlier concerns. According to this group, there is a "young," or "humanist," Marx, and a "mature," or "revolutionary," Marx, and the two are quite separate and distinct.

A second group of scholars stresses the continuity of Marx's thought, denying that the older Marx abandoned his youthful intellectual pursuits. According to this group, there is only one Marx who undergoes a process of intellectual development, restating the same basic themes while using different modes of expression.

After we have examined the thought of Young Marx and of Mature Marx, we shall return to an evaluation of this controversy.

Young Marx

The main source for understanding the Young Marx is his book titled *The Economic and Philosophical Manuscripts of 1844*, also known as the Paris Manuscripts (since Marx lived in Paris at the time). This work remained undiscovered until 1927. A German edition was published in 1933, an English (London) edition in 1963, and an American edition in 1966. This publication chronology may explain in part why some scholars are unfamiliar with the Young Marx. But given that an English edition has been available since 1963, lack of familiarity with the Young Marx becomes puzzling. Accordingly, one suspects, a main reason for the obscurity of the Paris Manuscripts is that they put Marx in a good light. He emerges as a humane or humanist philosopher, in sharp contrast to his more usual image as the bearded revolutionary.

Here as elsewhere Marx's elemental concern is human productive activity. Before we do anything else, Marx maintains, we human beings are creative and productive. Even our most routine activities (such as meeting as a class) require the collective efforts of those who created the classroom and the blackboard, as well as those who provide the light, the heat, and the chalk. In this process of productivity, we interact with ourselves (that is, with our physical and intellectual powers), with other humans (since we are not isolated beings), and with nature (as the source of the raw materials we need). In short, Marx's understanding of productive activity has many dimensions, but it is central to everything he has to say. Moreover, Marx seeks to know what happens to human creativity in various kinds of societies. Under what conditions, for example, is productive activity turned into oppression, exploitation, and alienation? So, the Young Marx is a romantic Marx, a philosophical Marx, an idealist Marx, who advances a series of propositions concerning human productive activity as it is and human productive activity as it ought to be. In juxtaposing the ideal and the real, he will be interested in exploring how one might go about changing the real in order to bring it closer to the ideal—the real as an approximation of the ideal.

The Young Marx is a complicated man, indeed. But I will try to summarize his arguments in terms of four central propositions.

Proposition 1

The human condition is a condition of labor, productivity, and creativity. Human beings, says Marx, are potentially wise, creative, and free. Human beings are by nature driven to creativity. We *must* work. We *must* labor. We *must* produce.

Now, everything in this whole argument is contingent upon understanding what Marx means by "labor" or "work." For Marx, labor is not holding a job. It is not making a living. It is not a nine to five. It is not a chore. It is not drudgery.

Labor is not just an aspect of human life. Labor, as Marx sees it, is the *whole* of life. Labor is the essence of human personality. One expresses oneself in one's labor. One realizes oneself in one's labor. One objectifies oneself in one's labor. One lives one's life in one's labor. Labor is any human activity, manual or intellectual. Digging ditches, painting landscapes, writing music—these are all expressions of human labor and human personality. In a word, labor is human fulfillment.

One need not be a Marxist in order to have such a conception of human labor. Pope John Paul II, for example, issued an encyclical in 1981 titled "On Human Work." (Encyclicals are periodic papal statements on the pressing issues of the day.) In this document, the Pope says:

> Through work man must earn his daily bread and contribute to the continual advance of science and technology and, above all, to elevating unceasingly the cultural and moral level of the society within which he lives in community with those who belong to the same family.
>
> And work means any activity by man, whether manual or intellectual, whatever its nature or circumstances, it means any human activity that can and must be recognized as work, in the midst of all the many activities of which man is capable and to which he is predisposed by his very nature, by virtue of humanity itself. Man is made to be in the visible universe an image and likeness of God Himself, and he is placed in it in order to subdue the earth. From the beginning therefore he is called to work.
>
> Work is one of the characteristics that distinguish man from the rest of creatures, whose activity for sustaining their lives cannot be called work. Only man is capable of work, and only man works, at the same time by work occupying his existence on earth. Thus work bears a

particular mark of man and of humanity, the mark of a person operating within a community of persons. And this mark decides its interior characteristics; in a sense it constitutes its very nature. . . .

Man's life is built up every day from work, from work it derives its specific dignity, but at the same time work contains the unceasing measure of human toil and suffering, and also of the harm and injustice which penetrate deeply into social life within individual nations and on the international level.

Proposition 2

Ideally, human work should be voluntary or spontaneous. If it is the case, as Proposition 1 argues, that labor is the essence of human personality, then it follows that human beings should have the opportunity to labor as they please. In other words, Proposition 1 states that labor is an expression of human personality; Proposition 2 modifies Proposition 1 to read, labor is the *voluntary* expression of human personality. In a famous passage in another work (*The German Ideology*, written with Friedrich Engels, 1845), Marx says that ideally human beings should have the freedom to fish in the morning, hunt in the afternoon, and read drama in the evening without having to be either fishermen or hunters or drama critics. (Now, this proposition raises all kinds of problems, but we will turn to an evaluation of Marx shortly.)

Proposition 3

In reality, however, human labor has never been voluntary, spontaneous, or free. Throughout history, work has involved compulsion and force. Throughout history, the potentially creative person has been oppressed, exploited, and brutalized. Throughout history, human creativity has led to human alienation. Instead of finding fulfillment in free and spontaneous labor, everywhere human beings have been alienated in compulsion and force.

Here we are, face to face with Marx's conception of alienation developed about a century and a half ago. When we use the word alienation, we generally mean estrangement or separation, as in, for example, from society. Marx uses the concept of alienation in a far more sophisticated fashion and at four levels. In the first place, he argues, human beings are alienated from the *activity* of their own labor, from what it is that they do, from the physical or intellectual energy they expend. One is set apart from oneself. One is alienated from oneself.

But why? Because, Marx responds, human work is no longer free and spontaneous. Because compulsion, force, oppression, and exploitation literally dehumanize man. (Note the philosophical fancy footwork: to be human is to work voluntarily. It follows, then, that as soon as voluntarism is taken away, human beings are, in the most literal sense, dehumanized.)

Second, says Marx, one is alienated from the *products* of one's labor. The products of our labor everywhere surround us but they appear strange and foreign to us. From the most sublime and towering achievement to the most mundane activities, the results of our work strike us as alien and hostile.

But why should this be the case? Because, in part, argues Marx, these products are not the outcome of voluntary labor; they are the products of forced labor. In consequence, we are no longer creative beings. We do what we are told to do: tighten a bolt here, a screw there. We have become appendages to the factory, the assembly line, and the machine. We have become a tool of our own tools. The division of labor destroys human creativity.

Moreover, according to Marx, we are alienated from the products of our labor because, presented on the open market, these products assume the form of money, profit, and greed. And no one has more contempt for money than Karl Marx. Capitalism, he sneers, is the "religion of money worship."

Third, Marx argues, we are alienated from the society in which we live. Human beings live in societies and interact with other human beings. But society now consists of a collection of dehumanized and alienated human beings engaged in forced labor. All human beings everywhere are alienated, according to Marx, only some are unconscious of this state of alienation.

Fourth, human beings are alienated from nature. Human beings interact with nature, they use nature's resources to augment life, and they tame nature. But we are not supposed to exploit, pillage, or despoil nature. We are not supposed to dissipate our natural resources in a wasteful fashion as, for example, in strip mining or in the building of products with built-in obsolescence or self-destruction.

So, to summarize, according to Marx's idealist argument, we are alienated from the activity of our labor, from the products of our labor, from the society in which we live, and from nature. Overall, then, we confront a fundamental disjunction, an elemental chasm between human essence and human existence. Human essence is one of voluntary and spontaneous creativity. Human existence is one of forced and alienated labor. The human condition is one of servitude and bondage.

Proposition 4

Our experience of bondage and alienation, Marx argues, can be broken only through a radical transformation of the social conditions under which we live. In this context, Marx talks about "communist action" and "communist revolution"—"communist" in the sense of man's attempt to end his experience of alienation, to return to his original self, to rehumanize himself.

According to Marx, once upon a time we lived as human beings in a state of voluntary, free, and creative labor. Then came private property, economic systems, and greed; and they dehumanized us. The task now is to recapture our original self, to undergo a process of rehumanization. "Communism" for Marx is man seeking community with his true and original nature—with his old self. Man seeks reunion with himself, a religious experience. And all of this can be accomplished by the simple act of abolishing private property. If private property is the equivalent of the original sin, as Marx believes, then the abolition of private property is sure to lead to a state of personal and social salvation.

Marx announces triumphantly: "Communism is the riddle of history solved, and it knows itself to be this solution."

Before evaluating Young Marx, we should examine some of the implications of the argument we have just considered. For one thing, you can see why some people have labeled Marx's thinking "godless theology." Marx tells a story that has certain parallels with the Bible—human innocence, sin, fall, suffering, salvation, redemption. The major difference being that for Marx, man is God. So, he says: "The criticism of religion ends with the precept that the supreme being for man is man." Elsewhere he says: "The foundation of the criticism of religion is this. Man makes religion, religion does not make man."

Although Marx speaks of human nature and human essence (in terms of voluntary creativity), he does not see human beings as isolated. In fact, he refers to us as "species beings"—we are all members of the same race. For practical purposes, then, we live in societies. We are social beings, creatures of the society in which we live. We are malleable, we change from one society to another. But insofar as for Marx the most important aspect of any society is its economic foundation, human beings are economic beings. We are a reflection of the economic system in which we find ourselves—feudal, capitalist, or communist. Accordingly, to change human beings, one should change the economic conditions under which they live. For this reason, communist countries can claim that they have created a new society and, literally, a new human being.

As for an evaluation of the Young Marx, we can simply ask: are all human beings wise, good, creative, and productive? If that is the case, then where and how do oppression, exploitation, and alienation come about? (Marx argues that we are all alienated, only some of us are not aware of it.) Does Marx have a preemptive definition of labor? And is all work creative and fulfilling?

How do we reconcile the need for individual creativity (to fish, to hunt, etc.) with the need for social order, especially in the larger and more complex societies? Is division of labor destructive of human creativity (as Marx argued) or is it an essential aspect of social integration (as Emile Durkheim believed)?

In short, Marx's argument is attractive—perhaps even beguiling—but the practical problems associated with it are too serious to be ignored.

Mature Marx

The centerpiece of Mature Marx's thought is his "materialist interpretation (or conception) of history." Friedrich Engels called it "dialectical materialism." Dialectic means conflict. Materialism refers to economic forces or classes. Therefore, in simplified terms, dialectical materialism is about class conflict. But let us pause for a moment. In order to understand Marx's conception of history one must first grasp three things:

1. Marx's conception of social reality in general, which we have discussed in another context in chapter 1;

2. Marx's conception of reality in relation to Hegel's; and

3. Marx's conception of value.

As we saw in chapter 1, Marx sees society as consisting of two dimensions: a substructure and a superstructure. The substructure or foundation, by far the most important dimension, consists of the economic structure of society, defined in terms of ownership of private property. Accordingly, in every society there is an owning class, which is small, and a nonowning class, which consists of the large masses of people. The owning class is also the ruling class, the oppressor class, the exploiting class, while the nonowning class is also the ruled class, the oppressed class, the exploited class. The germ of conflict, in other words, lies in private property.

Now, Marx makes two crucial statements about the substructure: (1) it is the most important, although not the only force in society, and (2) it gives rise to a superstructure that consists of everything else in a society. So that the culture of a society, the art of a society, the religion of a society, the social and political institutions and practices of a society, these are all determined by the substructure of a society—that is to say, by the dominant, ruling class in that society. In other words, the ruling class invents, propagates, and utilizes art, culture, politics, ideology, and the rest in order to keep the underclass in its place, to maintain itself, and to perpetuate its rule. Marx does not say that art, culture, politics, and so on are not important; obviously they are. Rather, Marx maintains since they are reflections of a much more basic economic foundation of society, they have no *independent* reality.

As for Marx's relationship to Hegel, the topic is a complicated one but I can summarize it in this way: Hegel was an idealist who stressed the importance of "ideas," spiritual and moral forces, in human society. He also stressed the conflict of ideas. Each idea (for example, "being") brings with it the idea that is its opposite ("nonbeing"). Out of the conflict emerges a third idea, "becoming," which embodies the elements of the two ideas and is superior to both.

For Hegel, the most important idea is that of the *Geist,* or universal spirit. The *Geist,* as the embodiment of freedom, has been unfolding itself in humans and human institutions, most importantly, the state. Specifically, the *Geist* has progressively manifested itself in four types of states: the oriental type of state (freedom in one individual, the ruler); the Greek type of state (freedom in a few); the Roman type of state (freedom in many); and the German type of state (freedom in all). Crucial here is an understanding of Hegel's conception of freedom. This idea, which is at total variance with the Anglo-American conception, conceives of freedom as a condition of being at one with the state, as giving oneself entirely over to the state. An individual is free to the extent to which he or she is totally immersed in, and subservient to, the state.

At this point Marx appears upon the scene, as it were, takes one look at Hegel, and accuses him of hopeless confusion and superficiality. Realistically speaking, he asks, how can we deal with "ideas," *Geist,* universal spirit, freedom, and the like? After all, all of these lie in the area of superstructure, which, according to Marx, has no independent reality, is derivative and secondary, betraying a more fundamental economic base. In short, Marx found Hegel standing on his head and proceeded to turn him right side up again.

And finally, Marx's conception of value or worth. According to Marx, labor alone creates value, and, therefore, all value lies in labor. Given this formulation, the value of a commodity should consist of the *quantity* of socially necessary labor that has gone into making it. If I create a commodity that is worth $10, I should receive the entire $10. This is creating value. (Marx does not take into account quality of labor, intellectual labor, creative initiative, and the like.)

But, of course, that is not the way things work. I may be paid $10, but the commodity I have created will go on the market for, say, $50; and the $40 difference goes into profits, administrative overhead, and the like. Marx calls this difference between the value made ($10) and the value returned ($50) aggrandizing value or creating surplus value, which in his view is "theft." Marx excoriates the capitalist for trying to increase surplus value (profit) either by prolonging the working day or by shortening the time necessary for the production of a commodity (through mechanization, for example).

The labor theory of value is not new with Marx, having been expounded upon previously by such bourgeois thinkers as John Locke, Adam Smith, and David Ricardo. What is new is the use to which Marx puts it: not as a means of scientific analysis but as one of moral protest.

Moreover, Marx is inconsistent in his use of the labor theory of value. In one place he says labor alone creates value. In another place he says labor plus land create value. In a third place he states that labor plus land plus capital create value. In a fourth place he insists that labor plus land plus capital plus nature create value. In other words, Marx has a fuller understanding of the theory of value than he lets on; it is just that his moral passion does not allow him to be more balanced and objective. He is much too anxious to condemn capitalism for greedy and immoral behavior.

We are now in a position to understand the materialist conception of history (or dialectical materialism). History—all of history, according to Marx's grand scheme—has undergone four stages of development, each characterized by a distinct economic base or foundation: (1) ancient tribal, Asiatic, or gens society, as in prehistoric Rome of 5000–6000 B.C.; (2) slave society, as in classical Greece and Rome, ca. 500 B.C.–A.D. 500; (3) feudal society, as in Europe, ca. the sixth through the sixteenth centuries; and (4) capitalist society, ca. the seventeenth through the nineteenth centuries. Each stage is marked by a distinct mode of production, a distinct set of classes, and conflict between those classes. Thus, the slave mode of production gives rise to two classes, master and slave; the feudal mode of production, to lord and serf; the capitalist mode of production, to the bourgeoisie and the proletariat.

The reader has noticed, no doubt, that we just skipped the first period of history: ancient tribal, Asiatic, or gens society (Marx uses the three terms interchangeably). The reason is that, according to Marx, in ancient tribal society the concept of *private* property does not exist. Since all property is communally held and controlled, the notion of private ownership does not arise. And with no distinction between owners and nonowners, classes and class conflict do not come into being. For Marx, then, the history of human society is the history of private property.

It is with slave society that the concept of private property begins, giving rise to a distinction between the few who own the means of production and the many who work it. The ownership of the land, the factory, or the assembly line enables the few to oppress and exploit the many for the sake of profit and power.

To proceed with the materialist interpretation, each phase of history is characterized by the existence of two classes that are in "dialectical" relationship to one another. The dialectic means, in its general usage, the simultaneous unity and struggle of opposites. Think, for example, of life and death (or night and day)—the two concepts are opposed to one another, yet also united because without the one the other would not be understood.

The three sets of classes, too, represent the simultaneous unity and struggle of opposites. *Unity* because the master class, for example, will literally bring into being an underclass (the slaves) who will handle the productive labor and the chores of the society; therefore, without the master class, the slave class would not come into being. *Struggle* because, due to oppression and exploitation, the underclass will eventually rise against its masters. The same with lords and serfs in feudal society. The same with the bourgeoisie and the proletariat in the capitalist stage.

All of which is to say that the dynamics of conflict are inherent in the nature of class society, and that classes are in a process of interminable conflict with each other. Accordingly, following a short prefatory statement, Marx and Engels open the *Communist Manifesto* with a ringing statement: "The history of all hitherto existing society is the history of class struggle."

According to Marx, then, history has a momentum all its own. It has its own locomotive, its own engine—classes and class struggle. In each phase of history, oppression and exploitation intensify. In each phase of history, class struggle becomes acute. In each phase of history, there is class polarization—a small minority that rules, the vast masses of the people who suffer. A point is reached when the underclass says "No more!" And it rises in revolutionary struggle to overthrow the dominant class.

This, Marx believes, is how history evolved. Slave society reached a height of development and was transformed into feudal society. Feudal society reached a peak of intensity and was transformed into capitalist society. Capitalist society is approaching maturation and will be transformed, in a short while, into socialist society. Each "lower" form of society gives birth to each "higher" society; each higher society develops in the "womb" of each lower society.

Marx makes a distinction between evolutionary change and revolutionary change. Evolutionary change takes place *within* each stage, so that we have more or less sophisticated capitalist economic systems, for example. Revolutionary change takes place *between* stages: one form of society cannot be transformed into another without massive upheavals.

Revolutions, then, according to Marx, have taken place throughout history, but the essential source of oppression and exploitation—that is to say, private property—has remained intact. On the other hand, the capitalist stage of history will witness a proletarian revolution that is altogether unique: its primary objective is the abolition of private property and, with it, classes, class struggle, oppression, and exploitation. Capitalist society will be replaced by a classless society of human brotherhood, peace, and abundance.

Before this utopia can be reached, however, we need a period of the "dictatorship of the proletariat." This dictatorship is a temporary measure whose function is to consolidate the revolution, eliminate the class enemies of the proletariat, prevent a counterrevolution, and undertake economic construction to set the stage for the age of abundance promised by the classless society.

So much for Mature Marx and his materialist conception of history. How valid is Marx's interpretation? Does it hold water? Not very much.

Marx barely discusses ancient tribal society, and for good reason. Even contemporary anthropologists and archaeologists do not know much about tribal societies existing in 5000 B.C. Rome. The slave stage also gets short shrift, even though we do know more about classical Greece and Rome.

Marx discusses feudal society in some detail but only to claim that it set the stage for the rise of capitalism. Specifically, he considers the French Revolution of 1789 as the pivot of transition from feudalism to capitalism. As we know, however, the French Revolution was not engineered by the feudal underclass, the serfs; it was carried on the shoulders of the middle class.

Marx's chief concern was with capitalist society. In particular, he focused on Britain, France, Germany, and the United States because they were the most developed and, therefore, closer in his view to a revolutionary breakthrough. Marx discussed capitalist society extensively—problems of value and surplus value, recurrent crises of overproduction and underconsumption, the rise of monopolies, the immiseration of the masses, and the like. As we have noted, however, far from being scientific analysis, this was an expression of the moral outrage that haunted Marx throughout his life. (We shall return to the problems of capitalist societies in the following chapter.)

We can highlight further problems of Marxist analysis by raising an additional series of questions about Mature Marx. Are material forces, in fact, the most important in society? Is it not the case that intellectual, political, and spiritual forces have a decisive bearing on the economic foundations of society? (In fairness to Marx, he did acknowledge this possibility, but only in passing and as a rare exception.) Is class an exclusively economic phenomenon, to be understood simply in terms of ownership or nonownership? Are class conflict, violence, and revolution always progressive, as Marx assumes, leading human society to higher and higher stages of development?

One Marx

We are now in a position to return to the issue of the continuity or discontinuity of Marx's thought. From an *interpretive* point of view, we can see that certain themes run through *all* of Marx's writings: human suffering, human odyssey, human destiny. In effect, he uses two different sets of concepts or categories of thought to convey two different versions of the human odyssey. Focusing on the condition of the individual (as "species being"), Young Marx employed such ideas as labor, productivity, creativity, and alienation. Focusing on the condition of society, Mature Marx used such concepts as substructure, superstructure, division of labor, class, and class conflict. In each case, he expressed the moral outrage that he seemed to feel so intensely.

From an *evidential* standpoint, if we accept the year 1845 as the date of demarcation between the "two" Marxes, as it is supposed to be, it would then logically follow that we would not expect to find any of the Young Marx's thoughts in his later works. This is not the case. In a major work, *The Grundrisse*, written in 1857 but not discovered until 1923 and not published in English until 1971, Marx set out to delineate the "first principles" or broad intellectual outlines of his future work. *The Grundrisse*, as it turns out, is a synthetic statement that contains as much about Marx's pre-1845 intellectual concerns as about his post-1845 ones. In short, as he grew intellectually, Marx underwent a process of "self-clarification" (to use his own terminology), deploying different modes of expression to convey his preoccupations, as he deemed appropriate.

The Significance of Marx

In this brief discussion of some aspects of the thought of Karl Marx, I have criticized him for a variety of shortcomings. If Marx is in fact so vulnerable on so many grounds, the question naturally arises as to why he is considered such an important figure in the history of Western thought, occupying as he does a most pivotal position.

First, Marx was a thinker on a grand scale, bringing together and synthesizing into a new mold a great deal of Western philosophy. In so doing, he gave an interpretation of human society for all time and all place. It is axiomatic that the more grandiose one's philosophizing, the more vulnerable one's position becomes.

Second, Marx offered a synthesis that is historically and dynamically based. As such, he was a philosopher of change, not of the status quo. In fact, according to Marx, the function of the philosopher is twofold: (1) to help explain change—that is, to be a thinker, and (2) to help bring about change—that is, to be an activist.

Third, Marx presented a dynamic historical analysis that is economically based, together with a thoroughgoing critique of capitalism.* Where Marx erred was in assuming, *on the whole*, the primacy of economic forces and in postulating a one-way relationship between economics and politics (as well as other aspects of society). The crucial lesson to be learned from Marx in this context is the *fusion* of politics and economics—their mutual interaction and reciprocal influence.

Fourth, Marx's central concern was not simply economic forces and conditions but the *human consequences* of economic activity. In this sense, his detailed discussion of human alienation is remarkably acute and timely.

Fifth, although Marx's claim to science remains only a claim, it is important to realize that he *understood* what it takes to be a scientist. The problem is that his moral passion routinely drowned his scientific intention.

Finally, one must bear in mind Marx's contribution to the theory and practice of revolution. As modified, changed, adjusted, and applied to various social contexts by Lenin, Mao, Ho, Castro, and others, Marx's thought has literally changed the face of the earth. This, of course, is the subject of following chapters.

The Framework Applied

The cognitive dimension of Marxism sees the world as made up of potentially productive and creative human beings who are everywhere and at all times brutalized and dehumanized for the economic self-aggrandizement of a few. The primacy of economic forces and the

---

*In order to avoid repetition, further aspects of Marx's analysis of capitalism will be covered in the following chapter.

institutionalization of ownership-as-the-arena-of-exploitation give rise to incessant class struggle, oppression, and alienation. Conflict, in other words, is inherent in the economic structure of society.

The overriding and unifying theme in Marxism, as we have seen, is moral outrage against the institutions and practices of Western capitalist societies. When combined with unceasing reminders of exploitation, brutalization, dehumanization, and alienation, this dimension provides one of the most potent emotional appeals in human history. Thus, to paraphrase, Marx's *Communist Manifesto* closes with the ringing exhortation: Workers of all countries unite. You have nothing to lose but your chains.

Ideally, the evaluative component of Marxism revolves around egalitarianism, communalism, and communal ownership and control of national wealth. All this is merely a step toward the realization of a classless society in some distant future—a society in which all conflict ends, peace and harmony prevail, human creativity finds complete fulfillment, and the formula, "From each according to his ability, to each according to his need," is promulgated.

The programmatic ingredient of Marxism is weak and untenable in that it calls for spontaneous and successful risings of the oppressed against the oppressor. As we shall see, however, this weakness was amply remedied by Lenin, Mao, Ho, and Castro, among others.

The social base of Marxism is, strictly speaking, fully internationalist: the proletariat, regardless of time and place. (In classless society, of course, all distinctions will presumably vanish into one harmonious human race.) In practice, however, as we shall see, Lenin, Mao, Ho, and Castro turned Marxism into national enterprises.

Selected Bibliography

Avineri, Shlomo. *The Social and Political Thought of Karl Marx.* Cambridge: Cambridge University Press, 1970.
————, ed. *Marx's Socialism.* New York: Atherton Press, 1973.
Bober, M. M. *Karl Marx's Interpretation of History.* Rev. ed. New York: Norton, 1965.
Bottomore, T. B., ed. *Karl Marx: Early Writings.* London: C. A. Watts, 1963.
Cohen, G. A. *Karl Marx's Theory of History: A Defense.* Princeton, N.J.: Princeton University Press, 1979.
Fromm, Erich. *Marx's Concept of Man.* New York: Frederick Ungar, 1961.
Gilbert, Alan. *Marx's Politics: Communists and Citizens.* New Brunswick, N.J.: Rutgers University Press, 1981.
Heilbroner, Robert L. *Marxism: For and Against.* New York: Norton, 1980.

Koren, Henry J. *Marx and the Authentic Man*. New York: Humanities Press, 1973.

Marx, Karl. *Collected Works* or *Selected Works*. Various editions and publishers.

————. *The Grundrisse*. 1857. Ed. and trans. by David McLellan. New York: Harper & Row, 1971.

McLellan, David. *Karl Marx: His Life and Thought*. New York: Harper & Row, 1974.

McMurtry, John. *The Structure of Marx's World-View*. Princeton, N.J.: Princeton University Press, 1978.

Meszaros, Istvan. *Marx's Theory of Alienation*. London: Merlin Press, 1970.

Ollman, Bertell. *Alienation: Marx's Conception of Man in Capitalist Society*. 2d ed. Cambridge: Cambridge University Press, 1976.

Tucker, Robert C. *The Marxian Revolutionary Idea*. New York: Norton, 1969.

————. *Philosophy and Myth in Karl Marx*. Cambridge: Cambridge University Press, 1961.

5

Leninism レーニンイズム

As Marx matured intellectually, he became increasingly interested in the analysis and critique of the capitalist economic system and in the projection of its early demise due to the many problems that beset it. Specifically, he called for "proletarian revolutions" in the most advanced capitalist countries, where the proletariat is numerous—namely, Britain, France, Germany, and the United States. Marx expected these revolutions eventually to spread to engulf the entire globe.

Several decades after Marx's projections, the first "proletarian revolution" did occur—not in an advanced capitalist country but in backward Russia! How does one "explain" this momentous, yet unanticipated event?

The burden of "explanation"—and much more—falls primarily on the shoulders of one Vladimir Ilyich Ulyanov, better known as Lenin (1870–1924). Lenin set out to give the world a historic lesson: rather than studying Marxism "in the abstract," one can apply it to the concrete conditions of specific countries. Given great determination and skill—and a large measure of luck—one might just succeed!

Marxism and the Russian Context

Lenin is the initiator of the movement that in the previous chapter we called totalitarian socialism, or communism. In the most general terms, Leninism rests upon three articles of faith: (1) social reality can only be understood as classes and class conflict based on material, economic interests; (2) the only way to resolve the problem of class conflict is through violent revolution; and (3) the only means capable of bringing about revolution are organization and leadership, embodied in the Communist party.

While the first and the second articles of faith are consistent with Marx's, the third is not. According to Marx, revolutions occur spontaneously; in advanced capitalist societies conditions grow so bad that the people simply rise in revolutionary upheavals. Organization, leadership, Communist party—these are strictly Lenin's innovations and virtually the defining characteristics of modern communism. In a nutshell, then: Marxism + Leninism = Communism.

Lenin makes a number of other changes in Marx as well, as we shall see. Accordingly, the issue arises: In what relation does Lenin stand to Marx? Is Lenin still a Marxist? What remains of Karl Marx once Lenin gets done with him?

Two points of view have been expressed in relation to this issue. One view, shared by most Communists, is that Lenin represents a development, an extension, and an enrichment of Marx. The other view is that Lenin represents a sharp departure and deviation from Marx; that Marx and Lenin are two entirely separate individuals, Lenin having abandoned Marx.

There is enough in Lenin to support either of the foregoing views. Generally speaking, the more pragmatic Marxists adopt the first point of view while the more purist Marxists lean toward the second. And the burden of the argument seems to favor the pragmatists.

Marx himself laid down the principle that theory or ideology is "a guide to action"—that is, theory must be tested in reality and adjusted to reality. Now, Marx's own writing focused on the most advanced capitalist countries of his time: Britain, France, Germany, and the United States. But since Lenin is not in the advanced capitalist countries, he must take the theory of Marx and apply it to the conditions of feudal, czarist Russia. Adapting Marxist theory to Russian reality means changing it, bending it, twisting it. The acid test is whether the theory *works* toward the objective of bringing down the house of the Romanovs. Later, Mao, Ho, Castro, and others will face a similar set of problems and arrive at similar solutions—that is to say, they will take the theory of Marx and Lenin and apply it to the specific conditions of China, Vietnam, and Cuba.

Ever fine-tuned to developments in Russia, Lenin seeks to interpret them through a Marxist perspective and to apply (bend, shape) Marxist theory to them. Let me give three illustrations and then elaborate them in the pages that follow.

First illustration, Russia in 1902. A large number of reformist and radical groups have been active on the Russian political landscape for some time but no significant political change has taken place. The Bolsheviks, the Mensheviks, the populists, the social revolutionaries, the left social revolutionaries, and others have failed to alter the czarist, feudal system. Why should this be the case? What is to be done if they are to have a significant impact on czarism and feudalism?

What Is to Be Done? is precisely the title of a pamphlet Lenin wrote in 1902, therein developing his ideas of organization and leadership. More specifically, Lenin teaches, all the foregoing parties and groups should come together under the auspices of the Communist party and present a united front to czarism and feudalism. The Communist party, in turn, must become a steely, single-minded, well-knit, and tightly disciplined organization of talented revolutionaries if it is to succeed in its self-assigned mission to overthrow the Romanovs of Russia.

Second illustration, Russia in 1905. On that dark Sunday in February, there was a spontaneous rising of workers, displaced peasants, unemployed former soldiers, and housewives in St. Petersburg. The masses attacked the Winter Palace in what was a textbook example of a Marxist revolution. But what happened? Did it succeed? No. The revolution was an abortive one, as the czar's forces put an end to the uprising in very short order.

In September 1905, Lenin wrote another pamphlet, *On the Two Tactics of Social Democracy in the Democratic Revolution*, summarizing the lessons of the February Revolution. His main conclusion is that Russia was not ripe for a Marxist-style revolution, in which the proletariat rises to overthrow its masters. Russia was a feudal society, one step removed from Marx's proletarian revolution. In Russia, the revolution had to employ "two tactics," as the pamphlet's title suggests. In the first tactic or stratagem, the Communist leadership would form a grand alliance with all social forces that want to overthrow czarism and feudalism; this happened in February 1917. In the second tactic, the Communist party, taking advantage of the unavoidable condition of instability and uncertainty, would stage its own takeover and establish a dictatorship; this happened in October 1917. Throughout, the Communist leadership should concentrate on appealing to people's nationalism. The one thing that *every* class intuitively understands—the one thing that unites peoples of all persuasions—is nationalism, not Marxism. Unbeknownst to Lenin perhaps, this combination of Marxism and nationalism was to emerge as the most explosive revolutionary ideology of the twentieth century.

Third illustration, Russia (and the world) in 1916. The document: Lenin's pamphlet, *Imperialism: The Highest Stage of Capitalism*. In the midst of the war that pitted the imperialist countries against one another and that deeply embroiled Russia, Lenin saw the roots of Marxist revolutionary movements on a global scale. Whereas Marx had focused on class conflicts pitting the proletariat and the bourgeoisie within capitalist countries, Lenin projected, in addition, the emergence of interstate conflicts on a worldwide scale. Lenin was very careful, however, to locate the genesis of global conflicts in unresolved problems and "internal contradictions" of capitalism within individual countries. Imperialism, according to Lenin, is "international capitalism."

Before pursuing these concerns in greater detail, let us place Lenin in the context of his time and place.

Lenin and His Times

Lenin was born in 1870 in the provincial town of Simbirsk, on the Volga, to an educated middle-class family. His father was a secondary school teacher who, after years of service, was appointed czarist school administrator for the province of Simbirsk, a position that carried a minor nobility title.

Lenin's childhood and early youth were "normal" by conventional standards. A good student, athlete, and chess player, he gave no sign of becoming a revolutionary. He was an avid reader, at home with Russian literary and political writing.

Two aspects of Lenin's early life deserve special attention. First, since the father's post involved quite a bit of travel, Lenin was deprived, at least partially, of the appropriate male role model which the current literature of child development considers crucial in a boy's proper upbringing. Accordingly, it may be that the father's absence from the home helped young Lenin to gravitate more and more toward his older brother Alexander, who was a radical and political activist.

Second, the father's travels brought him into close contact with the peasants and the wretched conditions under which they lived. The father brought home stories of how hard the peasants worked, how exploited they were, how little they had, how arbitrarily they were treated. These stories must have left an impression on the young Lenin, because he later came to see the peasants as a revolutionary force in the first of his two-stage revolutionary theory. (Marx did not pay much attention to the revolutionary potential of the peasantry.)

Lenin's tranquil youth was jolted by the death of his father in 1886. A second trauma was the arrest and execution, in 1887, of his older brother Alexander for plotting to assassinate the czar. This event, Lenin claimed, set him on a revolutionary course.

Admitted to the University of Kazan (near which the family had moved), Lenin was later arrested and expelled for participation in student protest activity. Determined to pursue his studies, however, he plunged into a program of intense independent work, took a series of "external examinations," and obtained a law degree from the University of St. Petersburg in 1891.

A lawyer, however, Lenin was never to be. By this time, he had become well steeped in Marxist and anarchist literature and had come into contact with a variety of radical groups in Kazan, St. Petersburg, and elsewhere.

Lenin was arrested in 1895 for conspiring to publish an illegal newspaper and exiled to Siberia, where he was kept until 1900. During this period, he devoted much time to the analysis of the situation in Russia and the strategy and tactics of engineering a successful revolution against the czar. His principal conclusion was that nothing could be accomplished until a well-disciplined Communist party was organized and prepared for action.

Forbidden to participate in political activity in Russia, Lenin went into exile in Switzerland in 1900, where he sought to organize such a party and draft a revolutionary program. After reentering Russia in 1905 for a few months of clandestine activity, he returned to exile in Finland, Switzerland, and other European countries, where he remained until 1917.

Lenin's years of exile were characterized by unceasing efforts, through friends, supporters, and intermediaries, to incite radical activity in major Russian cities, eliminate opposition parties and groups, and eventually topple the czar. As a result, even while in exile he became the best known of the many Russian revolutionaries.

Lenin paid particular attention to the activities of the Russian Social Democratic Workers' party. As early as 1903, under Lenin's prompting, the party had broken into two wings: the Bolsheviks (the "majority") and the Mensheviks (the "minority"). In 1912, the Bolshevik faction organized itself into a separate party under Lenin's leadership.

With its political ineptitude and financial bankruptcy exacerbated by the strains of World War I, the czarist regime collapsed in February 1917, to be replaced by a provisional government, which included Alexander Kerensky, a social democrat, who became premier in July. Having determined to return to Russia, Lenin and other Russian political émigrés obtained permission to travel through Germany and other countries in a sealed railway car, reaching the Finland Station in Petrograd in April. Following months of ceaseless agitation, Lenin led the Bolsheviks in the power seizure of October 1917. Having assumed the responsibilities of governing, Lenin faced a triple challenge: (1) to consolidate sufficient state power so as to forestall a counterrevolution or a countercoup d'état, (2) to build the Soviet economy and improve the condition of the people, and (3) to promote revolution in other countries. Lenin's relentless pace exacted a toll on his health, however. He suffered a mild stroke in 1922 and a debilitating one in 1923, leading to his death in January 1924.

The Ideas of Lenin

Concept of Imperialism

Lenin's primary purpose in writing *Imperialism: The Highest Stage of Capitalism* (1916) was to provide an explanation of why, contrary to Marx's expectations, capitalism had not collapsed. A related purpose was to reiterate and refine a thesis he had first developed in 1905 concerning the possibilities of communist revolutions in underdeveloped countries.

Writing in the 1840s, Marx had anticipated the imminent collapse of capitalism. Now, many decades after Marx's projection, capitalism was still very much alive. If anything, in fact, it was even stronger than in Marx's lifetime. Where did things go wrong?

Lenin's answer in a nutshell is that capitalism had undergone a major change, a metamorphosis Marx could not have foreseen. After all, in Marx's theory of knowledge, we can know only those things we have experienced. There is no way Marx could have known what course the development of capitalism would take.

What was this metamorphosis? Capitalism, says Lenin, had undergone a transformation by becoming international in scope. Capitalism was no longer a discrete, domestic, national economic system. It was now a global, international phenomenon. For Lenin, the shortest possible definition of imperialism is international capitalism.

Imperialism, then, is a new form of capitalism, its "highest stage," according to Lenin's subtitle. By "highest," Lenin means the most developed, the most sophisticated, to be sure. But he also means the last, the final.

Lenin develops his argument in the following steps: (1) as Marx said, capitalism is an economy of constant problems and crises; (2) the crises of capitalism necessarily lead to its internationalization; (3) the internationalization of capitalism will precipitate a series of wars and revolutions; and (4) these conflicts will spell the end of capitalism. Capitalism will self-destruct.

Capitalism, says Lenin, is an economy of perpetual difficulties, problems, and crises. Two of these crises are the crisis of overproduction and the crisis of underconsumption. Why should there be overproduction in a capitalist society? Because of capitalist greed, responds Lenin. In order to maximize profits, capitalism will produce more and more, by mechanizing the labor process, for example. And what about underconsumption? Because of increasing oppression and exploitation, people in a capitalist society will be unable to afford capitalist goods and commodities. So, the capitalist system will produce more and more while the people in that system can consume less and less. In short, the time will come in a capitalist society when the domestic market will be entirely saturated. It can take no more automobiles, no more washing machines, no more electric can openers. No more.

Simultaneously, capitalism faces another major crisis, the crisis of monopoly formation. The time will come, Lenin believes, when competitive capitalism will be transformed into monopoly capitalism. At that point, a handful of gigantic industrial enterprises will dominate the economic life of the country; smaller and medium-sized enterprises will be wiped out because they can no longer compete. Who can compete, Lenin might ask, with the likes of Ford, Chrysler, and General Motors? (Insofar as competition is the heart and soul of capitalism, Lenin is arguing, in effect, that capitalism will subvert its own essence—which echoes Marx's dictum that capitalists are their own "gravediggers.")

Moreover, the appearance of industrial monopolies will go hand in hand with the formation of monopolies in the field of banking and finance. But why, the reader asks? Lenin responds: Central to capitalist economic life is the phenomenon of credit. The ability to buy, the ability to expand, the ability to innovate—everything depends on the availability of credit. And who controls credit? Ford or Chrysler or General Motors? Of course not. It is the banking and financial institutions that control credit: Bank of America, Citicorp, Chase Manhattan, Morgan Guarantee Trust.

So, says Lenin, the time will come in capitalist society when a handful of gigantic financial institutions will hold the power of life and death over the industrial institutions and, in effect, control the whole of society. This union of financial and industrial institutions Lenin labels "finance capital": capital available to finance economic ventures.

So what, the reader may wonder? Lenin makes two important points. One, contrary to what we have been taught, capitalism is not a competitive economy; it is inherently monopolistic. Two, the domestic market is saturated not only in terms of goods and commodities, but in terms of credit as well. It does not pay Bank of America, Citicorp, or Chase Manhattan to extend credit to Ford, Chrysler, or General Motors. The domestic market is totally exhausted; it can absorb no more. That simple.

So, does capitalism come to an end? Will capitalism halt or stop? Of course not. Having exhausted the old market, capitalism will seek new markets. Having saturated the domestic market, capitalism will seek international markets.

Thus begins a search for overseas markets, overseas sources of raw materials, overseas sources of cheap labor, overseas sources of investment. This is the process of internationalization or globalization of capitalism.

Let us pause to take note of two important things. First, we have been talking as if there is only one capitalist economy that undergoes this transformation. In fact, however, there are many capitalist countries that, having had similar experiences, are in competition with each other over overseas territories.

Second, critical in the process of internationalization of capitalism is the role of the capitalist state. The primary function of the capitalist state, the reader will recall, is to maintain and perpetuate the ruling class. Accordingly, it is not the financial institutions that set out in search of overseas sources of investment, markets, raw materials, and cheap labor; it is the capitalist state that conducts these activities on behalf of the capitalist class.

Now, what is the most effective way of accomplishing these objectives? What is the most convenient and the most lasting way? Colonization, of course: laying claim to countries and territories. Thus begins, according to Lenin, the feverish hunt of the capitalist countries for colonies, or for what Lenin calls "unoccupied territories," that is, areas not claimed by other imperialist powers.

Having become international, capitalism confronts a series of conflicts, wars, and revolutions as a result of which it is going to collapse. Lenin identifies four kinds of conflict. First, says Lenin, eventually there will be wars between imperialism and the peoples of the colonies. Second, there will be wars between capitalist countries and socialist (or communist) countries; in the struggle between imperialism and the colonies, socialist countries will side with the latter.

Third, imperialist powers will be going to war against each other (as they had by 1916, the time of Lenin's writing). The reason is that as time goes on, there is less and less to colonize. Once the division of the globe among the imperialist powers has been completed, capitalist countries will be competing—and fighting—over the same colonies.

Fourth, says Lenin, we will have the development of Marxist revolutionary movements within individual capitalist countries. As people's misery increases, they will rise in revolutionary upheavals to overthrow their class enemies.

In short, capitalism is besieged on many fronts. Its energy is being sapped in many ways. Imperialism is the "highest stage of capitalism": the last and the final stage. Because of revolutions and wars, capitalism will collapse. Capitalism is inherently warlike. It has the seeds of its own destruction. Superficially, it is powerful; in reality, it is weak and vulnerable. It is going to fall on its own face. It is "a colossus with feet of clay."

Lenin's concept of imperialism, though it contains an obvious grain of truth, is afflicted by some serious weaknesses. Most centrally, it overlooks the fact that the twentieth century has seen an improvement (rather than a deterioration) in the condition of the working classes in capitalist societies, so that they *can* afford the goods and commodities the capitalist economy turns out.

Similarly, Lenin's discussion of monopoly formation ignores the emergence of antitrust laws, regulatory commissions, and government control of the economy. (In the United States, for example, the Interstate Commerce Commission was formed as early as 1887.) Generally, Lenin's critique is more appropriate for "pure" capitalism (if such a thing ever existed) than for modern, regulated capitalism.

Finally, the kinds of conflicts and wars Lenin projects have either not materialized or, if they have (as in the two world wars), capitalism has been able to weather them. On the other hand, as we have seen in chapter 2, Lenin was prophetic in his projection of conflict between imperialist powers and the peoples of the colonies (or wars of national liberation).

The significance of Lenin's concept of imperialism is threefold. First, it extends Marx's critique of capitalism by giving a fairly "reasonable" explanation of why capitalism did not collapse. This hardly requires elaboration.

Second, the theory represents an extension of Marx's interpretation of history. Marx said history has gone through four stages of development: ancient tribal, slave, feudal, capitalist. Lenin introduces a substage he calls imperialism, a transformation Marx could not have anticipated. In more recent times, the former Soviets talked about "militarism" as a further substage Lenin could not have foreseen: the capitalist economy, they argued, relies in large measure on the production and consumption of weapons of war and military hardware. (Never mind that the former Soviet economy was similarly dependent on military production.)

Third, Lenin's idea of imperialism extends Marx's conception of revolution by allowing for the occurrence of "proletarian" revolutionary movements in underdeveloped—that is to say, nonproletarian— countries. In the very act of colonizing the whole world, Lenin maintains, imperialism becomes, in effect, the instigating and the precipitating force of revolution. In the very act of seeking colonies, capitalism at the same time sets the stage for the development of revolutions in those countries.

Concept of Revolution

Communist revolutions in advanced countries, Lenin maintained, will be accompanied by revolutionary movements in underdeveloped or colonial lands because capitalism is now a global, rather than a national, phenomenon, and the colonies are its inseparable extensions. Lenin developed an analogy likening imperialism to a global chain having many links; and he argued that a revolution will occur in *any* country—advanced or colonial—that happens to be the "weakest link" in this chain of capitalism. In a word, according to Lenin, there are two types of communist revolutions: those occurring in advanced capitalist countries and those occurring in underdeveloped colonial lands.

Communist revolutions in advanced countries follow Marx's model: having reached sufficient consciousness, the proletariat presumably engineers a revolution and overthrows the bourgeoisie. Communist revolutions in underdeveloped countries follow a different path, going through two stages of development.

The first stage, labeled "bourgeois-democratic," sees the alliance of the proletariat (under the leadership of the Communist party) with all social forces, classes, and groups that for whatever reason oppose feudalism, czarism, or imperialism, as the case may be. In other words, the proletariat, being small, cannot engineer a revolution on its own strength alone. It must form "united fronts" with all social strata that, inspired by nationalist and democratic sentiments, oppose the status quo. Of primary importance in this regard are the middle-class nationalists (businessmen, merchants, shopkeepers, civil servants, intellectuals); of secondary importance, the peasantry. Although the middle class and the peasantry do not want a Communist revolution, they share certain interests with the Communists in their distaste for oppression and exploitation. Hence, they can be used and manipulated. With Lenin, the exploitation of the nationalist sentiment in the service of communism becomes a hallmark of Communist theory and practice.

Having engineered a "bourgeois-democratic" revolution and having consolidated sufficient power, the proletariat now turns on its former allies, persecutes and eliminates them (as necessary), and pushes the revolution to its second stage, the "proletarian-socialist"—better known as a Communist takeover. Hence, in Russia, for example, the Communists (Bolsheviks) formed an alliance with the Nationalists (Mensheviks), social democrats, liberals, and other "progressive" forces to overthrow czarism and feudalism in February 1917. In October of that year, they took over in an outright power seizure.

It is clear that Lenin's "two-stage" notion of revolution, as it is called, is a far cry from Marx's conception of a proletarian revolution. Rather, it is a "pragmatic" or opportunistic adaptation of Marxist doctrine subsequently imitated and applied by revolutionary leaders in many parts of the world. Revolutions in China, Vietnam, Cambodia, Laos, Algeria, Angola, Mozambique, Cuba, and Nicaragua are prime examples.

The genesis of the two-stage concept is to be found in the abortive February Revolution of 1905. On that "Bloody Sunday," after years of labor unrest, riots, and strikes (to which the czarist regime responded only with empty promises), the urban masses stormed the czar's palace (and other strategic centers) in St. Petersburg. Commanding overwhelming firepower, the czar's forces made short work of the uprising, killing hundreds (by some accounts, thousands) of people in the process.

Having begun as a textbook case of Marx's spontaneous revolution, the February event had a crucial impact on Lenin's thinking. Specifically, ever sensitive to developments in Russia, Lenin drew two principal conclusions. First, he thought, the Russian proletariat was too small and too weak to attempt a revolution on its own strength alone—hence, the necessity for alliances with all other social forces in a two-stage revolutionary movement. Second, Lenin asserted, having been manifestly demonstrated wrong, Marx's notion of revolutionary spontaneity had to be replaced by something far more concrete, something that had preoccupied Lenin for some years.

Concepts of Party and State

Rejecting Marx's idea of spontaneity outright, Lenin insisted that the proletarian revolution requires leadership, organization, planning, and hard work. The principal agent for engineering and pushing the revolution forward must be the Communist party.

Lenin's concept of the party was fashioned in *What Is to Be Done?*, a pamphlet written in 1902, and it remains the foundation of all Communist party building up to this day. The revolutionary party, Lenin insisted, must be an elitist organization: small, tightly knit, highly disciplined, and secret in character. At least in its initial stages, revolutionary struggle cannot be entrusted to everyone; one cannot toy with revolution. In order to move ahead with the tasks of organization, mobilization, and consolidation, revolutionary activity must be in the hands of those with talent, skill, and dedication. In short, to use his famous description, Lenin called for an organization of "professional revolutionaries"—that is to say, of those who have devoted their entire lives to revolution, who have turned revolution into a calling and a vocation.

Consisting as it does of the best-qualified revolutionaries, the party, according to Lenin, is the "vanguard"* of the proletariat in every sense. It is the only instrument capable of bringing political consciousness to the proletariat. (On its own, Lenin believed, the proletariat could develop only "trade-union consciousness.") It is the only instrument capable of organizing and mobilizing the proletariat. It is the only instrument capable of leading the proletariat in political struggle and armed struggle, legal struggle and illegal struggle.

It is obvious, then, that although elitist in nature, the Communist party cannot separate itself from the masses. On the contrary, the party must go among the masses, appeal to their self-interest and emotions, persuade them to identify the party's interest as their own, rally them to the cause, draw them into revolutionary action, deploy and coordinate their energies toward the realization of revolutionary objectives.

If it is to accomplish its goals, the party must have cohesion, solidarity, discipline, control, and, above all, unquestioned command and leadership. Factionalism and dissent cannot be permitted. The party, in other words, is a monolithic organization. Nonetheless, since minority views and challenges to leadership are likely to emerge from time to time, the party must periodically purge itself of all "opportunist" and "deviationist" elements. No challenges to party leadership can be allowed.

At the societal level, the Leninist principle governing party organization is "democratic centralism," a concept we discussed in detail in chapter 3. Briefly, the centralism of this concept means that the party is a rigid hierarchy extending from the national to the regional, provincial, and municipal levels. The "democracy" of democratic centralism means creating the illusion of participation and decision making, thereby keeping party members pacified, if not truly contented.

In any event, the most important objective of the Communist party for the immediate future is to plan, engineer, and execute the overthrow of the capitalist state. Having done this, it will establish a transitional political apparatus—the "dictatorship of the proletariat"—in

---

*Or "advance guard"—the military connotation is quite intentional.

order to eliminate all opposition and thwart any potential attempt at restoration of the old regime.

So far, Lenin's notion of the state is identical to that of Marx. Lenin departed from Marx, however, in arguing that the state as a political apparatus will continue to exist after the dictatorship of the proletariat has been completed. Specifically, he distinguished between "socialism" and "communism" (classless society), insisting that the state will disappear in the communist (not the socialist) stage.

The "socialist state" must exist in order to perform two important functions. First, said Lenin, the exploiting classes can be wiped out only gradually, not overnight—and as long as there are classes, there will be a state. Second, "socialism" is the first necessary step toward the construction of a communist society of abundance governed by the formula, "From each according to his work, to each according to his need." This task, too, requires the political power of the state.*

The Significance of Lenin

Lenin, it is by now clear, made a series of concrete changes in Marxist doctrine. He modified Marx's interpretation of history by adding a substage that he called imperialism. He changed Marx's conception of revolution to account for proletarian upheavals in both advanced and developing countries. He rejected Marx's idea of spontaneity by insisting on leadership, organization, and mobilization. He modified Marx's concept of the state by stipulating the continuing necessity for a "socialist" political apparatus. These changes, by the way, can be viewed either as an abandonment of Marx, as some maintain, or as a development of Marx, as others argue.

In any event, these changes are important enough in and of themselves. They are so important, in fact, that henceforth they turned "Marxism" into "Marxism-Leninism." Nonetheless, these specific changes do not address the overall significance of Lenin.

The overall significance of Lenin is to be found in two areas. First, whereas Marx had stressed the fusion of economics and politics while assigning primacy to economic forces, Lenin reversed the relationship by assigning primacy to the political sphere. Economic analysis was

---

*Subsequent Communist thinkers have abandoned altogether Marx's idea of the disappearance of the state. In fact, in all Communist countries today, the state plays the preeminent role in all societal spheres.

important to Lenin, to be sure, as seen in his concept of imperialism. But far more important were such political considerations as class alliance and united front, leadership and organization (chiefly the party), socialist stage, and socialist construction.

Second, Lenin *demonstrated* once and for all that Marxist ideology, far from being just another set of mental abstractions, can be put to work to overturn political regimes and change the lives of millions. In other words, his protestations to the contrary notwithstanding, Marx was basically a prophet and a philosopher; Lenin is the practitioner and the strategist. Lenin showed that Marxist philosophy is "doable"; that it can be used to bring down the 303-year rule of the house of Romanovs. This is Lenin's special place in the history of revolution and of communism. This is the "magic" of Lenin, and in the long run it becomes more important than any specific change or contribution he introduced.

The Framework Applied

The cognitive dimension of Leninism views the world as consisting of relatively few people of wealth, privilege, and status on the one hand, and the masses of exploited workers on the other. Class warfare is inevitable and persistent until such time as the whole system is overturned.

The affective component of Leninism appeals to all oppressed classes to unite in a common struggle for justice and revenge. The evaluative ingredient promises, literally, a new world in which all wrongs have been righted. The affective *and* evaluative dimensions of Leninism are potentially captured in the following lines from *L'Internationale*, the official song of the Communist International (Comintern), established by Lenin in 1919:

> Arise you prisoners of starvation,
> Arise you wretched of the earth,
> For justice thunders condemnation,
> A better world's in birth.
> No more tradition's chains shall bind us,
> Arise you slaves, no more in thrall,
> The earth shall rise on new foundations,
> We have been naught, we shall be all.

The programmatic component of Leninism rests on a two-stage urban revolutionary strategy stressing the indispensability of leadership, organization, and class alliance (particularly with middle-of-the-road nationalists). Only through hard work can the masses be mobilized. Only through mobilization can a revolutionary movement gain momentum.

In theory, the social base of Leninism is internationalist. In practice, however, Lenin turned Marxism into a national phenomenon resting primarily on the working class and secondarily on the peasantry, with leadership always coming from the middle-class intellectuals, who form the core of the Communist party. At some unspecified moment in the future, however, Lenin expected communism to become an international reality.

Selected Bibliography

Bunyon, James, and H. H. Fisher. *The Bolshevik Revolution, 1917–1918.* Stanford, Calif.: Stanford University Press, 1934.

Carr, Edward Hallett. *The Bolshevik Revolution, 1917–1923.* Vol. 1, New York: Macmillan, 1951.

Chamberlin, William Henry. *The Russian Revolution, 1917–1921.* 2 vols. New York: Macmillan, 1935.

Conquest, Robert. *V. I. Lenin.* New York: Viking, 1972.

Deutscher, Isaac. *Lenin's Childhood.* New York: Oxford University Press, 1970.

Fischer, Louis. *The Life of Lenin.* New York: Harper & Row, 1964

Hill, Christopher. *Lenin and the Russian Revolution.* New York: Macmillan, 1950.

Lenin, V. I. *Collected Works* or *Selected Works.* Various editions and publishers.

Meyer, Alfred G. *Leninism.* New York: Praeger, 1962.

Payne, Robert. *The Life and Death of Lenin.* New York: Simon & Schuster, 1964.

Shub, David. *Lenin.* New York: Doubleday, 1948.

Theen, Rolf H. W. *Lenin: Genesis and Development of a Revolutionary.* Philadelphia: Lippincott, 1973.

Trotsky, Leon. *The History of the Russian Revolution.* 1 vol. ed. New York: Simon & Schuster, 1936.

———. *Lenin: Notes for a Biographer.* New York: Putnam, 1971.

———. *The Young Lenin.* New York: Doubleday, 1972.

Ulam, Adam B. *The Bolsheviks: The Intellectual and Political History of the Triumph of Communism in Russia.* New York: Macmillan, 1965.

Wilson, Edmund. *To the Finland Station.* New York: Doubleday, 1940.

Wolfe, Bertram D. *Three Who Made a Revolution.* Rev. ed. New York: Dial Press, 1964.

Wolfenstein, E. Victor. *The Revolutionary Personality: Lenin, Trotsky, Gandhi.* Princeton, N.J.: Princeton University Press, 1967.

6

Guerrilla Communism

It is a commonplace of the twentieth century that the Communists preempted guerrilla warfare as the chief method of revolutionary warfare, Afghanistan being a glaring exception. Although guerrilla warfare is accorded a lengthy history in the annals of military affairs, both the name and the methods were formalized only in the Spanish resistance to the Napoleonic invasion of 1808–1814. A derivative of *guerra* (the Spanish word for war), the term "guerrilla" means, literally, "little war." Such a war was waged in the Spanish countryside by partisan fighters who continued to harass the French army after the regular Spanish troops had been defeated.

Guerrilla (or "irregular," "unconventional," "insurgency," "partisan") warfare has since become a central concern of military theorists of every persuasion. Writing in the 1820s, for example, Carl von Clausewitz devoted a portion of his classic work *On War* to the analysis of this type of military operation (Book 5, chap. 26: "Arming the Nation"). Primary responsibility for developing the theory and practice of guerrilla warfare, however, must be assigned to communist thinkers. As early as 1849, Karl Marx exhibited an acute understanding of the nature and potentialities of irregular warfare:

> A nation fighting for its liberty ought not to adhere rigidly to the accepted rules of warfare. Mass uprisings, revolutionary methods, guerrilla bands everywhere—such are the only means by which a small

For research assistance on a larger project of which this chapter is a part, I am grateful to Candace C. Conrad, James A. Davis, and William J. Nealon.

nation can hope to maintain itself against an adversary superior in numbers and equipment. By their use a weaker force can overcome its stronger and better organized opponent.

Lenin also drew a sharp distinction between regular and irregular warfare, repeatedly stressing the importance of the latter. Revolutionary struggle, he wrote in 1906, must pay particular attention to guerrilla warfare:

> Military tactics are determined by the level of military technique. . . . Military technique today is not what it was in the middle of the nineteenth century. It would be folly for crowds to contend against artillery and defend barricades with revolvers. . . . These [new] tactics are the tactics of guerrilla warfare. The organization required for such tactics is that of mobile and exceedingly small units, units of ten, three, or even two persons.

In a classic passage written in 1920, Lenin forecast the spirit and rationale of the military doctrine to be adopted by Communist leaders everywhere:

> To tie one's hand beforehand, openly to tell the enemy, who is at present better armed than we are, whether and when we shall fight him, is stupidity and not revolutionariness. To accept battle at a time when it is obviously advantageous to the enemy and not to us is a crime; and those political leaders of the revolutionary class who are unable "to tack, to maneuver, to compromise," in order to avoid an obviously disadvantageous battle, are good for nothing.

As it has evolved in the twentieth century, guerrilla communism has come to assume several interrelated characteristics. First, it has come to be associated almost exclusively with the underdeveloped countries of the world; in that sense, it represents an application of Marxist-Leninist ideology to "developing" and "colonial" countries. Second, guerrilla communism has come to have a rural, rather than an urban, orientation; it looks to the countryside, not the cities. Third, it has come to rely upon the rural peasantry, not an urban proletariat, for support. Fourth, it has come to rest upon protracted military conflicts undergoing distinct stages of development.

The foremost theoretician-practitioner of guerrilla communism was undoubtedly Mao Tse-tung.* He formulated an explicit and self-conscious statement of the ideology and practice of guerrilla communism, and he proclaimed it as a model for all developing countries. Accordingly, we shall begin by delineating the evolution of guerrilla communism in China and its chief components as identified by Mao. We shall then proceed to an analysis of guerrilla communism in two other revolutionary situations: the Vietminh Revolution, which, with some exceptions, closely followed the Chinese model; and the Cuban Revolution, which seriously challenged it.

Led by Ho Chi Minh, Vietnam experienced two revolutions in the postwar period: (1) the Vietminh struggle against the French, 1946–1954, and (2) the Vietminh and the Vietcong struggle against the Americans, 1954–1975. ("Vietminh" means, literally, independence seekers or, more conventionally, nationalists; "Vietcong" was a pejorative label for South Vietnamese Communists.) In this chapter we focus on the first revolution because it enables us to examine the genesis of Vietnamese nationalism and communism. Although space considerations do not allow the coverage of the second revolution, a synopsis will be provided at the end of the chapter.

Led by Fidel Castro, the Cuban Revolution spanned a relatively short time period, from 1953 to 1959. July 1953 marked Castro's attack on an army barracks that marked the formal beginning of the struggle. December 1959 brought a revolutionary takeover.

The overall objective of this chapter is to describe, compare, and contrast the conditions under which guerrilla communism took root in the three countries, the ideology that sustained it, and the strategy and tactics that were essential to its success. We begin our treatment of each revolution with a portrait of the man most closely associated with it.

China

Mao and His Times

Mao Tse-tung was born in 1893 in the village of Shao Shan, Hunan Province, a traditional hotbed of radical activity. Mao's father had

---

*I use the Wade-Giles system of romanizing Chinese names to maintain consistency with the bibliographical entries, all of which were published before the new system went into effect.

gradually risen from the status of a poor peasant to that of a rich peasant, which meant he owned land and was a grain merchant.

Mao's father was a tyrant who ran his business with a firm hand, maltreating, humiliating, and punishing anyone who disobeyed him. His harshness did not spare even Mao, who came to resent his father and rebelled against him. As a result, Mao's childhood was highlighted by a long series of family conflicts. Simultaneously, he observed in microcosm and at first hand the plight of the Chinese peasant.

Mao's formal schooling was minimal, but he was a voracious reader throughout his life and did a great deal of independent study. He read widely in Eastern as well as in Western literature and philosophy.

Mao lived in Peking in 1918–1919 and held a minor post at Peking University library under Li Ta-chao, a leading Marxist intellectual. In this capacity, Mao met a variety of other radical intellectuals and read extensively in Marxist literature. By the summer of 1920, Mao considered himself a Marxist.

Mao's radicalization must be seen in the context of Chinese history in the first few decades of the twentieth century. Briefly, these decades were ones of intense intellectual and political ferment, centering primarily on two groups, the Nationalists and the Communists. We must place Mao's role in its broader context.

Conditions in China

The key figure in the Nationalist movement was Sun Yat-sen (1867–1925). Educated in Hong Kong and Hawaii, converted to Christianity at age eighteen, impatient with Chinese traditions, Sun sought to create a new China representing a fusion of oriental and Western values—a China free of foreign rule, politically strong, and economically prosperous. His objectives were spelled out in the Three People's Principles: nationalism, democracy, and people's welfare.

The accidental explosion of a bomb in a warehouse in Hankow in October 1911 ignited a popular uprising that spread rapidly across many provinces and eventually marked the overthrow of the hated Manchu regime. Sun Yat-sen was inaugurated as provisional president of the Republic on January 1, 1912.

Throughout his life, Sun sought to unify China and create a viable national government. To these ends, he welcomed cooperation with the Communists, with whom he formed an alliance in 1924. Sun's efforts were ended by his death in 1925. Taking Sun's place was Chiang Kai-shek (1887–1975), an ultraconservative who was deeply hostile toward the Communists.

The formal beginning of the Communist movement in China may be dated with the founding of the Chinese Communist party (CCP) in 1921. By this time communism had become a familiar ideology to many Chinese intellectuals and many Communist study groups had been established in the major cities. Having represented his home province at the founding of the CCP, Mao returned to Hunan to assume the post of provincial party secretary.

In April 1927, Chiang Kai-shek staged a massive night coup in Shanghai, killing thousands of Communists and labor leaders, eliminating the labor movement in that city, and virtually destroying the proletarian base of the CCP. Although the experience was disastrous for the Communists, they learned the importance of military strength and their vulnerability to enemy attacks in the major cities.

In September 1927, Mao Tse-tung organized a peasant uprising to coincide with the autumn harvest in Hunan. The uprising failed, and he led a contingent of armed peasants into the rugged mountains of Kiangsi. There he created a revolutionary base, set up a worker-peasant government, and launched a program of land reform. For the next three years, in relative isolation from government troops, Mao and his associates concentrated on building their military forces and expanding their "liberated areas."

In 1934, Chiang Kai-shek launched the last of a series of five campaigns (the first four having failed) to wipe out the Communists and destroy their strongholds. Employing overwhelming military power and a policy of multiple blockades, he was able to overpower the Communist forces. The Communists faced the alternatives of either being completely destroyed or trying to crash through Chiang's lines. Thus they began, on October 15, 1934, the famous Long March from Kiangsi (southeast China) to Shensi (north-central China). Taking a year to complete, this epic adventure covered some six thousand miles of deserts, mountains, and rivers.

Committing military blunders and following a predictable course, the Communists suffered heavy casualties. Because of the severity of the situation, the top leadership group held a meeting in January 1935. Having consolidated power, Mao emerged as undisputed leader—a position he was to hold for about three decades.

When the Japanese launched a full-scale invasion of China in 1937, the Communists immediately stressed national unity and resistance to the outsider as taking precedence over all other tasks. Their continued appeal to Chinese nationalism vastly enhanced their popularity in northern China. And they capitalized on the enormous prestige of Sun Yat-sen by formally adopting his Three People's Principles as their "minimum program."

When the Japanese surrendered in August 1945, the Communists were fully prepared to turn the anti-Japanese war into a "people's war" against Chiang Kai-shek and his corrupt government. The balance of forces between the two sides rapidly changed in favor of the Communists. From 1947 on, Chiang's troops suffered consistent defeats at the hands of Mao's People's Liberation Army. Rapidly withdrawing from the major cities, Chiang Kai-shek finally retreated to Taiwan. Mao Tse-tung proclaimed the Chinese People's Republic on October 1, 1949. He remained the key charismatic figure throughout the turbulence of Chinese politics of the ensuing decades until his death in 1976.

The Ideas of Mao

Chinese communism consists, primarily, of Mao Tse-tung's attempt to apply to the feudal, colonial country of China a theory of revolution originally designed for advanced capitalist societies. This attempt is consistent with the communist assertion, first enunciated by Lenin, that Marxism must be integrated with the specific conditions of the country in which it is to be employed. Accepting this proposition, Mao insisted that Marxism-Leninism must be fused with specific historical conditions and given a "definite national form" before it could be put into practice. As early as 1938, he wrote:

> Being Marxists, Communists are internationalists, but we can put Marxism into practice only when it is integrated with the specific characteristics of our country and acquires a definite national form. The great strength of Marxism-Leninism lies precisely in its integration with the concrete revolutionary practice of all countries. For the Chinese Communist Party, it is a matter of learning to apply the theory of Marxism-Leninism to the specific circumstances of China. For the Chinese Communists . . . any talk about Marxism in isolation from China's

characteristics is merely Marxism in the abstract, Marxism in a vacuum. Hence to apply Marxism concretely to China so that its every manifestation has an indubitably Chinese character . . . becomes a problem which it is urgent for the whole party to understand and solve.

Mao's sinification of Marxism has three important constituents: (1) changing the locus of revolution from the urban centers to the rural areas; (2) forming a lasting alliance with the peasantry; and (3) reliance on a protracted struggle beginning with peasant guerrilla warfare and ending in large-scale conventional military confrontations. Also notable is the attempt to project to the global level the revolutionary strategy of Mao Tse-tung.

The Locus of Revolution

Until the time of Mao Tse-tung, revolutionary leaders (communist and noncommunist alike) had considered the urban centers the principal locations of revolutionary activity. They had uniformly stressed coordinated insurrections in the major cities, capturing the regime's key power centers and paralyzing the government literally in its "seat." In contrast to all this, Mao proposed to relocate the center of revolution to the countryside as the *necessary* first step toward eventual power seizure. The resultant "rural" revolutionary strategy is rooted in Mao's extensive analyses of the conditions of Chinese society and how best to apply Marxism-Leninism to that particular set of circumstances.

To begin with, Mao identified China as a semifeudal and semicolonial country. A semifeudal society is one in which elements of feudalism exist side by side with elements of capitalism. In such a country, there is a small but powerful big bourgeoisie (upper and upper-middle classes), just as there is a small but powerful landlord class. There is also a small and weak proletariat, a small middle (or national) bourgeoisie, a medium-sized lower (or petty) bourgeoisie, and above all, vast masses of peasants. The coexistence of a multiplicity of social forces suggests that the revolutionaries must develop the foresight and skill to exploit existing grievances and injustices and to form alliances with any social group that for whatever reason may support them.

A semicolonial country, according to Mao, is one under the simultaneous influence of several imperialist powers. In China, these powers included Britain, France, Germany, Japan, and the United States. Not only are competition and conflict bound to develop among the several imperialist countries, these frictions are also bound to be reflected in the reactionary domestic groups that support them because they benefit from their presence. Hence, the revolutionaries must become especially alert to exploiting all conflicts and rivalries to their own advantage. Moreover, given the sheer presence of the outsiders, the revolutionaries must do all they can to appeal to nationalist sentiments and emotions. Accordingly, Mao paid far more attention to fusing communism and nationalism than any revolutionary before him had done. And in so doing, he established a pattern for many colonial revolutions of the postwar era.

A semifeudal and semicolonial country is, by definition, a partially developed country. This means, in practical terms, that the power of imperialist, governmental, and other "reactionary" forces is concentrated in relatively few urban and industrial centers while the great expanses of the country remain beyond their interest or control, or both.

Hence, Mao concluded, since they are initially weak, the revolutionaries cannot take on the enemy in his strongholds and on his own terms. Rather, if they are to succeed, the revolutionary forces must retreat to inaccessible rural areas, wait out their time, mobilize and consolidate their strength gradually, and then surround the cities and strangle them.

This was a whole new strategy of revolution, successfully employed in China beginning in the late 1920s and culminating in the seizure of power in 1949.

Mao's rural strategy confronted vigorous opposition from the former Soviet Union, which, under Stalin, erroneously sought to impose the "Soviet model" on China. Mao also faced serious resistance within the Chinese Communist party, whose early leadership was dominated by pro-Soviet elements. By the mid-1930s, however, Mao Tse-tung was able to consolidate his position within the party, reject the Soviet line, and emerge as the undisputed leader.

The Peasantry as a Revolutionary Force

One of the chief characteristics of an unevenly developed country, as we have seen, is the presence of a large peasant population. Having come from a peasant background himself, Mao Tse-tung paid particular attention to the Chinese peasantry and its revolutionary potential.

Since Marx's focus was on advanced capitalist countries, he paid relatively little attention to the peasants as a revolutionary force. Lenin did stress the importance of the peasantry, but only in the first stage of the revolution, the "bourgeois democratic" stage; beyond that, he was contemptuous and distrustful of the peasants. By contrast, Mao's faith in the peasantry was total and unqualified: they remained allies from first to last.

As early as 1925, Mao turned his attention to investigation of class conditions in China. His early thinking was set forth in the pamphlet *Analysis of Classes in Chinese Society* (March 1926), wherein he sought to identify the "friends" of the revolution and to isolate its "enemies." Having analyzed the conditions of the various classes, he concluded that the proletariat (to the extent to which it existed), the peasantry, the petty bourgeoisie, and the national bourgeoisie were among the friends, while the landlords, the big bourgeoisie, and the imperialist agents were the chief enemies.

In 1926–1927, Mao conducted a specific study of peasant conditions in his home province and summarized the results in *Report on an Investigation of the Peasant Movement in Hunan* (March 1927). This was in effect an extension of his 1926 work, in which the role of the peasantry in the revolution was stressed and glorified. Mao saw the peasant movement as "a mighty storm," a "hurricane" that would soon sweep all forces of oppression before it. The importance of the rural areas and the key role of the peasantry remained the mainstay of Mao Tse-tung's revolutionary strategy.

From a "theoretical" point of view, then, Mao dramatized the role of the peasants. From a practical standpoint, however, he had no other alternative: a rural-based revolutionary movement has *only* the peasantry as its main force while it forms alliances with other friendly urban classes as well.

The Protracted Struggle

A rural revolutionary strategy is based on the explicit realization that, initially being weak, the revolutionaries must withdraw to secure and inaccessible but well-populated "base areas," gradually establish themselves among the local population, mobilize and win them over in greater and greater numbers, provide them with appropriate political and military training, and eventually deploy them to topple the existing regime. This process, Mao acknowledged, requires a great deal of time, patience, and hard work. Hence, the revolutionary struggle is necessarily protracted in nature.

Mao showed acute sensitivity to the political dimensions of revolutionary activity, constantly stressing the importance of political as well as armed struggle. Political activity consists, above all, of generating active sympathy and support among the country's population. The army, he said, is not only a fighting force but also a propaganda force and a working force: it must "educate" the people, help them in their daily chores, and protect them in every way. In a word, Mao called for a "people's army" to fight a "people's war."

Mao's untiring efforts to attain "unity between the army and the people" found expression in other ways as well. As early as 1928, for example, he issued (and subsequently reissued) the following set of guidelines—Eight Points for Attention—for the army's treatment of the local population:

1. Speak politely.
2. Pay fairly for what you buy.
3. Return everything you borrow.
4. Pay for anything you damage.
5. Don't hit or swear at people.
6. Don't damage crops.
7. Don't take liberties with women.
8. Don't ill-treat captives.

From the standpoint of the revolutionaries, a protracted struggle undergoes three stages of development: strategic defensive, strategic stalemate, strategic counteroffensive. In the first stage, the main function of the revolutionaries is to retreat, protect, and consolidate their forces; accordingly, their principal form of military action is guerrilla warfare. In the second stage, the revolutionaries gradually grow in numbers and strength, eventually reaching a condition of relative parity with the forces of the regime; accordingly, when it is advantageous to them, they engage in conventional (mobile) warfare as well. In the final stage, the revolutionaries have presumably attained decisive military superiority over the enemy; they then confront him in open warfare. In China, this process unfolded over a period of some two decades.

In a protracted struggle, it is clear, guerrilla warfare plays a crucial role: without it, no revolutionary movement can get under way. Thus, Mao Tse-tung devoted a great deal of attention to perfecting this form of military activity. In fact, he was the great architect of modern guerrilla warfare.

Mao summarized the basic operational principles of guerrilla warfare in a deceptively simple formula: "The enemy advances, we retreat; the enemy camps, we harass; the enemy tires, we attack; the enemy retreats, we pursue."

For one thing, the entire formula hinges on timely and strategic intelligence—that is to say, clear knowledge of the enemy, his movements and activities, his strengths and weaknesses. Second, the guerrilla does not hesitate to run away (in contrast to the idea of "fighting like a man"). He insists on holding the initiative and fights only on his own terms.

Third, guerrilla warfare stresses the importance of surprise, deception, and cunning. Luring the enemy into unfamiliar and hostile territory, laying ambushes, undertaking hit-and-run tactics, striking when and where least expected—these are essential and standard guerrilla operations. Fourth, when the guerrillas decide to strike, they: (1) locate the enemy's weakest flank; (2) hit the enemy with everything they have; (3) conduct the operation decisively, surgically, and with maximum speed; and (4) disappear as quickly as possible.

Despite all this, the principal function of guerrilla warfare is not to destroy the enemy but to harass him, confuse him, disrupt his lines of communication and transportation, force him to commit mistakes, and, above all, undermine his morale. The actual destruction of the enemy takes place in the third stage of protracted conflict, through conventional warfare. Thus, in China, Mao began guerrilla operations in the late 1920s and shifted to conventional warfare in the middle 1940s in order to destroy Chiang Kai-shek's military forces.

The Global Dimension of Mao's Strategy

The Chinese Revolution, Mao believed, was an integral aspect of an epoch of world upheavals that began with the Russian Revolution of 1917. The October Revolution, he claimed, changed the course of world history and heralded an era of revolutionary movements around the world.

The significance of the Chinese Revolution, according to Mao, lies not only in carrying forward the tradition of the October Revolution but also in its special attraction for, and applicability to, other colonial, semicolonial, and semifeudal countries. The Chinese Revolution, in other words, is a new model to be followed in all developing societies where similar conditions prevail. 王士孝 .

Taking this proposition a huge step further, Mao attempted to apply his entire revolutionary strategy at the global level. Specifically, he identified a "vast zone" of colonial and semicolonial countries that he hoped would unite to confront "Western imperialism."

The most extensive attempt to "globalize" Mao's revolutionary strategy was undertaken in 1965 by Lin Piao (1908–1971), then Mao's chosen successor. In a much publicized document entitled *Long Live the Victory of People's War!*, Lin insisted that:

> Mao Tse-tung's theory of establishment of rural revolutionary base areas and the encirclement of the cities from the countryside is of outstanding and universal practical significance for the present revolutionary struggles of all the oppressed nations and peoples.

He added:

> Taking the entire globe, if North America and Western Europe can be called "the cities of the world," then Asia, Africa, and Latin America constitute "the rural areas of the world." . . . In a sense, the contemporary world revolution also presents a picture of the encirclement of cities by the rural areas. In the final analysis, the whole cause of world revolution hinges on the revolutionary struggles of the Asian, African, and Latin American peoples who make up the overwhelming majority of the world's population. The socialist countries should regard it as their internationalist duty to support the people's revolutionary struggles in Asia, Africa, and Latin America.

Such is the attempt to universalize the revolutionary strategy of Mao Tse-tung. What worked in the domestic arena, it is contended, can be extended and put to work at the international level. This leaves aside the elementary problem of China's inability to control the foreign policies of other countries and dictate a common posture (or united front) vis-à-vis the imperialist powers. It overlooks the forces of nationalism within individual countries and the system of international relations that imposes constraints on what nations can and cannot do to maximize their self-interests.

Vietnam

Ho and His Times

A charismatic leader and superb organizer, Ho Chi Minh was born in 1890 in the village of Kim-Lein in Nghe-An Province of central Vietnam. Ho's grandfather earned the equivalent of a Master of Arts degree and was appointed a district governor, a post from which he was dismissed for insubordination. Ho's father, also the recipient of a higher degree, refused to accept a mandarin post and joined a dissident intellectual group instead. Arrested and imprisoned in 1907, he was placed under permanent house arrest following his release in 1910. Thereafter, he earned a meager living as a practitioner of Chinese medicine.

Ho Chi Minh attended a French lycée at Vinh but was expelled at the age of thirteen for anti-French activities. Having earned a lower degree in 1907, he was appointed as an elementary school teacher, a job he soon deserted to participate in nationalist activity.

From 1911 to 1913, Ho served as a mess boy on a French liner, traveling extensively in Europe, Africa, and America. This experience profoundly embittered Ho by providing him with firsthand knowledge of the oppression and exploitation practiced by the Western powers in colonial areas. The humiliation Ho experienced in his dealings with the Europeans personalized the colonial struggle for him.

In 1913 Ho settled in London for a few years, where he worked as a kitchen helper and shoveled snow for the London school system. He moved to France in 1917 and came under the heavy spell of French socialism and communism. Having joined the French Socialist party, he attended the 1920 party congress that approved the formation of the French Communist party. In 1922 he traveled to Moscow as a party delegate to the fourth congress of the Communist International. He returned to that city in 1923 and again in 1924 and remained there to study communism.

In 1925 Ho accompanied Mikhail Borodin to China, ostensibly to work as a Chinese translator at the Soviet consulate in Canton, but in reality to operate as a Comintern agent in Indochina. While in Canton,

Ho founded the Vietnam Revolutionary Youth League (Viet-Nam Thanh Nien Cach Menh Dong Chi Hoi). This organization was in fact a training school in Marxism-Leninism; later, Ho's students dispersed to introduce communism throughout Vietnam.

In 1930 Ho founded the Indochinese Communist party (ICP). At about the same time, he was appointed head of the Far Eastern division of the Comintern, which activity precluded his effective leadership of the Communist movement in Vietnam. Ho's whereabouts throughout the 1930s remain something of a mystery. He reappeared on the scene in 1941, however, to devote his entire attention to problems of communism in Vietnam. From a small political party, Ho forged an organization that eventually controlled North Vietnam, influenced the South Vietnamese, Laotian, and Cambodian Communists, and drove the French out of Indochina.

Conditions in Vietnam

The Vietminh Revolution of 1946–1954 was an intense nationalistic response to the long French domination of Indochina. Vietnam had been a unified and centralized nation since 1802. With the coming of the French colonial wars, which lasted from 1858 until 1883, however, Vietnam lost its name, unity, and independence. For approximately eighty years it was divided into Tonkin (the North), Annam (the Center), and Cochinchina (the South). Throughout this period, an incipient nationalism gathered momentum, and it finally burst forth in the World War II period. During the Vietminh assertion of control, the alternatives of the Vietnamese people were relatively clear: to follow nationalist, albeit Communist, leaders, or to remain under French colonial control.

A vast array of conditions—economic, psychological, social, political—coalesced to set the stage for the revolution. The major economic difficulties revolved around the French tax and land policies. Taxation was based more on French fiscal needs than on the native population's capacity to contribute. The French had a monopoly on alcohol, salt, opium, and tobacco; the taxes on these products provided a significant portion of the colony's revenues. The French settlers paid almost no taxes.

The French land policies were also poorly conceived. The output required of the peasants drove them into debt or into renting land they had previously owned. The rent and the interest on loans were so high that thousands of debt-ridden peasants were forced off their land.

As the condition of the peasantry progressively worsened, the resultant gap between expectations and achievement created serious psychological frustration throughout the countryside. Conditions were no better in the urban centers, where the educated native elite was confronted with a persistent discrepancy between political aspirations and political achievement. The denial of political power to the intelligentsia—and the resultant discrepancy between their socioeconomic status and political influence—was a most important source of discontent leading to revolution. Indeed, much of the impetus for the Vietminh Revolution came from the relatively small segment of the Vietnamese population that had experienced some social mobility and economic achievement through colonial institutions, but no commensurate political power.

Revolutions occur, in part, when large segments of an oppressed population anticipate relief through open defiance of the existing regime and an appeal to an alternative one. Such a realization probably did not become widespread in Vietnam until the Japanese occupation of World War II. The comparative ease with which the Japanese subjugated the French exploded the myth of French military invincibility. During this period, various nationalist groups merged into the League for the Independence of Vietnam, founded by Ho Chi Minh. Thus emerged the possibility of a viable indigenous alternative to French colonialism.

French colonialism was phenomenally inefficient and unresponsive in Vietnam. The oft-promised tax and land reforms never materialized. Ho Chi Minh observed that in eighty years of colonial rule, the French constructed dozens of prisons but only one university. Only a small fraction of the Vietnamese children got even an elementary education. Early attempts to create a University of Hanoi and a native high school system met with strong opposition from the French settlers, chiefly on the grounds that education might promote rebellion. Such measures as were taken (e.g., sending bright Vietnamese students to France) were too little and too late. The victory of Japan over Russia taught the Vietnamese that Western knowledge was a most important weapon for defeating the Western powers. As a result, many natives left for Japan, underground study groups and newspapers began to appear, and traveling lecturers began to stress the importance of an educated native elite. All were spurred by the realization that education had been denied as a means of suppression.

Vietminh Ideology

The most important component of the Vietminh ideology was national-ism. The leadership was Communist and Marxist, to be sure, but their motivation, as well as that of the masses, was first and foremost a desire for national autonomy and the elimination of French colonial-ism. The ideology was tied to a militant psychology and to communist guerrilla warfare. Communist propaganda untiringly condemned the French imperialists and their desire to keep all the peoples of Indo-china in slavery, stressed the brotherhood of all peoples and their com-mon cause against colonialism, projected an image of the Communists as ceaseless fighters for national independence and the people's wel-fare, and emphasized the army's love for the people and the people's love for the army.

By the middle of the 1930s, communist ideology was widespread throughout Indochina. Attempts were made to infiltrate local govern-ments and to form secret underground organizations where recruit-ment, training, and propaganda proceeded ceaselessly. At first, the inspiration for the Communist movement in Vietnam came from Rus-sia. However, since the Soviet emphasis on a proletariat was inappro-priate in Vietnam, the Communist orientation was altered in favor of the Chinese model.

With the outlawing of communism in Vietnam at the outbreak of World War II, many Vietnamese Communists fled to China. In May 1941, Ho Chi Minh held a conference in Kwangsi Province attended by former members of the Indochinese Communist party as well as by left-wing and nationalist organizations. The conference resulted in the formation of the League for the Independence of Vietnam (the Viet Nam Doc Lap Dong Minh Hoi), thereafter commonly known as the "Vietminh." Although from the start the Vietminh was led and domi-nated by the Communists, its declared objective was the freedom of Vietnam. Communist ideology was played down because the leaders were in Nationalist China and because they hoped for Chinese as well as American aid. Ho Chi Minh and his fellow Communists privately resolved, however, that the Vietminh would follow a communist doc-trine. The core of this doctrine was to wage a protracted war based on guerrilla warfare.

On August 7, 1945, a day after the bombing of Hiroshima, Ho Chi Minh announced the formation of the Viet Nam People's Liberation

Committee as his provisional government. Communist guerrillas, now some 5,000 strong, on that day assumed the title of the Viet Nam Liberation Army. Ho and his military commander, Vo Nguyên Giap, had patterned their forces on the Chinese experience, as described in Mao Tse-tung's writings on guerrilla warfare. This experience emphasized the need for internal political cohesion and solidarity, mobilizing and organizing the masses, and establishing and equipping secure base areas. Mao's Eight Points for Attention became a guideline in all military activity.

With the abrupt surrender of the Japanese, the Vietminh infiltrated quickly into Haiphong, Hanoi, and many other areas in the North in order to claim the powers of government. The Vietminh apparatus worked exceedingly well, and by the end of August 1945, Ho Chi Minh was in control of all Tonkin and northern Annam except for Hanoi and Haiphong. Ho's victories brought forth a ground swell of nationalist feeling. On September 2, 1945, having just dissolved the old provisional Liberation Committee, he proclaimed the existence of an independent Democratic Republic of Vietnam, and severed all ties with France. The French, however, reestablished control, banned the Communist party, and forced Ho to continue the struggle for national independence.

Vietminh Strategy and Tactics

The chief objectives of the Vietminh organization were to facilitate political control and to develop an effective military system. Political organization, as we have seen, played a key role in propaganda and mobilization, even though from 1945 to 1951 the party was outlawed and the Communists had to operate in a clandestine fashion. In 1951, Ho Chi Minh announced the formation of the Lao Dong (Workers' party), which was the first overt appearance of the Communist party since its "dissolution" six years earlier.

The military was from the start subject to political control and centralized authority. The political officers were the most influential element in the military structure, having veto power over decisions made by their military counterparts.

Gradually, as the revolution progressed and they became less necessary politically, non-Communists were eased out of the political-military structure. By the end of the 1940s, the Vietminh tightly controlled the political-military apparatus and actively pursued Communist objectives consistent with nationalist goals.

The Vietminh military operations were masterminded by General Giap, and their effectiveness rested on several interrelated factors. One set of factors related to Vietminh tactical principles. The first of these was speed of movement. Forces would concentrate rapidly, take position, strike quickly and decisively, and disappear almost instantaneously. Marching at night, the Vietminh would develop a position without alerting the enemy. The attack would take place early in the morning. The assault and the retreat would be executed with maximum speed. The Vietminh were seldom caught without a plan of retreat.

Another principle was that of surprise. A favorite device was to leak inaccurate information to the enemy in order to mislead him into an ambush; to this end, for example, fake documents were planted on double agents.

A further principle was undermining enemy morale. Communist agents would infiltrate French camps to encourage treason and to spread propaganda. Threats of violence and terror were made against pro-French elements, and on occasion bribes were offered for cooperation.

Finally, the Vietminh would attack only if the manpower ratio was in their favor or if, through surprise or ruse, they had gained a decisive advantage over the enemy. This involved an intelligence system of an efficiency the alien French could not command.

The Vietminh intelligence system was quite elaborate. The Quan Boa (Military Intelligence) was composed of party members especially chosen for their physical and mental qualifications and given special training. On occasion these agents used comparatively modern methods (e.g., radio intercept) to obtain information; more characteristically, however, they relied on direct interrogation of both the local civilians and enemy personnel, a task at which they excelled.

The detailed planning of the Vietminh can be seen in their offensive and defensive tactics. All military operations were based on Mao Tsetung's formula: "The enemy advances, we retreat; the enemy camps, we harass; the enemy tires, we attack; the enemy retreats, we pursue." Several considerations were important for an offensive: the right choice of time, a careful plan, adequate preparations, and high combat spirit. Guerrillas would watch a garrison over a period of time in order to discover when it was most susceptible to attack. Observers took note of when the guards were changed, which guards were lax in their duties, and when key officers would be absent. Communist intelligence also noted the weakest points of defense, installations to be neutralized, and the best routes of retreat.

The Vietminh usually attacked at night because the French were considered inferior night fighters and because their air and artillery support was less effective at that time. Usually the main effort was concentrated on a very narrow front while other, smaller groups created diversions. Ambushes were laid for enemy relief forces. As a relief column approached, it met a Vietminh force blocking the road. As the column halted, it was met with fire not only from this group, but also from two others located on either side of the road and one to the rear of the column.

The typical defense operation was based on Mao's principle of retreat and of luring the enemy into an isolated and hostile environment. Some of the best defense tactics were illustrated in the villages. Individual shelters and hiding places, usually underground and connected by tunnels, were constructed so that a defender could fire from one place, disappear into the ground, and then fire again from another spot. To add to French confusion, each village had a different defense pattern.

The battle of Dien Bien Phu was a most atypical operation in the Vietminh Revolution—totally at variance with the strategy of protracted warfare. It was a classic nineteenth-century battle involving a surrounded defense position that sustained constant attacks from artillery and land forces. The French decided to defend Dien Bien Phu because—having two airstrips and serving as an intersection for three roads—it could be used to block Vietminh movements in and out of Laos. Moreover, the French believed that General Giap could not divert the number of men necessary to take the fortress and that any positional welfare would hurt the Vietminh more than the French.

From January to May 1954, the Vietminh pounded the French positions while digging a huge trench around Dien Bien Phu. The French morale remained high, though they were jolted by the intensity and accuracy of Vietminh firepower. Psychological pressures mounted as Giap began to close in simply by digging from the encircling trench toward the fortress. The final series of assaults began on May 1. Gradually, French positions began to collapse, and French outposts were overrun by Vietminh forces. On May 7, the Vietminh broke through the heart of the defenses; the struggle ended that evening.

Fighting the battle of Dien Bien Phu was consistent with Giap's conviction that a decisive battle may shorten a protracted war. Having been wary of protracted sieges since a series of defeats at the hands of the French in 1951, Giap gradually concluded that a successful general offensive involving positional warfare would make the taking of Hanoi easier and would deal a blow—political, psychological, and military—sufficiently crippling to be felt in Paris and thus shorten the war. This is the chief modification introduced by the Vietminh in the Chinese model of guerrilla communism.

The Geneva negotiations began shortly after the fall of Dien Bien Phu. Giap and his troops had given the Vietminh negotiators a much stronger political and psychological posture via-à-vis the French.

Addendum: The South Vietnamese Revolution, 1954–1975

Following the battle of Dien Bien Phu, the Geneva negotiations of July 1954 divided Vietnam into North and South, giving the northern part to Ho Chi Minh and his forces and retaining the South for French control. (The partition was supposed to be temporary, subject to a reunification referendum that never materialized.) Since France was politically, economically, militarily, and psychologically exhausted in the postwar period, the United States effectively replaced France in South Vietnam.

Before long, Vietcong guerrilla forces, assisted by the Vietminh, began to make headway in South Vietnam, attracting popular support and expanding their territorial holdings. (We earlier clarified the meanings of "Vietminh" and "Vietcong.") Becoming alarmed, the United States began committing "advisers" and, later on, troops. By the time President John F. Kennedy was assassinated in November 1963, an estimated 16,000 American advisers were in Vietnam.

President Lyndon B. Johnson sharply escalated the U.S. presence in Vietnam. On the one hand, under a policy of "Americanizing" the war, an increasing number of U.S. troops were sent to Vietnam, reaching a peak of 550,000 personnel by the beginning of 1968. On the other hand, the United States undertook a systematic policy of saturation bombing of military and industrial targets in both North and South Vietnam. For a time, some American officials declared a policy of "bombing the Communists to the negotiating table."

On the ground, Communist strategy remained unchanged: another protracted conflict using peasant guerrilla warfare. Deliberately and systematically avoiding confrontation with superior American forces, the Vietminh and the Vietcong pursued a war of attrition stressing indirect attacks, ambushes, hit-and-run tactics, terrorist activity, and the like.

In South Vietnam, popular discontent with the government mounted on a daily basis. Government inefficiency and corruption continued. Economic problems (for instance, inflation and unemployment) spun out of control. Buddhist monks immolated themselves in protest of government policy. The government resorted to coercive tactics and terrorism as a means of containing or discouraging popular protest.

In the United States, the anti–Vietnam War movement picked up significant momentum as it spread to all segments of the American population. Dovetailing with the student movement, the civil rights movement, and the feminist movement, the Vietnam protest movement posed a major challenge for the Johnson administration. But the war went on.

After months of careful preparation, the Communists launched the Tet Offensive of February 1968. Tet (the Vietnamese New Year) was a series of coordinated assaults on some one hundred cities and military installations throughout South Vietnam. The focus of the attack was the capital city of Saigon (later renamed Ho Chi Minh City) and, within Saigon, the American embassy as the symbol of American power in Vietnam. Although they did not penetrate the central compound, the Communists controlled a portion of the embassy for a few hours, exchanging gunfire with the Marines in the embassy gardens.

The Tet Offensive, as it turned out, was the South Vietnamese equivalent of Dien Bien Phu, a frontal assault upon the enemy in conventional warfare. Whereas Dien Bien Phu had been a military success, however, Tet was a crushing military defeat as the Communists lost an estimated 25,000 personnel in a single night. Nonetheless, the political and psychological reverberations of Tet certainly favored the Communists. Once again, General Giap's calculations had proved correct. He had demonstrated the vulnerability of an enemy who had repeatedly predicted imminent victory.

The Tet Offensive, it is widely believed, was the turning point in the American involvement in Vietnam. In March 1968, President Johnson announced that he would not be a candidate for reelection as president. Having won the election of 1968, President Richard M. Nixon set out to "Vietnamize" the war. Although for a time he widened the war into Cambodia and Laos (to destroy enemy "sanctuaries" or military head-quarters), he pursued policies that eventually ended in the Paris peace agreement of 1973 and the American withdrawal of 1975. North Vietnam and South Vietnam were reunified a year later.

Cuba

Castro and His Times

Fidel Castro was born in the rugged village of Birán, Mayarí District, the Oriente Province, in 1926. Having immigrated from Spain, his father, Angel Castro y Argiz, was a farm worker who eventually became the prosperous owner of a sugar plantation. In an extramarital affair with his maid, Lina Ruz González, Angel fathered five illegitimate children; Fidel was the second of these children. Angel and Lina were subsequently married.

After attending a Roman Catholic school in Santiago, the capital of Oriente, Fidel graduated from Belén, a leading Jesuit school in Havana, where he developed a reputation as a debater and an athlete.

In 1945, Fidel entered the University of Havana to study law. Instead he became involved in radical politics and political violence.

In 1947, Castro joined a Cuba-based expedition by Dominican exiles and Cuban radicals to overthrow the government of Generalissimo Rafael L. Trujillo of the Dominican Republic. The plan was broken by the Cuban government, but the idea of invasion from another land left a lasting impression on Castro.

Castro returned to the University of Havana to receive his doctor of laws degree in 1950. He then joined the Ortodoxo party, a reformist group, and entered a race for the Cuban congress in 1952. A few months before the elections, Fulgencio Batista engineered his second coup d'état (the first was in 1933), suspending the constitution and the electoral process.

Within a year, Castro had organized a group of reformist and radical Cubans to bring down the Batista regime. On July 26, 1953, he led an attack on the Moncada army barracks in Santiago. The attack was a failure, but it gave "the 26th of July Movement" its name.

Arrested and imprisoned, Castro made an eloquent speech in his own defense. In this speech, titled "History Will Absolve Me," Castro attacked the illegal and corrupt rule of Batista and called for constitutional government and political liberties in Cuba. He was sentenced to a fifteen-year prison term but was released in 1955 under the terms of a general amnesty intended to repair Batista's image.

Castro fled to Mexico where he devoted the next year and a half to a planned invasion of Cuba. On December 2, 1956, he and a group of about eighty armed men landed on the coast of Oriente Province.

The landing had been delayed by a couple of days and, having been alerted, Batista's forces awaited the revolutionaries. In the struggle that ensued, most of the invaders were killed. Castro and about a dozen men fled into the Sierra Maestra mountain range in the Oriente Province. From this headquarters, they launched an offensive that toppled the Batista regime in the short period of three years. Essential to Castro's success was the help of the Oriente peasants, the support of the middle class throughout Cuba, and a deliberate policy of guerrilla warfare against the government forces.

Conditions in Cuba

By the middle of the 1950s—a few years after the 1952 coup d'état that had established the dictatorship of Fulgencio Batista—Cuba seemed ripe for revolution. Economically, Cuba was a semideveloped or partly developed country occupying an intermediate position between the advanced countries of Western Europe and North America on the one hand, and the developing areas of Asia and Africa on the other. Cuba's single-crop sugarcane economy was highly unstable, however, and several economic tensions created strain on the socioeconomic system. One of the main tensions was between the city and the countryside. The countryside lagged seriously behind the cities in housing, education, and employment; agrarian reform had no place in Batista's economic program. People in rural areas had so little to lose under the Batista regime that once it began to weaken, they hastily abandoned it.

A serious gap between organized workers and the rootless unemployed accentuated the unstable character of the Cuban economy. The organized workers were able to neutralize to some extent the adversity that accompanied the unstable economy, but the rootless unemployed were completely helpless. The chronic unemployment rate was about 9 percent, and the status of a substantial segment of the agricultural work force was dependent upon prices, supply, and demand abroad.

Another tension involved the aspirations of the new middle class for change and the resignation of the older middle class to the status quo. Although the older middle class was not content with the Cuban society of the 1940s and 1950s, it was hesitant to espouse or participate openly in revolution. By contrast, a rising generation of educated Cubans was determined to build a new Cuba and reform its socioeconomic system. It was necessary for the younger generation to convince the older middle class to embrace revolution.

The most serious precipitants of revolution in Cuba, however, were political, not economic. The political history of twentieth-century Cuba is a history of dictatorship, corruption, incompetence, and—not surprisingly—little social and economic reform. The Batista administration was no exception. Batista, who first came to power in 1934, remained the leading political figure until 1959, although he relinquished the presidency in 1944, regaining it by a coup in 1952. Indeed, the most instrumental figure in bringing about a revolution in Cuba was Batista, not Fidel Castro. The persistent tyranny and gross inefficiency of the Batista regime provided the catalyst that made it possible for a charismatic leader to bring together the various disaffected groups in Cuban society. The Cubans turned against Batista for various reasons: because he became overtly corrupt, because of his dictatorial policies, out of hopes for a revitalized Cuba. Batista's rule, in short, gave disaffected groups a focus for their frustrations.

Another condition of political revolution in Cuba was a progressive reaction against foreign domination and control. The United States was deeply involved—economically, politically, and militarily—in Cuban affairs. American investors had enormous holdings in Cuba's national wealth and dominated the Cuban economy. By the late 1950s, however, a trend toward greater Cuban economic autonomy appeared to be emerging. The U.S. control of the sugar industry, for example, had declined from about 70 percent in 1928 to about 37 percent in 1958. The United States continued to retain firm political control, however.

What particularly annoyed Cuban intellectuals and revolutionaries of the 1950s was the U.S. policy—under the Mutual Security program and Mutual Assistance pact—of training the Cuban army and providing extensive military assistance (planes, tanks, ships, missiles, etc.) to the Batista regime, all for the purpose of "hemispheric defense." The revolutionaries protested that U.S. arms were being used to suppress popular sentiment against Batista. Some believed that a secret agreement had been reached between Havana and Washington, according to which Batista was to create the façade of constitutional government in return for accelerated U.S. military support, together with a U.S. pledge to take action against Cuban revolutionary sympathizers soliciting funds and purchasing arms in the United States.

In many ways the actions of the U.S. government at this time helped create, or kindle, Cuban nationalism and make "yankee imperialism" a vital catchword. But the exact nature and extent of Cuban nationalism's role in the early stages of the revolution is not altogether clear. Some scholars maintain that, although the United States was the natural scapegoat for Cuban troubles, the relative well-being of Cuban society mitigated against the development of mass anti-American sentiment as a basis for revolutionary activity. Because the Cuban people in general understood the primary goal of the revolution to be the ouster of Batista rather than the eradication of American control, nationalism played only a small role in the *beginning* of the revolution. Still, many of those who participated in Castro's revolution were weaned on the belief that American imperialism was the major cause of Cuba's shortcomings. They equated socioeconomic reform with national economic independence, to be attained by eliminating foreign influence and remolding the existing system.

Cuban Ideology

Castro's special talent lay in his ability to guide a revolution rather than to articulate a well-defined revolutionary ideology. This is consistent with his own perception of himself as a man of action and not an intellectual. Castro's pragmatism permitted him the luxury of molding and remolding his programs to fit changing conditions in Cuba. His relative detachment from a definitive ideology gave him great latitude to maneuver and to adapt.

The amorphous character of Cuban revolutionary thought makes it difficult to identify *an* ideology of revolution. No single well-defined ideological premise dominated the revolutionary movement. There were various ideologies within the overarching ideology of nationalism, itself largely latent or submerged in the initial phases of the revolution. Scholars generally believe that Castroism is made up of elements from divergent traditions and movements. Specifically, Castro was a democrat and a nationalist before turning to socialism and Marxism-Leninism.

Throughout the 1950s, Castro consistently attacked the Batista regime and called for a democratic Cuba. He sought constitutional government, land reform, a wider distribution of the national wealth, and an end to corruption and ineptitude. His public appeals for democracy, freedom, and social justice generated popular support throughout Cuba.

Throughout this period the underlying dynamic of Castroism was a latent or submerged nationalism. However, just as Castro could not have come down from the Sierra Maestra in 1959 proclaiming himself a Marxist-Leninist, he could not, in the early stages of the revolution, have expounded nationalism as effectively as he did after attaining power. Although a majority of the Cuban people wanted Batista overthrown, they did not necessarily see Batista as an American puppet. While Castro and his colleagues may have seen the end of U.S. domination as a panacea for Cuba's problems, they apparently realized that the majority of the Cuban people did not share this view. In a word, nationalism played a dual role in the Cuban Revolution: it was the rallying cry of the revolutionaries, but for the Cuban people as a whole, it played a latent role—a role, however, that became manifest as the revolution progressed.

Castro rarely alluded to the works of Marx, Lenin, Mao, and others. As some writers have argued, it was probably advantageous to the Cuban Revolution that Castro did not become imprisoned by these works. What Castro needed was ideological flexibility more than commitment to any formal doctrine.

Soon after the assumption of power in December 1959, a definite change began taking place in the ideological posture of revolution. At a youth congress in Havana in August 1960, Ernesto ("Che") Guevara, then minister of industries, stated: "What is our ideology? If I were asked whether our revolution is Communist, I would define it as Marxist. Our revolution has discovered by its methods the paths that Marx pointed out."

At about the same time Castro seemed to have concluded that the goals of his revolution would not be attained unless the Cuban econ-

omy was socialized. Thus in October 1960, the Castro regime national-
ized most Cuban, American, and Cuban-American enterprises. In a
matter of days, virtually the entire Cuban bourgeoisie was eliminated.
Castro stated: "We ourselves don't know quite what to call what we
are building, and we don't care. It is, of course, socialism of a sort."

On December 2, 1961, Castro delivered his famous "I am a Marxist-
Leninist" address. The official adoption of Marxism-Leninism was
consistent with Castro's programs of extensive land reform, radical
redistribution of wealth, eradication of illiteracy and disease, and the
socialization of the economy. He legitimized Marxism-Leninism in
terms of the evolving needs of the Cuban society, not in terms of an
abstract commitment to that ideology.

Castro, then, used certain ideologies (democracy and nationalism) to
capture popular support and attain political power, and certain other
ideologies (socialism and Marxism-Leninism) to retain and solidify his
political control. Instead of adhering to any definite ideological posture, which would have restricted his freedom of movement and might
even have conflicted with the unique characteristics of Cuban society,
Castro subscribed to an amorphous ideological baggage.

Castro's Strategy and Tactics

As we have seen, following his release from prison for the Moncada
attack, Castro departed for Mexico, from where he organized an invasion of Cuba; he then landed on the coast of Oriente, and fled into the
Sierra Maestra. There he established his headquarters and sought to
develop support among the rural peasants while maintaining contacts
with the urban elements.

On March 12, 1958, Castro addressed the Cuban people over the
rebel radio, declaring "total war" against Batista and calling for a
general strike on April 9. The strike failed because, among other
things, the trade unions, which were prospering under Batista, refused
to participate. The abortive strike prompted Batista to initiate a policy
of massive terror against the revolutionaries, killing many innocent
Cubans and eroding middle-class and other support for the ruling regime.

The failure of the general strike propelled Castro toward guerrilla
warfare. Though some writers, especially Che Guevara, have made
guerrilla warfare into the key revolutionary activity throughout Latin

America, Castro accepted it only after other tactics had failed—and near the end of his struggle. Only after failing in conventional attack and the general strike did Castro "adopt" guerrilla warfare as his primary tactic.

Batista's response to guerrilla warfare was a more intensive program of governmental terror. The army and secret police struck indiscriminately and senselessly. An orgy of murders, tortures, and brutalities made life intolerable for the Cuban people. The working class, the middle class, and the intellectuals turned against Batista. Even the Batista army became demoralized and lost its combat effectiveness. By the middle of 1959, the revulsion against the Batista regime was virtually total.

Fidel Castro, Che Guevara, and Régis Debray have all attempted to theorize about the Cuban Revolution and to extend their generalizations to Latin America as a whole. Castro's basic insights are summarized as follows:

1. "The masses make history," but they must be "launched into the battle" by "revolutionary leaders and organizations."

2. The Cuban masses had been launched into the struggle by "four, five, six, or seven" guerrillas.

3. The "objective conditions" for such a struggle exist in "the immense majority of Latin American countries" and only the "subjective conditions"—that is, the "four, five, six, or seven" willing to launch the armed struggle—are lacking.

4. "Peaceful transition" may be possible, but there is not a single case of it on record, and in any event, armed struggle must take place in most Latin American countries.

Through such statements Castro stakes out—as did Mao Tse-tung before him—a claim both to the uniqueness of the Cuban Revolution and to its applicability to other Latin American societies where similar conditions exist.

Che Guevara derives three fundamental lessons from the Cuban Revolution, applicable to all Latin America:

1. Popular forces can win a war against the army.

2. It is not necessary to wait until all conditions for making revolution exist; the insurrection can create them.

3. In the underdeveloped America the countryside is the basic area for armed fighting.

The second point departs sharply from Mao's conception of the need for protracted warfare, especially a strategic defensive stage. According to Guevara, the "necessary minimum" for revolutionary activity is that the people "see clearly the futility of maintaining the fight for social goals within the framework of civil debate."

Perhaps the most far-reaching contribution to Cuban (and Latin American) revolutionary theory has been made by Régis Debray, a French philosophy student and an admirer of the Cuban experience. Debray's book *Revolution in the Revolution?* is purportedly based directly upon the Cuban experience and has been formally sanctioned by Fidel Castro himself.

According to Debray, the Cuban experience demonstrates that revolution in Latin America cannot follow the pattern established by either the Bolshevik or the Chinese revolutions. The Cuban Revolution is a "revolution in the revolution," different from all revolutions before it.

The relationship between the revolutionary party and the guerrillas, Debray maintains, is the most significant and novel concept in the Cuban Revolution. Not until the Cuban experience did anyone question the supremacy of the party in all matters of revolution. Since then Castro and other Latin American revolutionaries have embraced the belief that the Marxist-Leninist party need not necessarily serve as the political vanguard. As Debray states, "There is no exclusive ownership of the revolution."

Although theoretical and historical orthodoxy asserts the supremacy of the party over the army, Debray believes, "historical circumstances have not permitted Latin American Communist Parties, for the most part, to take root or develop in the same way." Just as Mao and Giap modified Lenin's theories to fit the conditions of China and Vietnam, it is Debray's contention that Castro had to modify the theories of Mao and Giap to fit Cuba. The Cuban example is a direct reversal of Mao Tse-tung's dictum that, under all conditions, "the Party commands the gun, and the gun must never be allowed to command the Party." Successful revolutionary activity in Latin America requires the opposite practice: the political apparatus must be controlled by the military. While the success of the revolution lies in the realization that guerrilla warfare is essentially political, the party and the guerrilla must become one and the same, with the guerrilla in command.

The successful execution of revolutionary policies demands a unified command responsible for maximizing the effective use of scarce resources. The guerrilla cannot tolerate a duality of functions and powers, but must become the political as well as the military vanguard of the people. In Latin America today, as the Cuban Revolution shows, it is necessary for the party and the military to become unified in the guerrilla movement: "The guerrilla is the party in embryo." This union of Marxist theory and new revolutionary practice is the most novel aspect of the Cuban Revolution, says Debray. The armed destruction of the enemy—the public demonstration of its fallibility—is the most effective propaganda for the local population. Consequently, in Latin America today, the chief concern must be the development of guerrilla forces and not the strengthening of political parties.

In Cuba, Debray points out, military and political leadership are combined in the person of Fidel Castro. He quotes Castro: "Who will make the revolution in Latin America? The people, the revolutionaries, with or without a party." Castro's thesis, Debray believes, is not that there can be a revolution without a vanguard, but that the vanguard need not necessarily be the Marxist-Leninist party. "In Cuba it was not the party that was the directive nucleus of the popular army, as it had been in Vietnam according to Giap; the Rebel Army was the leading nucleus of the party, the nucleus that created it." This, Debray concludes, is Cuba's "decisive contribution to international revolutionary experience and to Marxism-Leninism."

This deviation from orthodoxy can be explained and justified, according to Debray, by the unique conditions of Latin America. Each particular revolution must be sensitive to the contingencies forced upon it by the environment. Flexibility of response rather than the rigidity of doctrine must prevail. The Cuban example, and not the Russian or the Chinese, is the appropriate one for Latin America. Though there cannot be another Cuban Revolution, its lessons are of the most immediate relevance for Latin American countries.

Summary

The Russian Revolution established communism in Europe, the Chinese Revolution in Asia, and the Cuban Revolution in Latin America. Guerrilla communism as a revolutionary doctrine was first formulated during the Chinese Revolution, modified in the Vietminh experience, and challenged in Cuba. In all three countries the conditions of revolution were similar, except that economic factors played a less prominent role in Cuba than in China and Vietnam. The ideologies of revolution were nationalist and communist in all three countries, although the Cuban revolutionary ideology was much more amorphous than the others. The Cuban Revolution had an urban (or middle-class) component that was largely absent in China and Vietnam. All three ideologies left room for maneuver and compromise. Communism was regularly soft-pedaled to maximize popular support and avoid alienating hostile forces domestically and internationally. Each revolution gave birth to a political hero (Mao, Ho, and Castro) and a corresponding military hero (Chu Teh, Giap, and Guevara, respectively).

Mao Tse-tung's theory of guerrilla communism revolved around rural base areas, alliance with the peasantry, and the protracted military struggle. Since China was unevenly developed and the combined power of imperialism and the domestic reactionary classes was concentrated in the urban centers, the revolutionaries would have to retreat to the countryside, establish inaccessible bases in the most rugged areas, gradually consolidate and strengthen their position, surround the cities, and gradually choke the enemy to death. The core of his strategy was a protracted military conflict based on peasant guerrilla warfare, the mobilization and organization of the local population, the fanning of their patriotism and nationalism, and complete reliance on them for food, supplies, and manpower. Mao proclaimed this strategy as a model universally applicable to all colonial countries.

The Vietminh Revolution closely followed the Chinese pattern, though reliance on nationalism and anti-imperialism was probably more systematic and self-conscious in Vietnam than in China. The chief strategic departure from the Chinese model, crystallized in the battle of Dien Bien Phu, stemmed from Giap's conviction that a decisive battle at the right time and place would have sufficient political, psychological, and military impact to demoralize the enemy and shorten the duration of the revolution.

The Cuban leaders, in contrast, have posed a sharp challenge to the Chinese prototype of guerrilla communism. Castro, Guevara, and Debray all believed that revolution in Latin America could not follow the pattern established by either the Bolshevik or the Chinese revolutions. Just as Mao and Giap revised Lenin's theories to fit conditions in

China and Vietnam, the Cuban leaders changed the theories of Mao and Giap to fit conditions in Cuba. Specifically, they reversed the relationship between the military and the political leadership, and stressed the primacy of the military in guiding and directing the revolution. 補足的な

The Chinese and Vietminh models of guerrilla communism are highly complementary, with Giap's notion of the decisive struggle as a "pragmatic" modification where appropriate conditions prevail. These 勝つ models have been applied successfully to a number of revolutions, including those in Algeria, Angola, Cambodia, Laos, Mozambique, South Vietnam, and Zimbabwe.

Posing a direct antithesis, the Cuban model has had its adherents among some revolutionaries, particularly in Latin American countries (Bolivia, Colombia, and Guatemala, for example). Significantly, however, these movements have either been crushed or are in various stages of dormancy. Indeed, Che Guevara's 1967 failure in Bolivia demonstrates that—however dedicated to "freedom" and "humanity" a small guerrilla force may be, in an unfamiliar and hostile environment, isolated from a distrustful local population whose language it does not speak, and relentlessly pursued by a vastly superior government force trained in counterguerrilla techniques—such a force is doomed to defeat.

Accordingly, as early as 1974, Debray repudiated his own theory, admitting that he had mistakenly dissociated the military from the political leadership, and that political mobilization was of paramount importance. Indeed, it would appear that, beguiled by prospects of quick victory, Debray and others initially misinterpreted the Cuban revolutionary experience in asserting the supremacy of the military over the political and in advancing the argument that the military forces played an exclusive role in creating a revolutionary situation. In truth, such a situation existed to a large extent prior to the emergence of military power.

The Framework Applied

にんしまする

The cognitive dimension of guerrilla communism perceives the world in terms of a dual conflict on a grand scale: (1) the struggle between the oppressed peasants and workers, on the one hand, and the feudal lords and the big bourgeoisie, on the other; and (2) the warfare between colonial peoples and imperialist powers. Not until feudalism and imperialism are smashed can one rest.

The affective component of guerrilla communism calls upon peasants and workers to unite in a victorious struggle to liberate themselves and their nations from the twin evils of feudalism and imperialism. The evaluative ingredient promises an age of peace, harmony, and plenty. Incessant appeals to nationalist values and sentiments overlap the affective and evaluative dimensions.

The programmatic component of guerrilla communism calls for a rural or a rural-urban revolutionary strategy, masterminded and guided by skillful leadership. A protracted revolutionary struggle begins in small-scale guerrilla warfare and ends in a conventional takeover.

Having applied the theories of Marx and Lenin to the conditions of China, Vietnam, and Cuba, Mao, Ho, and Castro had no alternative but to seek their social base in peasants, workers, and middle-class nationalists. Once again, Marx's internationalism was turned into national enterprises.

Selected Bibliography

Bell, J. Bowyer. *On Revolt: Strategies of National Liberation*. Cambridge, Mass.: Harvard University Press, 1976.

Berman, Paul. *Revolutionary Organization*. Lexington, Mass.: Lexington Books, 1974.

Blackey, Robert. *Modern Revolutions and Revolutionists: A Bibliography*. Santa Barbara, Calif.: Clio Press, 1976.

Brandt, Conrad, Benjamin Schwartz, and John K. Fairbank. *A Documentary History of Chinese Communism*. Cambridge, Mass.: Harvard University Press, 1952.

Buttinger, Joseph. *Vietnam: A Political History*. New York: Praeger, 1968.

Chaliand, Gerard. *Revolution in the Third World*. New York: Viking Press, 1978.

Ch'en, Jerome. *Mao and the Chinese Revolution*. New York: Oxford University Press, 1964.

Cohen, Arthur A. *The Communism of Mao Tse-tung*. Chicago: University of Chicago Press, 1964.

Debray, Régis. *Revolution in the Revolution? Armed Struggle and Political Struggle in Latin America*. New York: Grove Press, 1967.

Downton, James V., Jr. *Rebel Leadership*. New York: Free Press, 1973.

Draper, Theodore. *Castroism: Theory and Practice*. New York: Praeger, 1965.

———. *Castro's Revolution: Myths and Realities*. New York: Praeger, 1962.

Fairbairn, Geoffrey. *Revolutionary Guerrilla Warfare: The Countryside Version*. Middlesex, U.K.: Penguin Books, 1974.

Fall, Bernard, ed. *Ho Chi Minh on Revolution*. New York: Praeger, 1967.

————. *Street without Joy: Insurgency in Indochina, 1946–1963*. Harrisburg, Penn.: Stackpole, 1964.

————. *The Two Vietnams: A Political and Military Analysis*. New York: Praeger, 1967.

Giap, Vo Nguyên. *People's War, People's Army*. New York: Bantam Books, 1968.

Guevara, Ernesto. *Guerrilla Warfare*. New York: Vintage Books, 1961.

————. *Reminiscences of the Cuban Revolutionary War*. New York: Grove Press, 1968.

Hoang Van Chi. *From Colonialism to Communism: A Case History of North Vietnam*. New York: Praeger, 1964.

Hodges, Donald C., and A. E. Abu Shanab. *National Liberation Fronts, 1960/1970*. New York: William Morrow, 1972.

Honey, J. P. *Communism in North Vietnam*. Cambridge, Mass.: MIT Press, 1963.

Huberman, Leo, and Paul M. Sweezy. *Cuba: Anatomy of a Revolution*. New York: Monthly Review Press, 1961.

Johnson, Chalmers A. *Peasant Nationalism and Communist Power: The Emergence of Revolutionary China, 1937–1945*. Stanford, Calif.: Stanford University Press, 1962.

Laqueur, Walter. *Guerrilla: A Historical and Critical Study*. Boston: Little, Brown, 1976.

Lin Piao. *Long Live the Victory of People's War!* (September 1965). Peking: Foreign Languages Press, 1966.

McAlister, John T., Jr. *Viet Nam: The Origins of Revolution*. New York: Alfred A. Knopf, 1969.

Mao Tse-tung. *Selected Works of Mao Tse-tung*. 5 vols. Peking: Foreign Languages Press, 1961–77.

Matthews, Herbert L. *Castro: A Political Biography*. London: Allen Lane, 1969.

O'Ballance, Edgar. *The Indo-China War, 1945–1954*. London: Faber & Faber, 1964.

Rejai, Mostafa. *The Comparative Study of Revolutionary Strategy*. New York: David McKay, 1977.

————, ed. *Mao Tse-tung on Revolution and War*. New York: Doubleday, 1969.

Rejai, Mostafa, with Kay Phillips. *Leaders of Revolution*. Beverly Hills, Calif.: Sage Publications, 1979.

Schram, Stuart, ed. *The Political Thought of Mao Tse-tung*. New York: Praeger, 1963.

Schwartz, Benjamin I. *Chinese Communism and the Rise of Mao*. Cambridge, Mass.: Harvard University Press, 1952.

Snow, Edgar. *Red Star over China*. New York: Grove Press, 1961.

Suarez, Andres. *Cuba: Castroism and Communism, 1951–1966*. Cambridge, Mass.: MIT Press, 1967.

Tanham, George K. *Communist Revolutionary Warfare: From the Vietminh to the Viet Cong*. New York: Praeger, 1968.

7

Democracy

For twenty-five hundred years, political thinkers have been concerned with "democracy" as a form of sociopolitical organization. The concept, and ideology, did not become the subject of sustained popular discourse, however, until the nineteenth century (note its association with the French Revolution in chapter 2). The present century has witnessed a singular concern with democracy. Fresh attempts have been made, particularly in the postwar period, to throw light on a topic of immense complexity.

Analytically, democratic ideology has two fairly distinct features. On the one hand, it deals with certain definitional components, or core concepts; on the other, it is concerned with certain conditions deemed essential for the emergence and flourishing of democratic political order. The two aspects are closely interrelated, the conditions often being treated as integral parts of the definition. As we shall see, it is an index of the resiliency of democratic ideology that it can subsume such doctrines as conservatism and liberalism or that it can be fused with either a capitalist economy or a socialist one.

Before examining any of these topics, it would be helpful to consider briefly the evolution of democratic ideas in the West, beginning with their initial appearance in ancient Greece. The historical sketch that follows is necessarily selective, treating only the most important concepts. Moreover, the discussion excludes various conceptions of "democracy" expounded in the Eastern world because, with rare exceptions (India, for example), these concepts are predemocratic or pseudo-democratic, propagated primarily for their propaganda function. I shall return to this topic in a later section.

The Evolution of Democracy

Early Ideas of Democracy

Coined by the Greek historian Herodotus (ca. 484–425 B.C.) in the fifth century B.C., "democracy" combined two Greek words: *demos*, meaning "the people," and *kratia*, meaning "to rule." Thus, the original meaning of democracy was, in the literal sense, "rule of the people"; among its specific features, Herodotus included equality before the law, popular participation in decision making, and popular control of public officials.

With rare exceptions, however, other Greek thinkers did not look with favor upon democracy. Although they denounced tyranny and stressed respect for constitution and law, Greek thinkers were typically elitist—that is, they believed in the rule of the few and, presumably, the best. Plato's famous *Republic*, for instance, is openly hostile to democracy, depicting the ideal society as a fine hierarchy in which various groups of citizens perform the functions for which they are best suited and trained.

After the Hellenic period, sustained discussion of democracy became a rarity in political thought. Nevertheless, over the centuries many democratic ideas did emerge.

Rome's major contribution to democratic government consisted in the further development of the concept of constitutionalism and in the emphasis on law as a system of norms that binds the ruler as well as the ruled. The Romans' fascination with legal matters was a consequence of their attempt to identify a concrete basis for governing the far-flung empire.

Such a basis was found in the concept of "natural law," whose principal author was the Roman lawyer, thinker, and statesman Cicero (106–43 B.C.). Although the genesis of natural law goes back to the Greek Sophists, Cicero made the concept a permanent fixture in political thought.

A series of concrete propositions will serve to summarize Cicero's discussion of natural law:

1. The cosmos is rational and governed by an underlying principle of order.
2. The cosmic process is moral and founded in supernatural reason.

3. Natural law is an expression of supernatural reason; it precedes the state and is superior to all legislation.

4. Being moral and rational, human beings can discover and comprehend natural law and govern their lives accordingly.

5. Before the law of nature all persons are equal and enjoy equal rights; natural law applies equally to all individuals because they are equally possessed of reason and equally capable of virtue.

6. Natural law endows individuals with certain rights that are "natural"; these rights precede the state because natural law precedes the state.

Cicero, in short, not only systematized the concept of natural law but also formulated explicitly, for the first time, the idea of natural rights.

The Middle Ages hold a dual significance for our purposes, one religious (associated with Christianity), the other sociopolitical and economic (associated with feudalism). To begin with, some parallels between Christian and Roman ideas were potentially conducive to democratic government. These included the conception of a moral law of nature, the quest for a universal society, and the belief in the dignity of the individual. Moreover, Christianity stressed, obedience to political authority is conditional, not absolute. Thus, if the ruler exceeds his earthly authority and violates the law of God, he may be lawfully overthrown.

The great synthesizer of the Middle Ages was St. Thomas Aquinas (1225?–1274), who gave natural law a distinct religious flavor. The law of nature was viewed as the reason of God, the law of creation, the plan of divine wisdom by which the entire world is governed. It is eternal because God's rule is eternal. It represents, at the same time, participation of all rational creatures in comprehending God's rule. Human beings, by virtue of their rationality, can participate in divine providence; they must grasp the law of God and order their lives accordingly. Natural law was viewed as the final arbiter of human conduct; it applied to the ruler and the ruled alike.

Feudalism was essentially a series of relationships between the king, the lord, and the vassal or serf. Too weak to control his land in its entirety, the feudal king distributed its largest portion among the lords in return for loyalty and fidelity. Each feudal unit consisted of a territorial entity in which the lord exercised complete authority. Each lord in turn divided his land among a number of vassals, thereby creating a network of interpersonal relationships. The central institution from which "feudalism" derives is *feudum*, or the fief: a grant of land by the lord to the vassal in return for services (generally, agricultural production). The vassal pledged loyalty to the lord, in return for which he was granted protection and a small portion of what he produced. This exchange of services for protection is the very essence of feudalism. Emerging from it are ideas of contract and mutual obligation. These contractual relationships were at first informal and revocable by the lord; later, they became formalized and institutionalized.

The network of feudal relationships was institutionalized in the court system, through which everyone, including the king, theoretically, was subject to law. The two types of courts, the lords' courts and the kings' courts, each emphasized trial by equals. The lords' courts were composed of a number of vassals who tried other vassals accused of breaches of contract. The kings' courts were composed of a number of lords who tried other lords. The king, as *primus inter pares*, was considered morally obliged to honor his commitments.* In case of violation or noncompliance, however, there was no effective remedy. The feudal court system has generally been regarded as the forerunner to kings' councils, representative assemblies, and parliaments.

The Protestant Reformation was the religious counterpart of a multitude of social, political, and economic changes all pointing toward individualism. The Reformation stressed the primacy of personal conscience and the possibility of direct relationship between man (or woman) and God. It meant, particularly for Martin Luther (1483–1546), elimination of the church as the intermediary between the individual and the Creator. It provided all people with the opportunity to interpret the scriptures for themselves.

John Calvin (1509–1564) considered salvation a question of individual effort and hard work. Success in this world, he maintained, particularly in the economic field, was a concrete indication of the possibility of redemption. Herein lies the coalescence between Protestantism and the growing capitalist economic system: Protestantism not only sanctified individual initiative and exertion, it rationalized the human acquisitive impulse into a moral duty and a calling.

Calvinism found its most vigorous supporters in the growing indus-

*As the feudal lords gained in power, the position of the king was gradually reduced to that of "first among equals," and, presumably, he could be tried by the lords.

trial, commercial, manufacturing, and business classes, whose interests could best be advanced in an orderly but fairly permissive political environment and whose existence was eventually deemed necessary for the emergence of democratic government. In other words, Protestantism was congenial to the development of capitalism, which in turn was conducive to the emergence of the type of democracy that prizes individualism and liberty.

The Renaissance witnessed the intensification of optimism about the future of humankind; it led to further expressions of individualism, particularly in the intellectual and artistic fields. At the core of the Renaissance was the discovery of the human being and the emphasis on self-expression, self-realization, and self-fulfillment. Only the Renaissance could have produced the "universal man," who took it upon himself to develop his potential fully and give expression to all aspects of his personality.

One of the central contributions of the Renaissance was the concept of the secular state. Its chief theoretician was Niccolò Machiavelli (1469–1527), whose main objective was the unification of Italy, a goal he believed had been undermined by the church. The major theme of Machiavelli's work is the stability and instability of political orders; its main concern is the creation of a stable, secular state.

A host of later writers, including Jean Bodin (1530–1596), Hugo Grotius (1583–1645), and Thomas Hobbes (1588–1679), further developed the concept of the state. When combined with the notion of "sovereignty," the state became a definite impediment to the development of democratic government. Sovereignty referred to the quality of final, absolute, and ultimate power in the hands of the ruler or the state. The conception of ruler-as-sovereign or state-as-sovereign fitted neatly into the scheme of monarchical absolutism.

Social Contract and After

The seventeenth and eighteenth centuries witnessed serious challenges to such notions as sovereignty or absolutism. The scene was England and France, and the principal challengers were John Locke (1632–1704) and Jean-Jacques Rousseau (1712–1778).* The idea of "social contract" proved to be of crucial importance for the development of democracy.

---

*Though born in Switzerland, Rousseau spent most of his life in France.

The starting point for both Locke and Rousseau was that before there ever was a government or a society, human beings lived in a "state of nature." The state of nature is stipulated to be the presocial and prepolitical condition of human beings in a distant past. No specific time referent is given because, rather than being an actuality, the state of nature is used as an analytical device. In other words, Locke and Rousseau maintain, in order to understand what government is really like, it is necessary to imagine a condition in which government does not exist.

Both Locke and Rousseau stressed the intrinsic value of the individual, although in the latter the individual has often been interpreted as submerged in the collectivity. Both emphasized that the key to political order lies in agreement among individuals. Rousseau in fact goes a step further by insisting that mere agreement is too passive and that what is required is active and voluntary participation of each person in the creation of political society.

The Lockean theory of the social contract is based explicitly on natural law as a moral, universal, and eternal phenomenon, comprehensible to all men of reason. The law of nature is seen to impart certain rights that are natural, inalienable, and absolute—including "life, liberty, and estate." For Locke, men are "by nature all free, equal, and independent"; they are born "with a title to perfect freedom." As such, no man may legitimately subject another to his will, nor may he be subjected to the will of another. The formation of political society is a consequence of man's desire to eliminate certain "inconveniences" or "wants" of the state of nature—particularly the want of a "common judge" as the arbiter of disputes. The purpose of the state is to provide the kind of protection not available in the state of nature. The "great and chief end" of men in forming governments, according to Locke, is the preservation of their property—"property" defined so broadly as to include "lives, liberties, and estates." The political society is a "trust" and government is an agent of the governed: it merely does what it is told to do. It follows that if the ruler exceeds his political authority and violates the trust, he may be rightfully overthrown through revolution and violence.

For Rousseau the central problem of political life is spelled out in the opening sentence of Chapter 1, Book I, of *The Social Contract:* "Man is born free; and everywhere he is in chains." Rousseau's declared objective is to identify the conditions under which the chains may be legitimized. He attempts to do this by constructing a political utopia in which the nature of man and the functions of government are harmonized, a society in which there is no compulsion and force. Rousseau's argument is that the transition from the state of nature to civil society takes place through a social compact that is the product of man's act of willing: through the contract, the moral man voluntarily chooses to live in society. Unable to live alone, man wills to be a part of a larger system of social and emotional commitments. In and out of society, in other words, man obeys himself.

The formation of the political society coincides with the creation of the "General Will." In constructing a political society, Rousseau argues, each and every man surrenders himself completely. Each man contributes all of his rights toward the creation of the General Will: "each man, in giving himself to all, gives himself to nobody." The surrender of rights is total; the recipient is the General Will.

Although the vaguest concept in Rousseau, the General Will appears to refer to the collective moral entity that emerges from the contract. It is infallible, flawless, always for the common good, and never wrong. Above all, it is the supreme embodiment of man's act of willing. Its very existence justifies the change from nature to society and makes the "chains" legitimate.

Rousseau considers sovereignty, which is lodged in the people, to be an attribute of the General Will. Sovereignty, he says, is "nothing less than the exercise of General Will." It is absolute, limitless, indestructible, indivisible, and inalienable. In specifying the people as the source of sovereignty, Rousseau seeks to reverse the traditional relationship between the ruler and the ruled.

Rousseau's overall emphasis is on an ethical, moral, and perfectly unified community. He envisions the complete psychological and emotional identification of the individual with the collectivity. Man obeys the state because the state is the embodiment of the General Will. Thus, in obeying the state, man obeys himself. It is in this sense that he may be "forced to be free." And it is for this reason that Rousseau is sometimes interpreted as the forerunner of "totalitarian democracy."

The idea of social contract gained immense popularity for many reasons. It was an assertion of human freedom and dignity. It was an expression of revolt against absolutism, tyranny, and monarchical rule. It was an assertion of the consent basis of government and a justification for obedience and authority. It viewed government as a means to human betterment, not an end in itself.

The English, American, and French revolutions of the seventeenth and eighteenth centuries gave concrete reality to the social contract idea and popularized and legitimized democratic government throughout the Western world. The systematization and elaboration of democratic ideology throughout the eighteenth and nineteenth centuries were primarily the work of American, English, and French writers and political leaders: Thomas Jefferson (1743–1826), Alexis de Tocqueville (1805–1859), Abraham Lincoln (1809–1865), Jeremy Bentham (1748–1832), Edmund Burke (1729–1797), and John Stuart Mill (1806–1873). The first two, together with Locke and Rousseau, are generally known as the "classical" theorists of democracy.* In the pages that follow, I shall clarify this concept and use it as a basis for comparing earlier doctrines of democracy with their modern and contemporary counterparts.

Conceptions of Democracy

Definitions of democracy are legion. Since it would be impossible to review—or to remember—all definitions, I shall instead group them into three types: (1) *direct, or classical*, conceptions of democracy, which have been associated primarily with ancient Greece, particularly Athens, and the New England towns; (2) *indirect, representative, or pluralist* ideologies of democracy, which emerged and flourished in the nineteenth and twentieth centuries; and (3) *participatory* democracy, which originated in the 1960s and later, a child of Vietnam and Watergate. As can be seen, analytical as well as historical imperatives characterize the three types. Each type will be examined in terms of (1) its major premises and principles; (2) the major difficulties it confronts; and (3) the implications following therefrom.

Direct or Classical Democracy

Although Herodotus, Locke, Rousseau, Jefferson, and de Tocqueville all have many differences among themselves, each nonetheless has

---

*Although de Tocqueville greatly admired American democracy, his personal sentiments were aristocratic, not democratic.

contributed many ideas to the classical conceptions of democracy.

The first principle of classical democracy is self-rule: popular participation in decision making, "government of the people, by the people, for the people." A second, related principle holds that the purest manifestation of self-rule is to be found in small towns or communities. Thus, for instance, Jefferson maintained that the political organization of American society should find expression at four levels: federal, state, county, and ward. The "ward republics"—Jefferson's idealized means of self-government—were to be sufficiently small to permit personal participation of every individual in the affairs of the community. De Tocqueville's praise for grassroots democracy was even more lavish. The town, he wrote, "seems to come directly from the hand of God." It is characterized by a high degree of "spirit" and excites "the warmest of human affections."

A third principle of classical democracy, attributed mainly to Rousseau, is that democratic government is a method of realizing the "common good" as expressed in the "common will." A fourth principle, derived from the tradition of natural law, stresses the rights and liberties of individuals: "natural," "self-evident," and "inalienable," to use Jefferson's wording. Finally, all classical formulations of democracy have in common the assumption of the ordinary individual's goodness and rationality. Without this assumption, all other stipulated views would lose their significance. What, for instance, would remain of government by the people, if the "people" were not good, rational, and capable of self-rule?

The classical expressions of democracy came under heavy assault from many sources. Although there were other opponents, by far the most trenchant critics of democracy were a group of European intellectuals commonly called the "elitists" and including Vilfredo Pareto (1848–1923), Gaetano Mosca (1858–1941), and Roberto Michels (1876–1936). A detailed analysis of the various attacks upon classical democracy is beyond the scope of the present chapter. I shall briefly outline, first, the general arguments against the classical conceptions and, then, the particular critique of the elitists.

The general arguments include the following: First, it was pointed out, available evidence overwhelmingly negates the notion that "government by the people" has ever been—or is ever likely to be—a reality. People, it was suggested, cannot—in the literal sense—rule themselves, regardless of the size of their communities. It has been repeatedly found that even Athenian democracy and the New England towns were dominated by minority interests.

Second, such conceptions as "common will" and "common good" are mystical, intuitive notions, incapable of demonstration and proof. There is no *one* policy, no *one* "good," that can benefit every member of a society. To be sure, such "goods" as defense and education are of general benefit, but they cannot be the distinguishing marks of democracies, because they are provided by *all* countries. In other words, it would be impossible to sort out democratic from nondemocratic government by these criteria.

Third, "natural law" and "natural rights" are assumptions neither verifiable nor necessary to political life. The validity of a natural law proposition cannot be demonstrated or tested, and there is no society in which human rights are "natural" or absolute. Fourth, liberty and equality, if interpreted in rigid and literal terms, emerge as contradictory values, incapable of attainment in any society. A moment's reflection reveals that if individuals are free, they are not necessarily equal; if they are forced to be equal, they are no longer free. Finally, it was suggested, the underlying premise of classical democracy—its faith in human rationality—is untenable, particularly in the light of findings of modern psychology.

Following up on this point, the elitists, under the strong influence of Freudian psychology, insisted that a significant portion of human behavior is motivated and sustained by irrational and nonlogical drives lying well below the level of consciousness. Human conduct is governed as much by unconscious habit as by deliberate choice.

The elitists' analysis of historical evolution established to their satisfaction that human society at all times has been characterized by a fundamental division between a minority that rules and a majority that is ruled, between elite and mass. They saw politics as perpetual conflicts among contending groups for position and power, democratic politics being no exception. In these power struggles, moreover, the elites routinely resort to myths, lies, and ideologies in order to manipulate and control the masses, rationalize and legitimize themselves, and perpetuate their rule. Moreover, the masses have a psychological *need* for leadership: lacking the necessary capabilities and skills, they *want* to be guided and ruled.

The elitists concluded, therefore, that democracy is not only an unrealizable form of government, it is irrational and undesirable as well.

The masses are incompetent and incapable of self-government. The elite will always rule.

Confronted with such an overpowering critique, and recognizing the validity of much of the argument, the modern defenders of democracy set out to revise and update classical democracy in such a way as to overcome its weaknesses. The result has been a transformation in democratic thought: the emergence of indirect, representative, or pluralist democracy.

Indirect, Representative, or Pluralist Democracy

The reformulation of democracy has been the work of many philosophers and theorists—from Jeremy Bentham and John Stuart Mill in the nineteenth century to Joseph A. Schumpeter, E. E. Schattschneider, Robert A. Dahl, and Seymour Martin Lipset in contemporary times. The operating assumption of these writers is that democracy must be defined not as a constellation of idealized values but in terms of a series of propositions, practices, actions, and institutions that can be observed and verified in actuality. The gap between the ideal and the real, as created by the classical writers, must be closed.

The starting premise of indirect, representative, or pluralist democracy is that people in a democratic society have limitations as well as capabilities. One such limitation is that they do not and cannot directly rule themselves, if for no other reason than the sheer weight of their numbers. Instead, they choose representatives and leaders who rule on their behalf.

Given this premise, the main principles of indirect, representative, or pluralist democracy revolve around the existence of many institutions, practices, and safeguards. What is needed first and foremost is the existence of social and political competition, or pluralism. "Social pluralism" refers to the existence in a democratic society of a multiplicity of interest groups, civic organizations, voluntary associations, artistic and cultural institutions, scientific and professional groups, business and labor organizations, and the like; these overlapping power centers prevent power monopoly in any one source. "Political pluralism" requires the continued presence of two *or more* political parties to offer alternative candidates (leaders), platforms, policies, and programs.

Before proceeding, we should note the trade-offs between two-party and multiparty political systems. Put directly, the two-party system is high on stability but low on representation (of either the extreme right or left); a multiparty system is high on representation but low on stability. Practically speaking, this means that in a two-party system, one or the other party is certain to capture a majority of the votes cast and become the governing party. This political system is predictable and stable within the parameters of the two parties.

In a multiparty system, by contrast, very rarely does one party capture a majority of the votes cast. Rather, several parties capture parliamentary pluralities and form coalitions to become governing parties. These coalitions are frequently unstable, especially as they confront major policy issues. Italy is the best example of this genre, having elected, on the average, a new government each year throughout the postwar period.

Second, representative democracy stipulates, the people must have the ability—through elections and referenda, for example—actually to choose (as well as dismiss) leaders and programs. (This obviously requires information and education, a subject to which we shall return.) Third, it is not enough that there simply exist alternative parties and leaders; over a period of time, there must be actual changes in rulership (rotation in office). Fourth, parties, leaders, and governments so elected must remain responsive and responsible to the electorate: they must be answerable and accountable for their actions; they must be willing and able to meet reasonable popular demands.

Finally, it is clear, a democratic political system cannot operate in the absence of liberty and equality—but in a relative, not an absolute sense. This means, for example, that one person's freedom is limited by the equal freedom of all other persons. It also means that we must avoid absolute equality because it would be destructive of human creativity, that is to say, people's expression of intellectual and physical prowess, initiative, entrepreneurship, and the like. A democratic society encourages the expression of human potentialities (within the limits of civilized society) rather than stifling them.

In more general terms, as we have already noted, liberty and equality are incompatible values: the more you have of one, the less you have of the other. That is why French democracy, for example, stresses not just the values of liberty and equality but fraternity also. Brotherhood—that condition of concern, respect, and caring for other human beings—was intended to mitigate the extremes of liberty and equality.

Indirect, representative, or pluralist ideologies of democracy were variously refined and reformulated, but their essential principles remained unchallenged for a long time. Vietnam and Watergate changed all that by demonstrating, among other things, that a democratic government can be corrupt, unresponsive, and irresponsible.

More specifically, the "radical" and "revisionist" intellectuals of the 1960s and later launched a series of nearly crippling attacks upon pluralist democracy. Among other things, they pointed to a series of gaps between concept and reality. First, they argued, pluralist democracy claims to be objective, based on observable and verifiable facts of democratic political life. In reality, however, by stressing political competition and rotation in office, the pluralist writers express a conservative ideology of preference for stability, harmony, balance, predictability, status quo.

Second, in theory, pluralist democracy emphasizes political competition and popular participation, whereas in reality democratic societies are dominated and run by elites of all sorts: political, economic, industrial, military, scientific. Other than pro forma voting for preselected candidates, the radicals asked, what effective role do the people play? There are (at least) two ways of looking at representative democracy, the critics maintained. Looked at from the inside and from the top down (that is, from the standpoint of the members of the elite stratum), one sees political competition, change, and alternating governments. But looked at from the outside and from the bottom up (that is, from the standpoint of the masses in a society), no amount of rotation at the top suggests popular influence, let alone control, down below.

Third, in theory, pluralist democracy stresses responsiveness and responsibility, whereas in reality the elites are to a large extent autonomous and beyond the reach of the public. Finally, thanks to advances in communications media, public relations, and effective "packaging," contemporary elites have vastly improved their ability to manipulate and dupe the people.

Pluralist democracy, the "radicals" and "revisionists" concluded, is a façade. The gap between concept and reality persists. What we need, they contended, is a new alternative. This alternative they labeled "participatory democracy."

Participatory Democracy

The ideology of participatory democracy is not nearly as comprehensive or elaborate as the two we have just examined. Its central premise calls for maximum popular participation in and control over candidates, policies, and programs. Or, as the slogan of the times went, "Power to the People."

Stripped to bare essentials, participatory democracy calls for at least two things: (1) decentralization of political power and decision making, and (2) direct popular involvement in political affairs. The first principle calls for devolution of power from the center (Washington) to the periphery (local communities): political decisions should be made as near to the affected source as possible. The second principle stresses the involvement of ordinary citizens in the making of these decisions. Stated differently, participatory democracy calls for the involvement of "citizen politicians" in contrast to the traditional, professional politicians.*

The exponents of participatory democracy claim a number of advantages on its behalf. To begin with, they argue, participatory democracy limits governmental abuse of power. Moreover, decision making under participatory democracy is bound to be "better"—that is, more responsive to local needs and conditions. Even if not better, it is said, the legitimacy of decisions—and hence confidence in government—is seldom called into question, since the community is bound to accept common responsibility for its own actions. Finally, in the processes of deliberation and decision making, participatory democracy provides education, learning, and enrichment for the entire community.

The problems associated with participatory democracy are no less severe than those associated with classical and pluralist ideologies. For one thing, although the radical and revisionist critique of pluralist democracy carries much validity, the suggested alternative—participatory democracy—is not a coherent ideology in its own right; in fact, it is weak, vague, and incomplete. In this sense, participatory democracy was more of a *reactive* phenomenon: an outrage against the abuses of Vietnam and Watergate. For another, participatory democracy is incompatible with contemporary reality, for it overlooks the simple problem of increasing societal complexity on many fronts. How can, one is bound to ask, some of the most pressing issues of our times—arms

---

*The reader may remember that, taking advantage of the climate of opinion, both Ronald Reagan and Jerry Brown of California first presented themselves as citizen politicians.

control, the economy, pollution, poverty—be addressed at the local level? Where and how will ordinary citizens obtain the expertise necessary for handling global, national, and regional problems?

Finally, although admittedly romantic and attractive, participatory democracy is afflicted with a fatal flaw: it seeks to return to direct or classical democracy without having resolved the elemental problems that besieged its centuries-old predecessor.

On the whole, participatory democracy seeks perfection and utopia while political reality is by definition imperfect. Consequently, for all its shortcomings and flaws, indirect, representative, or pluralist democracy is the only realistic arrangement available to us today. As Winston Churchill is supposed to have said, democracy is a bad form of government—until one begins to contemplate the alternatives.

The Conditions for Democracy

Democratic governments do not grow in a vacuum, in any time and place, under any set of circumstances. Although the particular mix will vary from country to country, a series of concrete conditions must coalesce before democratic regimes emerge and flourish. For the sake of convenience, I shall group these conditions under three headings: socioeconomic, political, and psychocultural. Some of the stipulated conditions, as will be seen, are mutually contradictory, which leaves it to the reader to decide the best or the most reasonable position.

Socioeconomic Conditions

The socioeconomic requisites of democracy stipulate the existence of material affluence, urbanization and industrialization, a middle class, literacy and participation, media of communication, and a network of voluntary groups and associations.

Economic development—which incorporates affluence, a middle class, urbanization, and industrialization—is the most widely discussed condition of democratic government. Only in a relatively prosperous society in which a reasonably fair distribution of the national wealth has taken place do people have the leisure, information, and education necessary to participate in political affairs. Only such a society can produce a significant middle class whose interests are best pursued in a permissive and stable environment. A middle class acts as a buffer between the extremes of poverty and wealth, and it tends to discourage extremist ideologies, whether of the right or the left.

A democratic society is a participant society in which the practice of participation is institutionalized in voting, elections, referenda, initiatives, and petitions. The evolution of a participant society, in turn, hinges on the development of literacy and media of communication.

The importance of a network of voluntary groups and associations (social pluralism) for democratic politics has been emphasized by many writers. Acting as structures of authority in their own right, groups and associations help prevent concentration of power in the government.

Political Conditions

Among the more distinct political conditions of democracy, the following are most frequently included: effectiveness, legitimacy, an effective political opposition, and agreement (or disagreement) on "fundamentals" or "rules of the game."

Effectiveness refers to the ability of democracy to perform the basic functions of government, to respond to popular demands, and to provide the necessary services. Legitimacy refers to the capacity of the system to promote and retain popular support for the overall maintenance of the system. The relationship between the two is reciprocal: legitimacy enhances effectiveness, effectiveness reinforces legitimacy. Together, they ensure political stability.

The existence of effective opposition parties and groups is frequently regarded as a crucial criterion of democratic government. Some scholars, in fact, view it as *the* most distinctive feature of democracy, considering that its absence indicates the absence of democratic government. As we have seen, opposition parties and groups provide political competition and prevent monopolization of power in a few hands.

Agreement on "fundamental principles," or the "rules of the game," has long been a point of contention between those who insist that such agreement is essential to democracy and those who maintain that democracy means, among other things, agreement to disagree. On the one hand, it is argued, the various components of democratic government—the executive office, the legislature, the judiciary, bureaucracy, political parties, and so on—all must play their roles in a way that is consistent with the "principles" or the "rules." On the other hand, it is maintained, any insistence on such conformity is unnecessary and undesirable; indeed, any demand for such agreement would be antidemocratic, since democracy thrives on diversity and dissent.

Psychocultural Conditions

Democratic government rests upon a "political culture" and a "political personality" that evolve over a period of time and that are virtually inseparable. It goes without saying that democratic culture and personality are markedly different from authoritarian ones. I shall briefly summarize the main contrasts.

Democratic culture and personality are receptive to divergent points of view; authoritarian culture and personality are intolerant of variety and seek to impose their own views upon others. Democratic behavior is characterized by openness to change, itself resting on a feeling of security on the part of the individual; authoritarian behavior is marked by rigidity and insecurity associated with status-ridden personalities who are obsessed by fear of losing face and position. Democratic behavior integrates a variety of interests, values, and goals; authoritarian behavior is guided by rituals.

Democratic behavior is marked by "empathy": the ability to put oneself in another person's situation and see things from his or her point of view; authoritarian behavior is callous and aloof. Democratic personality is a participant personality and senses some degree of control over events and situations; authoritarian personality is a subject personality, subservient to superiors who will provide guidelines for all actions. Democratic personality is marked by the ability to play multiple roles; authoritarian personality lacks the ability to incorporate new roles and handle new situations.

In short, democratic personality is characterized by openness, security, tolerance, empathy, adaptiveness, and flexibility; authoritarian personality is marked by closedness, insecurity, intolerance, callousness, rigidity, and inflexibility.

Summary

This discussion has, it is hoped, clarified some of the conditions necessary for the emergence and survival of democratic government. Although we cannot identify a precise, uniform, and inflexible set of conditions that obtain in *all* democracies, we do know that *some* mix of conditions must prevail.

This discussion also demonstrates why, much as we might wish, democracy is unlikely to appear in underdeveloped countries: the necessary conditions simply do not exist. A world racked by poverty, hunger, and ignorance is more likely to fall under the spell of tyrants, dictators, and juntas than democratic regimes. Thus, while for political purposes from time to time the United States sets out to thrust democracy upon another country (Vietnam or El Salvador, for example), we should not expect much by way of positive outcomes.

Conservatism and Liberalism, Capitalism and Socialism

Although democratic government does not grow at any time, in any place, or under any set of conditions, it is nonetheless sufficiently flexible to accommodate a variety of ideological postures and economic systems. Thus, for instance, conservatism and liberalism have always been variants or subsidiaries of democratic ideology, even though they have undergone dramatic transformations over time.

The initial statement of conservatism by, say, Edmund Burke rested on a pessimistic view of human nature and of human ability to introduce constructive societal change. Accordingly, Burke glorified a country's tradition and called for structures of authority—political, religious, familial—to maintain order and stability. By contrast, the initial statement of liberalism by, say, John Stuart Mill was based on an optimistic view of human nature and of human reason. Accordingly, Mill called on human beings to exercise their liberty—within civilized social constraints—in order to improve their condition and bring about progress.

We should take care not to confuse liberalism and democracy. Liberalism stresses individual rights and it places limits on government to protect these rights. There is a tendency to view government, if not as a necessary evil, at least as something that should be relied on only when there is widespread consensus on a course of action.

Democracy, on the other hand, stresses government that is responsive to the majority of the people. There is a strong implication that government is a useful means by which people can achieve ends that a majority deems in the public interest.

Over the ages, liberalism and conservatism have undergone radical changes. Specifically, in our time, conservatism has come to stand primarily for liberty and individualism; liberalism, for equality and social welfare. At times, in fact, conservatives are called "classical liberals," and liberals, "modern collectivists."

Similarly, the democratic ideology can be fused with either a socialist or a capitalist economy, thus giving us a democratic socialist government or a democratic capitalist one. As we saw in chapter 4, "socialism" in its generic sense embodies three main principles: (1) relative egalitarianism, based on the assumption of the fundamental dignity of all human persons; (2) communalism, resting on the primacy of the welfare of the community as a whole; and (3) communal ownership and control of the basic wealth of the community in the interest of the whole. Correlatively, the three core principles of capitalism would be liberty, competition, and individual (or corporate) ownership and control. Put crudely, democratic capitalism would say: "What is good for General Motors is good for the country." Democratic socialism would retort: "What is good for the country had better be good for General Motors." It is an index of the resilience of democratic ideology that it can incorporate two contrasting sets of principles.

To reiterate a point made in chapter 4, socialism in its generic sense is not the same as Marxist socialism or Leninist socialism or Maoist socialism or any other kind of socialism. Marx, Lenin, Mao, and others accepted the three core principles but introduced all sorts of additions and modifications of their own.

There are actually two types of democratic socialism. The first type draws its inspiration from Marx but rejects Marx's ideas of violence and revolution, arguing, in effect, that democratic socialist goals can be achieved through gradual, peaceful means. This version of democratic socialism can be found in most European countries, especially France, Italy, and Germany. On the other hand, the second type of democratic socialism rejects Marx outright, maintaining that socialism does not need a Marxist component. This variety of democratic socialism can be found in England and Sweden, for example. Indeed, such African intellectuals as former President Julius Nyerere of Tanzania and former President Léopold Sédar Senghor of Senegal take a huge step farther by maintaining that there was homegrown and indigenous socialism in Africa thousands of years before European writers formalized it into a self-conscious ideology.

The Framework Applied

The cognitive dimension of democracy perceives the world as consisting of rational and capable human beings (both the ruler and the ruled) who can live harmoniously without unnecessary coercion and force. Majority rule, representation, and constraints on government assure the continuation of this state of affairs. That not all persons equally enjoy the blessings of democracy is balanced out, in the long run, by the interests of the whole.

In its beginnings as a revolutionary ideology, democracy shared some of the same powerful emotional appeals of nationalism. It began as an outrage against tyranny and absolutism, glorifying peoples and nations instead. This is as true of the American Revolution as it is of the French. Consider, for example, the haunting appeal of the Tricolor, the Stars and Stripes, or the Statue of Liberty.

As Western democracy reached a condition of maturity, however, rationalism and pragmatism overtook the preoccupation with affect, although emotions periodically make dramatic reappearances, as in the American experience with the Vietnam War and the Iran hostage crisis. Even under normal conditions, however, emotive appeal is not altogether absent. In the last couple of decades, for instance, the people of the United States have been presented with a whole series of attractively packaged and popularized promises: New Frontier, Great Society, Generation of Peace, Human Rights. And the "National Interest," of course, has been there for invocation at every whim and convenience.

The evaluative component of democracy is well encapsulated in "Liberty, Equality, Fraternity" (France) and "Life, Liberty, and the Pursuit of Happiness" (the United States). Other values are so much a part of the democratic heritage that they do not require discussion: human dignity, popular sovereignty, consent, legitimacy, obligation.

The programmatic ingredient of democracy is all too familiar to need belaboring. Briefly, democracy requires contending leaders and parties, election and representation, popular participation, education and information. It also rests on popular control to assure responsibility, responsiveness, and accountability of public officials. On a personal level, democracy calls for openness, tolerance, empathy, and flexibility.

At times, the programmatic dimension of democracy has entailed an expansionist element as well. Thus, for instance, when Woodrow Wilson set out "to make the world safe for democracy," his hope and ideal were, in effect, to universalize the values of the American civilization.

The social base of democracy incorporates the entire citizenry, except the fringe groups on the very right and the very left. Seldom, however, do we expect the "entire citizenry" to agree on any major issue. As a result, as is commonly known, democracy is a political system in which conflicting issues and demands are settled by peaceful means. Violent exceptions do take place from time to time, however, as seen in the convulsions of Western democracies in the 1960s.

Selected Bibliography

Almond, Gabriel A., and Sidney Verba. *The Civic Culture: Political Attitudes and Democracy in Five Nations*. Princeton, N.J.: Princeton University Press, 1963.
————, eds. *The Civic Culture Revisited*. Boston: Little, Brown, 1980.
Bachrach, Peter. *The Theory of Democratic Elitism*. Boston: Little, Brown, 1967.
Benello, C. George, and D. Roussopoulos, eds. *The Case for Participatory Democracy*. New York: Viking, 1971.
Burke, Edmund. *Reflections on the Revolution in France* (1790). Various editions and publishers.
Burnheim, John. *Is Democracy Possible? The Alternative to Electoral Politics*. Berkeley: University of California Press, 1985.
Cnudde, Charles F., and Deane E. Neubauer, eds. *Empirical Democratic Theory*. Chicago: Markham Publications, 1969.
Connolly, William E., ed. *The Bias of Pluralism*. New York: Atherton Press, 1970.
Cook, Terence E., and Patrick M. Morgan. *Participatory Democracy*. New York: Harper & Row, 1971.
Dahl, Robert A. *Democracy and Its Critics*. New Haven, Conn.: Yale University Press, 1989.
————. *Dilemmas of Pluralist Democracy*. New Haven, Conn.: Yale University Press, 1982.
————. *Polyarchy: Participation and Opposition*. New Haven, Conn.: Yale University Press, 1971.
————. *A Preface to Democratic Theory*. Chicago: University of Chicago Press, 1956.
————. *Who Governs?* New Haven, Conn.: Yale University Press, 1961.
De Tocqueville, Alexis. *Democracy in America*. 2 vols. 1835, 1840. New York: Alfred A. Knopf, 1945.
Diamond, Larry, Seymour Martin Lipset, and Juan J. Linz. *Democracy in Developing Countries*. Vol. 1. *Persistence, Failure, and Renewal*. Boulder, Colo.: Lynne Rienner, 1988.
Domhoff, G. William. *Who Really Rules?* New Brunswick, N.J.: Transaction Books, 1978.
Downs, Anthony. *An Economic Theory of Democracy*. New York: Harper & Row, 1957.

Dye, Thomas R. *Who's Running America?* 2d ed. Englewood Cliffs, N.J.: Prentice-Hall, 1979.

Fukuyama, Francis. *The End of History and the Last Man.* New York: Basic Books, 1992.

Guinier, Lani. *The Tyranny of the Majority: Fundamental Fairness in Representative Democracy.* New York: Free Press, 1994.

Held, David. *Models of Democracy.* Stanford, Calif.: Stanford University Press, 1987.

Huntington, Samuel P. *The Third Wave: Democratization in the Late Twentieth Century.* Norman: University of Oklahoma Press, 1991.

Kariel, Henry S. *Open Systems: Arenas for Political Action.* Itasca, Ill.: Peacock Publishers, 1969.

———, ed. *Frontiers of Democratic Theory.* New York: Random House, 1970.

Lipset, Seymour Martin. *The First New Nation.* New York: Basic Books, 1963.

———. *Political Man: The Social Bases of Politics.* New York: Doubleday, 1960.

Locke, John. *Two Treatises of Civil Government* (1690). Various editions and publishers.

Lowi, Theodore J. *The End of Liberalism.* New York: Norton, 1969.

Macpherson, C. B. *Democratic Theory.* Oxford: Clarendon Press, 1973.

———. *The Life and Times of Liberal Democracy.* New York: Oxford University Press, 1977.

———. *The Real World of Democracy.* Oxford: Clarendon Press, 1966.

Mansbridge, Jane J. *Beyond Adversary Democracy.* New York: Basic Books, 1981.

Margolis, Michael. *Viable Democracy.* New York: Penguin Books, 1979.

Martin, Rosco C. *Grass Roots.* Tuscaloosa, Ala.: University of Alabama Press, 1957.

Mill, John Stuart. *On Liberty* (1859). Various editions and publishers.

———. *Representative Government* (1861). Various editions and publishers.

Mills, C. Wright. *The Power Elite.* New York: Oxford University Press, 1957.

Parenti, Michael J. *Democracy for the Few.* 4th ed. New York: St. Martin's Press, 1983.

Pateman, Carole. *Participation and Democratic Theory.* Cambridge: Cambridge University Press, 1970.

Pennock, J. Roland. *Democratic Political Theory.* Princeton, N.J.: Princeton University Press, 1979.

Plamenatz, John. *Democracy and Illusion.* New York: Longman, 1977.

Powell, G. Bingham, Jr. *Contemporary Democracies: Participation, Stability and Violence.* Cambridge, Mass.: Harvard University Press, 1982.

Rejai, Mostafa, ed. *Democracy: The Contemporary Theories.* New York: Atherton Press, 1967.

Rousseau, Jean-Jacques. *The Social Contract* (1762). Various editions and publishers.

Sartori, Giovanni. *Democratic Theory.* Detroit: Wayne State University Press, 1962.

Schattschneider, E. E. *The Semisovereign People.* New York: Holt, Reinhart & Winston, 1960.

Schumpeter, Joseph A. *Capitalism, Socialism, and Democracy.* New York: Harper & Row, 1942.

Weber, Max. *The Protestant Ethic and the Spirit of Capitalism.* 1904. Reprint. New York: Scribner, 1958.

Wolfe, Alan. *The Seamy Side of Democracy.* 2nd ed. New York: Longman, 1978.

8

Feminism

The Meaning of Feminism

Originating principally in the United States and Great Britain—and gradually spreading throughout much of the globe—feminism means, in its most generic sense, political, social, and economic equality of women with men. Until recent times, women had been regarded as inferior to men physically and intellectually. Both law and religion had sanctioned their subjection. Women could not possess property in their own names, engage in business, control the rearing of their own children, or divorce their husbands. As a result, they were assigned to such traditional roles as teachers, nurses, librarians, secretaries, and the like.

The principal reasons for the inferior status of women were sex role socialization and gender stereotyping. Sex role socialization means that men are brought up to be fighters and lovers and to look after the affairs of the state. By contrast, women are brought up to be wives and mothers and to look after family and children. In other words, men are socialized to be tough and macho; women, to be emotional and submissive. The result was a systematic undermining of the female self-esteem.

Recent research has established that sex role socialization has been a practice invented by men in order to maintain a masculine status quo; that men and women are not all that different; that while men stress

---

In addition to Kay Phillips's contribution, noted in the table of contents, I draw especially on the works of Deckard, Donovan, and Tong listed in the bibliography for this chapter.

172

independence and autonomy, women stress interdependence and affiliation; that women are guided by the ethics of justice and fairness more than men. In short, to use the title of Carol Gilligan's famous book (see bibliography), women speak "in a different voice."

Gender stereotyping has had equally deleterious effects on women, the general assumption being that women lack the necessary attributes, skills, attitudes, and motivations to compete in a man's world. The male stereotype portrays men as dominant, assertive, independent, competitive, risk-taking, task-oriented, and with a high need for power and achievement. The female stereotype pictures women as passive, submissive, interdependent, emotional, expressive, cooperative, person-oriented, and with a low need for power and achievement.

Recent research has found that these stereotypes are without scientific foundation. The only established differences are that women rank higher than men on expressiveness and lower on advanced mathematical ability; that men rank higher on task orientation and women on person orientation; that men are more confrontational and women more indirect; that assumptions of female inferiority are to be found in situational and organizational contexts, task environments, group composition, and power structure. It has also been found that gender differences are due to men's better access to social, political, and economic resources.

To summarize, gender differences have been overexaggerated; men and women are not that different; human behavior is a function of context or situation, not gender.

In this section, we have outlined the most general meaning of feminism and some traditional issues blocking women's advance in various areas of social, political, and economic endeavor. However, current feminism takes a variety of forms and we shall discuss some of these forms in a subsequent section.

The Evolution of Feminism

The genesis of the feminist movement traces to the philosophers of the Enlightenment (particularly Voltaire and Rousseau) and the French Revolution of 1789, which made "Liberty, Equality, and Fraternity" bywords throughout France. In 1789 the French National Assembly adopted the "Declaration of the Rights of Man and Citizen." In 1791 Olympe de Gouges issued a "Declaration of the Rights of Woman," in which she sought to establish gender equality.

In 1792 the English writer and activist Mary Wollstonecraft wrote the epochal book, *A Vindication of the Rights of Woman*. Thoroughly influenced by Voltaire, Rousseau, and John Locke, Wollstonecraft was responding to the ultraconservative attack by the English philosopher Edmund Burke, who in his *Reflections on the Revolution in France* (1790) had unleashed a full-scale assault on everything the French Revolution stood for. Wollstonecraft argued that the teachings of the Enlightenment philosophers were equally applicable to men and women and that women's liberation must become a primary concern of all civilized society. She further argued that human limitations are not given by nature but by social environment, and that men and women can learn anything if they are given the opportunity to do so. Wollstonecraft's book found an immediate following in Britain and North America, and today it is considered a landmark of the feminist movement. Over three-quarters of a century later, some of Wollstonecraft's themes were echoed in the English philosopher John Stuart Mill's essay, "The Subjection of Women" (1869), which also specifically challenged men's alleged intellectual superiority and which became another major document of early feminism.

In the United States, the feminist movement may be said to go back to Abigail Adams, who in the 1770s urged her husband to allow for women's representation and participation in the projected new constitution. But Abigail's admonition went unattended for nearly a century.

The mid-nineteenth century witnessed the emergence of three women as pivotal figures in the resurgence of the feminist movement in the United States: Lucy Stone, Elizabeth Cady Stanton, and Susan B. Anthony. During the 1840s, the 1850s, and the 1860s, these three did much to promote the cause of women, particularly in the northern part of the United States. In particular, under Stanton's leadership, 1848 saw the formation of a women's convention in Seneca Falls, New York. The convention issued a declaration of independence for women, demanding full legal equality, full educational and economic opportunity, equal compensation, and the right to vote. Women's suffrage became a fact in the Nineteenth Amendment in 1920. But beyond that, the combined forces of the Civil War, Reconstruction, the Great Depression, and the two world wars pushed the feminist agenda to the background.

The feminist movement emerged in full force in response to the social upheaval and political activism of the 1960s. The National Organization for Women (NOW) was founded in 1966 and soon developed hundreds of local chapters.

Under feminist leadership, the Equal Rights Amendment was approved by the United States Congress in 1972. The amendment simply read: "Equality of rights under the law shall not be denied or abridged by the United States or by any State on account of sex." That such a commonsensical measure failed ratification by the states is testimony to the deep entrenchment of sexism and inequality still prevalent in American society.

Among the most influential early documents of the postwar feminist movement are Simon de Beauvoir, *The Second Sex* (1949), Betty Friedan, *The Feminine Mystique* (1963), Kate Millett, *Sexual Politics* (1969), and Germaine Greer, *The Female Eunuch* (1971).

The feminist movement resulted in millions of women moving into the workplace and assuming subnational, national, and professional positions of leadership. Today, feminist issues include access to employment, education, child care, contraception, abortion, equality in the workplace, changing family roles, redress for sexual harassment, pornography, and the need for equal political representation.

Varieties of Feminism

Some scholars consider feminism simply as an extension of democracy. But feminism has found expression in three *principal* forms: liberal feminism, radical feminism, and socialist feminism. Liberal feminism is compatible with democracy. Radical feminism challenges many traditional aspects of democratic government as practiced in the United States. Socialist feminism rejects democracy altogether. Insofar as these varieties of feminism are by now familiar to many readers, I offer brief sketches below. For detailed treatment of these and other varieties of feminism, see the Donovan and Tong books listed in the bibliography.

Liberal Feminism

Liberal feminism fits the general definition of feminism with which this chapter opens. As represented by NOW, liberal feminism seeks to bring women into full participation in the mainstream of American society, exercising full privileges and responsibilities of citizenship in genuinely equal partnership with men. Most of NOW's members are middle-of-the-road, middle-class women. NOW's tactics represent mainstream politics: setting up task forces, bringing suits, lobbying government officials. The goals of NOW have included: adoption of an Equal Rights Amendment (ERA) to the Constitution, enforcement of laws banning sex discrimination in employment, maternity leave rights, child-care centers, equal education, and the right to abortion.

Radical Feminism *challenges many traditional aspects of democratic government.*

During the activist days of the 1960s, women involved in the civil rights movement became aware that, NOW notwithstanding, they were still second-class citizens, their principal roles limited to the office, the kitchen, and the bed. They became convinced that American society considered their grievances to be trivial.

Radical feminism of the 1960s allied itself with such New Left organizations as the Students for a Democratic Society (SDS) and the Student Non-Violent Coordinating Committee (SNCC). In 1968, radical feminists staged "The Burial of Traditional Womanhood" in a torchlight parade at Arlington National Cemetery. They protested the Miss America Contest. They set up a Freedom Trash Can into which they threw bras, girdles, curlers, and other symbols of female servitude. They protested male chauvinism and the oppression of women as a fundamental political practice wherein women are treated as inferior based upon their gender. They called for a radical transformation of American democracy.

Radical feminism has become much more elaborate and sophisticated since the 1960s, though the basic tenets remain unchanged. Given a male-dominated world, however, the objectives are far from attainment.

Socialist Feminism *rejects democracy altogether.*

Socialist feminism finds a ready and convenient ideology in the works of Marx and Engels. Subordination of women, Marx and Engels believed, is an inescapable outcome of class society. Marxism treats women as the appendage of the exploited class, the proletariat. The economic oppression of women is but one component of the economic oppression of capitalism as an economic system. It follows, then, that

付属

in order to free women, one must first undermine, if not destroy, the class base of capitalist society. A socialist revolution is the necessary prerequisite to full liberation for women. Some critics of socialist feminism maintain, however, that socialism subordinates the concerns of women to those of class.

Radical and socialist feminism attracted many lesbians who were in search of an outlet for self-expression. Oppressed both for their sex and for their sexual orientation, such women readily saw the need for organization and action. Unable to rely on men to support them, they felt the brunt of job discrimination. Many had rejected the feminine role because of its oppressiveness and its absurdity. They energized the feminist movement by gradually coming out of the closet.

More assertive than radical and socialist feminists, the lesbian component has at times created tension and friction within the feminist movement. In fact, some lesbians have altogether separated lesbianism from feminism.

Feminism and Psychoanalysis

Because it has been so influential and because it is so condescending toward women, psychoanalysis has always constituted a major bone of contention within the feminist movement.

Feminism is directly antithetical to psychoanalysis, particularly as formulated by Sigmund Freud. According to Freud, the "normal" woman is passive, masochistic, and inferior. Women's inferiority is anatomically based: to use his famous dictum, "Anatomy is destiny." Woman is incomplete because she lacks a penis.

Freud believed that early childhood development is similar for both sexes until about age six. At that time children enter the phallic stage of development, characterized by singular preoccupation with their own genitals and those of the opposite sex.

The phallic phase coincides with the development of the Oedipus complex in the boy. He experiences sexual desire toward his mother, accompanied by a desire to kill his main rival, his father. Realizing that the father is more powerful than he, the boy fears that, learning of his sexual fantasy, the father will sever the boy's penis. The fear of castration resolves the boy's Oedipus complex.

Meanwhile, the superego has begun to develop. The superego (conscience) embodies the social and moral code of a society, including a set of standards by which to judge oneself and one's behavior. The development of the superego coincides with the development of civilization.

The girl's experience is quite different. Observing that she lacks a penis, she imagines that she has been castrated and develops penis envy. The "normal" girl eventually substitutes her desire for a penis with a desire for a child.

As a result, women do not develop strong superegos. They develop an inferiority complex and become passive and masochistic. A woman who wants actively to participate in the world outside the home is abnormal and neurotic. She still carries the burden of penis envy.

In short, according to Freud, women are innately inferior because of their anatomy. They have no place in the world of politics, art, literature, culture, or the professions.

Though highly influential, the central problem of psychoanalytic or Freudian theory is that it is entirely speculative, lacking any scientific foundation whatever. Psychoanalytic terminology is not amenable to scientific definition, testing, and replication. It is more mystification than fact. Accordingly, Freud's biological determinism must be rejected.

Feminism and Racism

African American (and other minority) women in the United States face a "double jeopardy." On the one hand, like all women, they endure oppression on account of their sex. On the other, along with men of their race, they experience oppression due to race. Compounding the problem is the fact that African American women meet with sexism in political groups organized to combat racial injustice and racism in white feminist organizations.

Like white feminists, many African American women came to feminism through the realization that they were being treated as second-class citizens within the civil rights movement of the 1960s. However, the American feminist movement has been predominantly white and middle-class. How to get more African American (and other minority) women involved in the movement has been a constant topic of conversation in women's groups. Socialist feminist groups concerned about building a class movement have been especially worried about their white, middle-class membership.

Many African American and other minority women have been re-

repelled by the racial and class composition of the women's movement. Especially during the early years, they felt they had little in common with movement women and that the movement did not address problems of central concern to them.

Many African American and other minority women still feel that they must choose: they can either become feminists or support their brothers. They must decide whether their basic identity is racial or sexual. Most have chosen to work within the African American movement.

However, ideological tendencies within parts of the African American movement recently led many African American women to decide that an African American feminist movement was necessary. This was in part due to the fact that some African American men had accepted basic tenets of white establishment ideology. The African American woman who was economically and socially oppressed for both her sex and her race, who made less money and might be unemployed, who frequently had to rear her children alone, was seen as a problem, not a sister.

The African American movement's position on birth control and abortion disturbed many women. African American male radicals charged that white America planned genocide. Forced sterilization and the availability of birth control and abortions were all part of the plan. African American women should refuse to use these methods; they should breed and rear warriors for the revolution.

Many African American women felt that neither the white women's movement nor male-dominated African American organizations addressed their basic concerns. An African American woman's organization was the obvious solution. Thus in August 1973 activist African American women formed the National Black Feminist Organization. NBFO has fluctuated in membership and activism; today it remains a relatively minor force on the political landscape. Women's liberation has taken a back seat to African American liberation.

Feminism Ascendant 支配, 優位

The postwar period has witnessed the emergence of women as leaders at the subnational, national, and professional levels. The United States being no exception, today we find women leaders at all strata of American society. Geraldine Ferraro, the unsuccessful Democratic vice-presidential candidate in the 1984 U.S. presidential election, reached the highest level of political leadership ever occupied by an American woman.

Setting aside the United States for the time being, in this section I focus on twelve women who have risen to positions of national leadership, either as presidents or prime ministers. These women are not necessarily feminists, but their rise was certainly facilitated by the feminist movement. The twelve women are: Corazon Aquino of the Philippines, Benazir Bhutto of Pakistan, Gro Harlem Brundtland of Norway, Kim Campbell of Canada, Edith Crésson of France, Violeta Chamorro of Nicaragua, Tansu Çiller of Turkey, Indira Gandhi of India, Golda Meir of Israel, Isabel Perón of Argentina, Hanna Suchocka of Poland, and Margaret Thatcher of Great Britain.

Elected women political leaders, such as Aquino, Bhutto, and Gandhi, achieve positions of national prominence in a political world almost totally dominated by men. What allows such women to come to power? It is by now a truism that the most significant difference between men who rise to positions of national leadership and those who choose to mount revolutionary upheavals is purely and simply access to political power. Such diverse revolutionary figures as George Washington and Fidel Castro have visions of a better and more just world they can achieve only through political power. Thwarted in their quest for access to those positions of power, they rely on violence as a way of contesting the established system. Washington, unsuccessful in his bid to expand his landholdings, came into direct conflict with English law. He was also personally affected by the Stamp and Navigation acts. Failing to reform the system to advantage himself and others in his situation, he embraced the radicalism that led to the American Revolution. Similarly, were it not for the Batista coup of March 1952, which suspended the Cuban constitution and political processes, Castro, who at the time was campaigning for a parliamentary seat in the upcoming June elections, might have turned out to be a regular politician.

To take a more contemporary case, George Bush, by contrast, had access to political power from early in his career. Appointed to high office by several presidents, Bush was elected vice-president of the United States in 1980. His successful presidential candidacy in 1988 simply and unequivocally documents the role of access in political ascendancy.

As is well known, women have been thwarted by the long-standing tradition that favors male political leadership, by socialization patterns that negate the cultivation of traits and attributes that prepare them for leadership roles, and by life patterns that do not place them into positions of potential access to political power. Despite these setbacks, some women do achieve legitimate leadership positions. How do they overcome tradition and gender socialization patterns? How do they reach national political leadership? A review of the paths to power for contemporary women is in order.

Some women, such as Margaret Thatcher of Great Britain, Kim Campbell of Canada, Edith Crésson of France, Gro Harlem Brundtland of Norway, and Hanna Suchocka of Poland, are elected to political office in ways that follow paths of access to power typically associated with men. Each of these women, mostly from the more industrial nations of the world, appears to be selected through a path of coalition building and electoral politics without the advantage of family position or favor. These few women function in societies that, more than most in the world, have had paths to political leadership open to women for some time. These opportunities for women, to use an old phrase, are few and far between. Yet in some cases one finds, upon investigation, these women have experienced nontraditional political socialization. For example, while most media speak of Margaret Thatcher's father as a grocer, further exploration shows that Alfred Roberts was politically active all of his adult life, rising from school governor to the position of mayor of his city, Grantham. Thatcher's father encouraged her to move into political activity early in life; she responded by marrying a wealthy man whose resources released her from the usual household and maternal duties. Without the burden of child care and housework, Margaret Thatcher was free to pursue a public career. Needless to say, most women cannot expect to rise to positions of national prominence; the chances are infinitesimally small.

Other women who hold positions of national leadership, particularly in modernizing countries, have risen to power as a result of the mantle or cloak of family prominence passing to them from father or husband. Usually one of the only surviving family members of a dead or martyred political leader, the woman who is of the appropriate age or possesses the minimal requisite skills for leadership cultivates the followers associated with her dead family member to maintain and perpetuate his power.

Corazon Aquino was elected president of the Philippines following the assassination of her husband, Benigno Aquino. A leader of the opposition to Ferdinand Marcos (autocratic leader of the Philippines for two decades), Benigno Aquino had remained outside of the Philippines for years prior to his death. After his assassination, his followers and others appealed to Corazon Aquino to challenge Marcos in the upcoming election. A quiet and traditional woman, Corazon Aquino would never have been interested personally in high political office, but accepted the political role to perpetuate the beliefs, ideals, and following of her dead husband. Supported by the United States, her candidacy was successful.

Similarly, Benazir Bhutto of Pakistan accepted the mantle of leadership from her martyred father, Zulfikar Ali Bhutto, former prime minister of Pakistan, to challenge the power of General Mohammed Zia ul-Haq, who had ruled under martial law for eleven years. When pursuing a political career as a single woman became a liability, Benazir Bhutto accepted an arranged marriage with Asif Zardari. (Even women politicians at the national level must maintain their legitimacy within their societies.) Campaigning on the appeal of the memory of her martyred father, Benazir Bhutto became the first woman to head a contemporary Muslim state and the youngest head of a fledgling democracy.

By her own account, Violeta Chamorro, widow of Pedro Joaquín Chamorro, slain owner of the newspaper *La Prensa* and one of the most active opposition figures in Nicaragua until his assassination in 1978, considered her life's work to be the care of her husband, her children, and her home. Encouraged to take up candidacy for the presidency, Violeta Chamorro coalesced sufficient support as a result of her husband's martyrdom and American backing to be elected president of Nicaragua in February of 1990. A measure of her socialization to roles ill-suited to the exercise of political power at the national level is the widely accepted belief that her son-in-law, Antonio Lacayo, is the real power behind the presidency.

One of the most famous women political leaders of the late twentieth century, Indira Gandhi of India was carefully trained by her father, Jawaharlal Nehru, India's first prime minister. Many of Nehru's hopes for the political future of India were placed upon his daughter, an only child, although he asserted publicly that he wanted no role in choosing his successor. After the sudden death of Prime Minister Shastri in

1966, the Congress party president Kamaraj chose Indira Gandhi for succession. Her ascendancy to the position of prime minister was not without an open contest, but the overwhelming vote for Gandhi was illuminated by the cries of the crowd: not only "Long live Indira," but also "Long live Jawaharlal."

Isabel Perón of Argentina held elected political office in her own right prior to ascendancy to the paramount office. Elected vice-president to her husband, President Juan Perón, she succeeded him as president upon his death in 1974. Without her husband's support, one would not have expected Isabel Perón to have been elected vice-president of Argentina. Possessing only a sixth-grade education and political experience limited to that available to the wife of a prominent national leader, Isabel Perón was an unlikely candidate for the presidency of one of the largest countries in South America. That she was the symbolic leader of the Peronist party until 1985 speaks more to her political abilities after her short presidency (1974–1976) than before. But pathway to political power is the theme of this section, not exercise of power. How women and men use leadership positions—their similarities and differences—awaits another essay.

The newly elected prime minister of Turkey, Tansu Çiller, deserves note at this point, for she is an anomaly in the line of women leaders documented above. An American-trained economics professor, Çiller entered politics only three years ago, and her family has no history of involvement in politics. As economics minister prior to her election as prime minister, Çiller represents a new kind of leader in a rapidly modernizing country. She is able to bring vision and experience to the position, yet faces considerable difficulties dealing with what is considered Turkey's most serious immediate problem: the economy.

To summarize, these twelve leaders have established once and for all that women are fully capable of the highest achievement at the national level. Although some came from political families, they have nonetheless exploded the myth of male dominance in political leadership.

Feminism and the Future

In her recent book *Fire with Fire* (see bibliography), feminist writer Naomi Wolf argued that the feminist movement has emerged—or is about to emerge—as victorious. Wolf's optimism notwithstanding, the feminist movement faces a series of problems in the foreseeable future.

First, women continue to face antagonism from men who are fiercely protective of their status and power and who passionately resist the feminist movement.

Second, in America and elsewhere, many women are perfectly satisfied with their traditional roles as wives, mothers, and homemakers. The antagonism of traditional women toward feminism is well illustrated by the likes of Phyllis Schlafly and by the founding in California in the 1960s of an organization pointedly called "The Pussycats."

Third, the feminist movement experiences fragmentation within. All is not well among the liberal feminists, the radical feminists, the socialist feminists, and the lesbian feminists. It will take time, to say the least, to forge a unified movement.

Finally, the feminist movement is characterized by a fundamental means/ends inconsistency. Even the most basic feminist value, equality, has been denied, as the ERA experience demonstrates. And it is unlikely that peaceful means will attain even this elemental goal.

In short, hurdles remain to be overcome, the glass ceiling is firmly in place, and it will be decades or epochs before women everywhere attain genuine equality of opportunity. Nonetheless, leadership roles at various levels are open to most women so that by adhering closely to their goals, by patiently waiting to advantage their cause when opportune, and by their own determined action, women will make a difference in their societies.

The Framework Applied

The cognitive dimension of feminism perceives a world in which men dominate all the political, economic, social, and cultural spheres, and in which women are oppressed, exploited, and pressed into positions of subordination. Human behavior, feminists believe, is a function of context or situation, not gender differences. Women demand equality, full participation, equal compensation, control over their reproductive functions, child care, and freedom from any form of harassment.

The affective dimension of feminism appeals to justice, fairness, and the necessity of reversing centuries of mistreatment at the hands of men. Women are capable of any masculine-type accomplishments, if only given the opportunity. The main impediment standing in the way of the feminist movement is male chauvinism.

The evaluative dimension of feminism centers on the idea of equality, particularly equality of opportunity. Women believe that they are capable of any accomplishment, were it not for a repressive and male-dominated society. Beyond this, women are guided by the principles of justice and fairness to a greater extent than men.

The programmatic dimension of feminism stresses the necessity of rejecting sex role socialization and gender stereotyping. In the last three decades women have emerged upon the political, economic, social, and cultural scene, advocating their causes, lobbying the political system, and running for political office. On both the national and international levels, women have amply demonstrated a successful activist posture. Although the Equal Rights Amendment fell short of ratification, it is likely to be reintroduced in the near future.

Theoretically, the social base of feminism embraces all women. In reality, however, some women are perfectly satisfied with their traditional roles as lovers and mothers; other women have limited social, political, and economic objectives; and still others reject the status quo altogether. Until such time as a unified feminist movement emerges, women will face difficulty achieving the goals for which some have struggled for so long.

Selected Bibliography

Alvarez, Sonia. *Engendering Democracy*. Princeton, N.J.: Princeton University Press, 1990.

Banks, Olive. *Faces of Feminism: A Study of Feminism as a Social Movement*. Oxford: Martin Robertson, 1981.

Barber, James David, and Barbara Kellerman, eds. *Women Leaders in American Politics*. Englewood Cliffs, N.J.: Prentice-Hall, 1986.

Beauvoir, de Simone. *The Second Sex* (1949). Translated and edited by H. M. Parshley. New York: Knopf, 1953.

Carrol, Susan J. *Women as Candidates in American Politics*. Bloomington: Indiana University Press, 1985.

Deckard, Barbara Sinclair. *The Women's Movement: Political, Socioeconomic, and Psychological Issues*. New York: Harper & Row, 1975.

Donovan, Josephine. *Feminist Theory: The Intellectual Traditions of American Feminism*. New York: Frederick Ungar, 1985.

Dworkin, Andrea. *Ice and Fire*. New York: Weidenfeld & Nicolson, 1987.

———. *Intercourse*. New York: Free Press, 1987.

Elshtain, Jean Bethke. *Public Man, Private Woman: Women in Social and Political Thought*. Princeton, N.J.: Princeton University Press, 1981.

Flamming, J. A., ed. *Political Women*. Beverly Hills, Calif.: Sage, 1984.

Firestone, Shulasmith. *The Dialectic of Sex: The Case for a Feminist Revolution.* London: Jonathan Cape, 1971.
Freeman, Jo. *The Politics of Women's Liberation.* New York: McKay, 1975.
Friedan, Betty. *The Feminine Mystique.* New York: Norton, 1963.
Frye, Marilyn. *Willful Virgin: Essays in Feminism.* Freedom, Calif.: The Crossing Press, 1992.
Genovese, Michael A., ed. *Women as National Leaders.* Newbury Park, Calif.: Sage, 1993.
Gilligan, Carol. *In a Different Voice: Psychological Theory and Women's Development.* Cambridge: Harvard University Press, 1982.
Greer, Germaine. *The Female Eunuch.* New York: McGraw-Hill, 1971.
Heller, Trudy. *Women and Men as Leaders.* New York: Praeger, 1982.
Jaggar, Alison M. *Feminist Politics and Human Nature.* Totowa, N.J.: Rowman & Allanheld, 1983.
Jaggar, Alison M., and P. S. Rothenberg, eds. *Feminist Frameworks.* New York: McGraw-Hill, 1984.
Kelly, Rita Mae, and Mary Boutilier. *The Making of Political Women: A Study of Socialization and Role Conflict.* Chicago: Nelson-Hall, 1978.
Kirkpatrick, Jeanne. *Political Women.* New York: Basic Books, 1974.
Levy, Marion F. *Each in Her Own Way: Five Women Leaders of the Developing World.* Boulder, Colo.: Lynne Rienner, 1988.
Millett, Kate. *Sexual Politics.* New York: Simon & Schuster, 1969.
Mitchell, Juliet. *Woman's Estate.* Harmondsworth, U.K.: Penguin, 1971.
Morgan, Robin, ed. *Sisterhood Is Powerful.* New York: Vintage Books, 1970.
Okin, Susan Moller. *Women in Western Political Thought.* Princeton, N.J.: Princeton University Press, 1979.
Phillips, Kay, and Mostafa Rejai. "Women as Leaders: A Research Note." Unpublished manuscript. Miami University, 1994.
Rowbotham, Sheila. *Women in Movement: Feminism and Social Action.* New York: Routledge, 1992.
Tong, Rosemarie. *Feminist Thought: A Comprehensive Introduction.* Boulder, Colo.: Westview Press, 1989.
Wolf, Naomi. *Fire with Fire: The New Female Power and How It Will Change the 21st Century.* New York: Random House, 1993.
Young, Iris Marion. *Justice and the Politics of Difference.* Princeton, N.J.: Princeton University Press, 1990.

9

Environmentalism

The Meaning of Environmentalism

Environmentalism is an ideology and a movement to protect the quality and continuity of human life through population control, conservation of natural resources, prevention of pollution, and control of land use. Environmentalism is distinctive in its unwillingness to maximize economic advantage for its own adherents or for any other social group. Environmentalism requires accepting limits to unrestrained economic development, and those limits are universally applicable. Environmentalists readily accept the unavoidable inconveniences of public transport, highways, and airports in the interest of the broader public good. But on the whole, environmentalism has minimal appeal by way of personal economic gain.

The first principle of environmentalism is that the earth as a whole, for all time, must be seen as a "commons." Accordingly, the basic building blocks of an environmentalist ideology are the triple issues of population control, conservation, and pollution. All three rest on an understanding and appreciation of nature and ecology, and all three require that one see human society intertwined with the ecological web of life. Environmentalists accept that virtually every economic benefit has a measure of environmental costs and that often the sum total of such costs, particularly in affluent societies, exceeds the value of the benefits. And some environmental costs are not worth bearing regard-

---

I draw especially on the works of Dunlap and Mertig, Paehlke, and Rosenbaum listed in the bibliography for this chapter.

less of the benefits they may bring. Environmentalists see enormous possibilities for continued human development without the continually expanding use of materials and energy.

Put in a nutshell, the principal concerns of the environmentalist movement include: (1) population control; (2) preservation of wilderness, endangered species, and wildlife habitat; (3) pollution; (4) availability of enough food for everyone; (5) long-term adequacy of energy supplies; and (6) threat of war in a nuclear age. We shall return to these and related concerns presently.

The Evolution of Environmentalism

Environmentalism has its historical roots in the conservation movement that began in North America in the mid-nineteenth century. The importance of nature, the appreciation of nature, and the need to preserve nature and wilderness were articulated by such figures as James Audubon (1785–1851, founder of the National Audubon Society) and Henry David Thoreau (1817–1862). The early conservationist movement was largely concerned with the efficient use of natural resources; it did not have a broad ecological perspective. Its central concern was the scientific management of natural resources; it wished to avoid waste.

A second group of conservationists, led by John Muir (1838–1914, founder of the Sierra Club), took conservation a step further, applying an ecological perspective to the activities of human beings. This laid the groundwork for the environmental movement of the 1960s and beyond. The transition from conservationism to environmentalism began with a renewed emphasis on preventing the pollution of air, water, and land. Later another concern was added: that of resource depletion. Both conservationists and environmentalists saw that resource depletion and pollution are two sides of the same coin, but the latter movement broadened the emphasis to include forest, water, and soil resources—that is, the whole resource base of industrial society.

The environmental movement is political and ideological in perspective in that it has an antitechnological dimension. Moreover, environmentalism is not concerned only with forests and wilderness but with the viability of the global biosphere in its entirety. Beyond this, environmentalism questions the logic of private investment decisions and the conventional models of production expansion to generate economic growth and profit. Finally, environmentalism harbors a strong asceticism embedded in doubts about the extravagant North American and Western European consumer life-styles.

Public concern with nuclear pollution, air pollution, water pollution, noise pollution, solid waste disposal, dwindling energy resources, radiation, pesticide poisoning, and other environmental problems engaged a broadening number of sympathizers and culminated in the Earth Day demonstrations of April 22, 1970, and its twenty-fourth anniversary on April 22, 1994.

In the 1980s, under presidents Ronald Reagan and George Bush, many environmental issues were downgraded, suppressed, or ignored. This, in turn, created a backlash in which environmentalist groups expressed their frustration and outrage in various forms of public protest. The Clinton administration promises to be much more sympathetic to environmentalism.

The environmental neglect of the 1980s gave impetus to the emergence of the Green Movement, which sought to push environmental issues to the forefront of the national agenda. Alarmed by the multitude of environmental problems and crises that beset us (see below), the Green Movement argues for the urgent adoption of constructive national and global environmental policies. At risk, it argues, is nothing less than the fate of the human species: we need a new environmental ethics.

On the international level, concern for environment was the subject of a United Nations conference in Stockholm in 1972, attended by 114 nations. Out of this meeting developed the United Nations Conference on Environment and Development of 1992. Known as the Earth Summit, this meeting was held in Rio de Janeiro, Brazil, to discuss the global conflict between economic development and environmental protection. Representatives of 172 countries agreed to work toward the sustainable development of the planet, although most of the agreements were not legally binding. (Sustainable development is the growth of population, industry, and agriculture in a way that will allow the present generation to meet its own needs without damaging those of future generations.) Two binding declarations—to minimize global climate change (global warming or greenhouse effect) and to stem the depletion of the world's inventory of biological diversity—were signed by more than 150 countries. Led by the United States, which saw these measures as detrimental to capitalist economic development, some of the developed countries declined to sign the declarations.

To summarize, factors expediting the rise of environmentalism include: (1) threat of nuclear war and nuclear pollution, which energized many formerly inert groups; (2) postwar economic affluence, which lowered concern with materialism and focused attention on the quality of life; (3) the 1960s, which gave rise to an activist culture that encouraged people, especially youth, women, and minorities, to take action to solve society's problems; (4) scientific knowledge about environmental problems (for instance, smog), which began to grow as did media coverage of such problems and such major disasters as the 1989 *Exxon Valdez* oil spill in Prince William Sound in Alaska; (5) a rapid increase in outdoor recreation, which brought many people into direct contact with environmental degradation and heightened popular commitment to preservation; (6) the broadening of their focus to encompass a wide range of issues by many of the environmental organizations (see below), enabling them to mobilize increased support for environmental causes.

The Political Stance of Environmentalism

Because it is not an ideology of self-interest, and because self-interest is deeply ingrained in American society, economy, and polity, environmentalism does not easily attract an intensely committed mass following. It appeals most to those with a reasonable degree of economic security (as distinct from wealth), and only rarely does it appeal to the economically insecure.

As time has progressed—and as pressures of nuclear and other pollution became immediate—environmentalism has crossed class lines. Not everyone has the time and money to appreciate nature, but everyone eats, drinks, and breathes. Antipollution environmentalism developed a broad political appeal.

The central value assertions of environmentalism are inherently appealing to most reasonable and informed people. These value assertions are as follows: (1) appreciation of all forms of life; (2) a sense of humility regarding the human species in relation to other forms of life and to the global ecosystem; (3) a concern with the quality of human life and health; (4) a global rather than a nationalist or isolationist perspective; (5) preference for political and population decentralization; (6) an extended time horizon and a long-term point of view; (7) a sense of urgency regarding the survival of life on earth; (8) a revulsion toward waste in the face of human needs; (9) a preference for simplicity without rejecting modernity; (10) an aesthetic appreciation of season, climate, and nature; (11) an attraction to autonomy and self-management in human endeavors; (12) an inclination to more democratic and participatory practices.

Given these value assertions, it goes without saying that environmentalism faces opposition from the political right. This opposition thrusts environmentalism toward an alliance with the progressive forces of the moderate left. Many persons who articulate environmentalism in North America and Western Europe place themselves in sympathy with the moderate political left. A conservative environmentalism is a theoretical possibility, but in actuality it has never existed.

The most obvious point of similarity between environmentalism and the moderate left is their shared willingness to intervene in a market economy on behalf of values that do not necessarily promote uncontrolled economic expansion. The moderate left, moreover, has traditionally favored improving the distribution of expanding social and popular benefits.

Some Problems of Environmentalism

While in passing I have mentioned some of the urgent problems of environmentalism, it is now time to consider the most pressing ones in some detail. Since it is difficult always to be precise about the relative importance of these problems, I present them more or less in chronological order.

Population

By far the overall and the most pressing problem for the environment is population growth. Population growth taxes the earth's resources, necessitates economic growth and infrastructure development, and creates industrial and human waste.

The world's population stood at about 5.5 billion in 1994. The United Nations estimates the current world population will double around 2050. As population growth increases, the possibility emerges that the earth may not be able to sustain future generations. Some new Malthusians estimate that the world's population will soon outstrip the world's food supply.

The population problem is particularly urgent in third world countries. As health and sanitation measures are introduced, the death rate declines while the birth rate remains relatively high, leading to a veritable population explosion.

Population explosion engenders resource scarcity. Resource scarcity, in turn, sets the stage for the emergence of conflict at several levels: interpersonal, communal, national, international.

Nuclear Pollution

Nuclear pollution is a matter of major concern at several levels. To begin with, many nuclear plants are in routine operation, producing electricity and other forms of energy. The safety record of these plants is far from perfect, the most publicized accidents having taken place at Three Mile Island in 1979 and at Chernobyl in 1986.

More important, although the cold war has ended, the threat of nuclear war has by no means disappeared. About a dozen countries possess nuclear weapons today. The United States alone possesses enough nuclear power to destroy the globe about twenty times over. Then there are the former Soviet republics (Russia, Ukraine, Belarus, Kazakhstan), Britain, France, China, India, Israel, and South Africa, not all of which are entirely stable. Nuclear proliferation could endanger human life as such unpredictable countries as Iran, Iraq, North Korea, and Pakistan strive to develop their own nuclear arsenals. In short, humanity continues to face the threat of nuclear incineration and pollution for the foreseeable future.

(In a January 1994 trilateral agreement with the United States and Russia, Ukraine agreed to dismantle its nuclear arsenal. Belarus and Kazakhstan declared their intention to follow suit. When these laudatory pronouncements will find actual implementation remains to be seen. Even if fully implemented, however, these measures make relatively little difference in the nuclear danger facing humankind.)

Air Pollution

The Clean Air Act of 1970, as amended in 1990, seeks to regulate six "criteria pollutants" and eight "hazardous air pollutants." These pollutants are emitted by mobile sources, mostly cars and trucks, and by stationary sources such as industrial concerns and commercial electrical power plants.

These fourteen pollutants and their major health effects are as follows:
Criteria Pollutants: (1) ozone—respiratory tract problems, (2) par-

ticulate matter—lung diseases, (3) carbon monoxide—impaired ability of blood to carry oxygen, (4) sulfur dioxide—respiratory tract problems, (5) lead—mental retardation and brain damage, and (6) nitrogen dioxide—respiratory and lung damage.

Hazardous Air Pollutants: (1) asbestos—a variety of lung diseases, (2) beryllium—lung diseases and a variety of cancers, (3) mercury—brain disorders, (4) vinyl chloride—lung and liver cancer, (5) arsenic—cancer, (6) radionuclides—cancer, (7) benzene—leukemia, and (8) coke oven emission—respiratory cancer.

While the last quarter of a century has seen some improvement in air quality, many cities and major urban centers remain dangerously polluted.

Water Pollution

Both surface water and ground water remain dangerously polluted as we approach the twenty-first century. Our surface waters—streams, rivers, lakes, and the sea—constitute our most visible water resources. They are also the most used and the most exploited, as they account for a very high proportion of all recreation activities, commercial fishing grounds, industrial water resources, and industrial dumping. The rapid degradation of the nation's surface waters generated congressional action in the 1960s and the 1970s. Nonetheless, the Environmental Protection Agency and the Council on Environmental Quality have consistently rendered ambiguous verdicts on the nation's water resources.

Ground water is as essential as surface water to the nation's existence and far more abundant: the annual flow of ground water is fifty times the volume of surface flows, and most lies within one-half mile of the earth's surface. Almost 50 percent of the U.S. population and 95 percent of our rural residents depend on ground water for domestic use. However, because it is not as visible as surface water, ground water is widely and dangerously degraded. Sources of ground contamination include septic tanks, underground storage tanks, agricultural activities, landfills, oil and gas intrusions, mining activities, waste sites, and the like.

In addition to surface and ground waters, the quality of our country's drinking water is also emerging as a major issue, inasmuch as drinking water is dependent on surface water and ground water.

Virtually all Americans daily drink water drawn from surface or ground sources. The Environmental Protection Agency continues to insist that America's drinking water is free of serious pollutants. By all objective measures, however, America's water quality is in need of significant improvement.

Hazardous and Toxic Substances

Toxic and hazardous substances penetrate our air, water, and earth, including radioactive waste, gasoline from leaking storage tanks, and pesticide residues on food. Widespread media coverage of hazardous chemical spills, newly discovered abandoned toxic waste sites, and other dangerous substances have forced attention upon hazardous and toxic substances and imparted an air of urgency to resolving the problems.

Most hazardous and toxic substances are an inheritance of the worldwide chemical revolution that followed the Second World War. The creation and manufacture of synthetic chemicals and pesticides have grown at an alarming rate, far beyond popular or even scientific expectations. Some of these chemicals are carcinogens seriously endangering public health.

It is to be noted that hazardous and toxic wastes potentially pose a greater threat to humans and their environment than that posed by chemicals used in the workplace or at home. The disaster at Love Canal (1978) is only a small reminder of this danger.

Consumer Waste

Since World War II consumer waste has emerged as a pressing problem of the age. Americans are the world's most prolific producers of consumer waste: they produce more than one thousand pounds of consumer trash annually per capita, including landscaping and gardening waste, books and magazines, corrugated cardboards, beer and soft drink cans and bottles, food, and glass. Household waste consists of cellophane, plastic, paper, styrofoam, and other materials.

Disposal of consumer waste is increasingly difficult because the land available for garbage dumps is fast disappearing and other methods of disposal are often hazardous and expensive. More than 80 percent of the nation's consumer waste is still buried in landfills, while only 10 percent is recycled and another 10 percent is incinerated. The nation's municipalities are so rapidly consuming land for garbage dumps that more than half of the cities will exhaust their landfills in the 1990s.

Global Climate Warming (Greenhouse Effect)

By the mid-1980s, many scientists had become convinced that a global warming effect was well under way. In 1988, James E. Hansen, director of NASA's Goddard Institute for Space Studies, testified to the members of the Senate Energy and Natural Resources Committee that it was "99 percent certain" that global warming was a reality. That announcement instantly caught the attention of the Congress, the media, and the American people. Suddenly, global warming was no longer speculation; it bore the imprimatur of NASA science. Thus Hansen did the environmental movement a great service.

Since then, predictions of global climate warming have become persuasive, and the Bush and Clinton administrations promised measures to mitigate its impact. Since the United States is the leading producer of the carbon dioxide emissions believed to be the leading cause of climate warming, the U.S. initiative is essential to any worldwide scheme to address the problem.

Predictions of an impending global warming are based on data demonstrating that the amount of carbon dioxide in the atmosphere has been steadily increasing since the beginning of the Industrial Revolution. Until the middle of this century, fossil fuel combustion, mostly from worldwide coal burning and motor vehicles, was the principal source of these emissions. In the last several decades, deforestation (particularly in the tropics) is estimated to have been related to additional carbon dioxide emissions of up to 50 percent of those released by fossil fuel combustion. The "greenhouse" theory asserts that the increasing levels of carbon dioxide will progressively trap more of the earth's heat, gradually warming the global climate as much as three to nine degrees Fahrenheit. This warming will accelerate polar icecap melt and alter world climate zones.

Any effective strategy for mitigating the adverse impacts of a global warming would require global cooperation among all nations burning fossil and wood fuels. But developing countries often blame the industrialized nations for global climate pollution and expect these developed countries to assume the major responsibility—and economic burden—for environmental restoration. Many developing nations like China, India, and Brazil perceive U.S. admonitions to reduce their air or water pollution as an attempt to keep them economically weak by inhibiting their industrialization.

Acid Rain

Recent public opinion polls have found that the vast majority of the American public (as high as 80 percent) consider acid rain a serious problem. In other words, there is very little disagreement among public officials, the public, the scientific community, and affected economic interests about the existence of acid rain. But disagreement persists about many other aspects of the matter, including how much industry, utilities, and the automobile each contributes to the acid rain problem; how injurious acid rain is to humans and the environment; and who should bear the costs for abating air emissions causing acid rain if, in fact, any action is necessary.

Some acid rain occurs naturally, and scientists have been aware of this for quite some time. In recent years, however, acid rain has become increasingly widespread and more acidic. It now occurs throughout much of the world as well as the United States, and it is as high as thirty times more acidic than it would naturally be in many American industrialized regions. Scientists attribute most of this increase to growing fossil fuel combustion, particularly by electric utilities and industry. The United States, currently discharging well over forty-one metric tons of nitrogen and sulfur oxides annually, is the global leader. But acid rain is a world issue because all industrialized nations and many developing ones discharge significant amounts of the ingredients.

Currently, the acid rain problem affects not only North America, but Eastern and Western Europe, Scandinavian countries, central Africa, and parts of South America. Yet governments have been slow to act because of political, economic, scientific, and bureaucratic impediments.

Atmospheric Ozone Depletion

Scientists first suggested in the mid-1970s that the worldwide use of chlorofluorocarbons (CFCs) and halons (the ingredients in fire extinguishers) could be destroying the ozone in the thin but important stratosphere encircling the earth at about 43,000 feet. In 1982 British scientists for the first time documented the existence of a large hole in the ozone layer over Antarctica, which had been predicted earlier. Further research has largely confirmed that atmospheric ozone is being chemically depleted at an alarming rate, and this depletion is occurring across an area far larger than the Antarctic. By the mid-1980s scientists were predicting that a large ozone hole also existed over the Arctic and that rapid depletion might also be found in more temperate regions.

When NASA scientists announced in 1988 their estimate that 3 percent of the atmospheric ozone had been depleted between 1969 and 1986, the findings startled many people around the world. Suddenly, ozone depletion became a serious matter of debate by governments, industry representatives, and researchers everywhere.

Because tropospheric ozone is a natural shield against the sun's ultraviolet rays, any significant depletion of the ozone layer could mean increased human exposure to ultraviolet light, yielding significantly increased risks of skin cancer and eye damage (cataracts). A depletion of 1 percent of the atmospheric ozone is estimated to create millions of new cases of skin cancer and cataracts. Increased global exposure to ultraviolet rays could produce serious derangements in existing ecological balances, including a major depletion of ocean plankton, which constitutes the foundation of the ocean's food chains.

Some Solutions of Environmentalism

Solutions to environmental problems can emanate from two possible sources: governments and environmental organizations. I consider each in turn.

Governmental Solutions

As intimated in the foregoing pages, governmental solutions to environmental problems have been slow in coming. There are several reasons for this. First, many (if not all) environmental problems are regional, national, and international in scope, requiring the cooperation of many governmental units and decisions on expenditures of public funds. Governmental cooperation is hard to come by because of jurisdictional disputes, assignment and acceptance of responsibility, and cooperative action.

Second, most industrial concerns have shown a singular lack of inclination to accept responsibility for environmental problems they cause. The fact that in many countries industrial concerns work in close cooperation with governments only helps compound the problem.

Third, assuming the cooperation of government and industry, science may be unable to address many of the environmental problems that have emerged in the postwar period. In other words, it may be that some environmental problems are intractable. It may be that human ingenuity has dug us into holes out of which we cannot easily climb.

Environmental Organizations

Environmental organizations are of two sorts: lobbying and nonlobbying. Although many of these organizations have local, state, regional, and international components, in the interest of space we shall limit discussion to national organizations only.

Twelve prominent national environmental organizations engage in extensive lobbying activities and constitute the core of the national environmental lobby. These organizations are: Sierra Club (1892), National Audubon Society (1905), National Parks and Conservation Association (1919), Izaak Walton League (1922), The Wilderness Society (1935), National Wildlife Federation (1936), Defenders of Wildlife (1947), Environmental Defense Fund (1967), Friends of the Earth (1969), Natural Resources Defense Council (1970), Environmental Action (1970), and Environmental Policy Institute (1972). It is apparent, as we intimated earlier, that the 1960s and the 1970s provided special impetus to the development of the environmental movement. Although these organizations engage in other activities as well (education, research, litigation), they are distinguished from other national environmental organizations by the fact that they openly lobby for the development and implementation of environmental legislation. Together, these organizations command well over three million members.

Nonlobbying organizations focus on research, litigation, educational programs, grassroots organizing, land purchase and maintenance plans, and (in a few cases) even direct action on behalf of environmental goals. Among the most important of these organizations are: Planned Parenthood Federation (1917), the Nature Conservancy (1951), World Wildlife Fund (1961), Union of Concerned Scientists (1969), Zero

Population Growth (1970), Greenpeace (1971), Sierra Club Legal Defense Fund (1971), Sea Shepherd Conservation Society (1977), Citizens' Clearinghouse for Hazardous Waste (1981), Earth Land Institute (1982), National Toxics Campaign (1984), Rainforest Action Network (1985), and Conservation International (1987). These organizations command a combined membership of about four million persons.

As suggested earlier, in general three basic tactical options are available to the environmental organizations: education, direct action, and policy reform. Education is stressed by the older organizations (for instance, the Nature Conservancy). Direct action is a phenomenon of the 1960s and 1970s (for example, Greenpeace). Lobbying and legislative action (for instance, Sierra Club) have become increasingly important in the 1980s and the 1990s. All environmental organizations—lobbying and nonlobbying—have become progressively professional in nature, relying on experts and consultants to advance their work.

The environmental movement has generated extensive legislation, notably the National Environmental Policy Act (NEPA) of 1970, which established an Environmental Protection Agency and a Council on Environmental Quality; the Clean Air Acts of 1970 and 1990; the Water Pollution Control Act, as amended in 1972; other laws regulating noise, pesticides, toxic substances, and ocean dumping; and laws to protect endangered species, wilderness, and wild and scenic rivers.

NEPA requires all federal agencies to file impact statements assessing the environmental consequences of proposed federal projects such as highways, jet runways, bridges, dams, and nuclear power plants. Moreover, the new laws provide for pollution research, standard setting, monitoring, and enforcement. Citizens are empowered to sue both private industry and government agencies for violating antipollution standards. Subsequent legislation includes the Safe Drinking Water Act of 1974; the Resource Conservation and Recovery Act of 1976; the Comprehensive Environmental Response, Compensation, and Liability Act (the Super Fund) of 1980; and the Super Fund Amendment and Reauthorization Act of 1984.

Although national environmental organizations have experienced much success over the last few decades, a great deal remains to be done. The extent to which environmental problems are amenable to political, bureaucratic, and scientific solution remains to be seen.

Vice-President Albert Gore concludes his best-selling recent book on the environment (see bibliography) by calling for a Marshall Plan for the earth, paralleling the massive economic and political reconstruction of Europe after World War II. However, while postwar European problems were in principle amenable to solution, it is not at all certain that the same can be said of our environmental crises. For humanity's sake, however, one earnestly hopes that Gore's projections will ultimately prevail.

The Uneven Burden of Environmentalism

Environmental problems impose inherently uneven burdens on those subject to them, whether at the international or individual level. At the international level, environmental problems are particularly acute for developing countries that face problems of overpopulation, pollution, toxic and consumer waste, global warming, acid rain, and ozone depletion because of two conditions: (1) many of these problems are the legacies of the development of advanced industrial societies; and (2) developing countries by definition lack the resources to begin to address these problems. Moreover, as we have noted, the developed countries routinely discourage the advancement of developing countries because such advance would only exacerbate the problems just mentioned.

At the individual level, problems of hunger, homelessness, and poverty notwithstanding, the typical middle- or upper-class citizens of advanced industrial societies enjoy privileges and amenities not even imagined by their counterparts in undeveloped lands. The former drive their air-conditioned automobiles (or private jets) to their air-conditioned offices and return to their air conditioned homes or villas in the suburbs, thereby circumventing—in the short haul, at any rate—the everyday problems of overpopulation, pollution, and global warming. Citizens of undeveloped lands are trapped in intractable dilemmas, many of which are not even of their own making.

At times, the foregoing conditions have generated charges of "environmental racism."

The Framework Applied

The cognitive dimension of environmentalism concentrates on protecting the quality and continuity of human life through the rational conservation of natural resources. Environmentalism focuses on problems of overpopulation, pollution, hazardous and toxic substances, human waste, global warming, acid rain, and ozone depletion. Environmentalism imposes limits to unrestrained economic development, and those limits are seen as universally applicable. Environmentalism sees human society as intertwined with the ecological web of life of past, present, and future generations.

The affective dimension of environmentalism stresses the finite nature of the universe and calls upon human beings to appreciate that finiteness and to engage in acts of conservation rather than waste. Environmentalism appeals to people's public-regardingness rather than self-regardingness and pursuit of personal interest. The global biosphere is deserving of everyone's respect and veneration.

The evaluative dimension of environmentalism includes an appreciation of all forms of life, a sense of humility regarding the human species in relation to the global ecosystem, a concern for quality of human life, a global rather than an isolationist perspective, a long-term point of view of the global biosphere, a revulsion against waste of all kinds, and an aesthetic appreciation of season, climate, and nature.

The programmatic dimension of environmentalism consists of a wide variety of groups and organizations—both lobbying and non-lobbying—that have appeared upon the American scene, going back to the Sierra Club of 1892. These organizations engage in grassroots mobilization, education, research, litigation, and lobbying on behalf of the environment. Environmental organizations have succeeded in generating extensive legislation, the most important being the National Environmental Protection Act of 1970; the Clean Air Acts of 1970 and 1990; and the Comprehensive Environmental Response, Compensation, and Liability Act (the Super Fund) of 1980. The twenty-first century is likely to see further developments along these lines.

The social base of environmentalism has significantly broadened in recent times. Because it is not an ideology of self-interest—and because self-interest is deeply ingrained in our capitalist society—initially environmentalism appealed to persons with a reasonable degree of economic security, that is, the middle class. As time progressed, and as pressures of nuclear and other pollution became immediate, environmentalism crossed class lines. The activism of the 1960s focused in part on the environment and galvanized youth, women, and minorities to work on behalf of social issues. As problems of global warming, acid rain, and ozone depletion come into sharper focus, people from all social strata will take a fresh interest in environmental concerns.

Selected Bibliography

Anderson, Walt, ed. *Politics and Environment: A Reader in Ecological Crisis.* Pacific Palisades, Calif.: Goodyear, 1970.

Bell, Garret de, ed. *The Environmental Handbook.* New York: Ballantine Books, 1970.

Bramwell, Anna. *Ecology in the Twentieth Century: A History.* New Haven, Conn.: Yale University Press, 1989.

Brown, Lester. *Building a Sustainable Society.* New York: Norton, 1981.

Bullard, Robert D., ed. *Confronting Environmental Racism: Voices from the Grassroots.* Boston: South End Press, 1993.

Carson, Rachel. *Silent Spring.* Boston: Houghton Mifflin, 1962.

Commoner, Barry. *Science and Survival.* New York: Viking Press, 1963.

Devall, Bill, and George Sessions. *Deep Ecology: Living as If Nature Mattered.* Layton, Utah: Gibbs M. Smith, 1985.

Dunlap, Riley E., and Angela G. Mertig, eds. *American Environmentalism: The U.S. Environmental Movement, 1970–1990.* Washington, D.C.: Taylor & Francis, 1992.

Gore, Albert. *Earth in the Balance: Ecology and the Human Spirit.* Boston: Houghton Mifflin, 1992.

Milbraith, Lester W. *Environmentalists: Vanguard for a New Society.* Albany: State University of New York Press, 1984.

Nash, Roderick Frazier. *The Rights of Nature: A History of Environmental Ethics.* Madison: University of Wisconsin Press, 1989.

National Staff of Environmental Action. *Earth Day—The Beginning.* New York: Bantam Books, 1970.

O'Reardon, T. *Environmentalism.* 2d ed. London: Pion, 1981.

Paehlke, Robert C. *Environmentalism and the Future of Progressive Politics.* New Haven, Conn.: Yale University Press, 1989.

Porritt, Jonathan. *Seeing Green: The Politics of Ecology Explained.* Oxford: Blackwell, 1984.

Rosenbaum, Walter A. *Environmental Politics and Policy*, 2nd ed. Washington, D.C.: Congressional Quarterly Press, 1991.

Roszak, Theodore. *Person/Planet.* New York: Doubleday Anchor, 1978.

Schell, Jonathan. *The Fate of the Earth.* New York: Knopf, 1982.

Schumacher, Ernest F. *Small Is Beautiful: Economics as If People Mattered.* New York: Harper & Row, 1973.

Vig, Norman J., and Michael E. Kraft, eds. *Environmental Policy in the 1980s: Reagan's New Agenda.* Washington, D.C.: Congressional Quarterly Press, 1984.

Worster, Donald. *Nature's Economy: A History of Ecological Ideas.* New York: Cambridge University Press, 1977.

Part III

Recapitulation

10

Comparing Political Ideologies

In chapter 1, we developed a framework for the comparative analysis of political ideologies in terms of five interrelated components: cognition, affect, valuation, program, and social base. In chapters 2 through 9, we examined the eight most significant political ideologies of the nineteenth and twentieth centuries: nationalism, fascism and nazism, Marxism, Leninism, guerrilla communism, democracy, feminism, and environmentalism. At the end of each chapter, we saw how a particular ideology can be analyzed, dissected, and understood in the light of our comparative framework. I shall now recapitulate our efforts by summarizing and highlighting the fit between all our ideologies and the analytical framework.

As noted in chapter 1, some overlap between the five dimensions of our framework is unavoidable. Moreover, as we have seen, nationalism and democracy share some elements of the affective and evaluative dimensions. (In fact, insofar as all our ideologies, explicitly or implicitly, appeal in *practice* to nationalist feelings and sentiments in one way or another, nationalism emerges as the most pervasive and influential political ideology of recent times.) Finally, needless to say, any attempt at recapitulation involves some repetition. But given the pedagogical objectives of this introductory text, I believe that such repetition is defensible. Nonetheless, in order to *minimize* repetition, I have decided to: (1) stress the most essential points, leaving aside much detail, and (2) lump together Marxism, Leninism, and guerrilla communism when feasible and appropriate, particularly since the latter two are considered variations upon the first.

The Cognitive Dimension

The world views of all our eight ideologies involve elements of knowledge (fact) as well as of belief (fiction). Nationalism rests on the assumption of the relative superiority of one people and the relative inferiority of all others. Accordingly, a nationalist ideology seeks to establish, maintain, and enhance a country's economic, political, military, diplomatic, and cultural status.

The cognitive dimension of fascism and nazism views the world in terms of a permanent struggle involving individuals, groups ("folks"), nations, and states. In such a world, only superior power, strength, and force will prevail. Violence is not only necessary and unavoidable, it is its own justification.

Marxism/Leninism/guerrilla communism perceives the world as made up of productive human beings who are everywhere and at all times exploited and oppressed for the economic benefit of a few. The resultant class struggles end in successive revolutionary upheavals culminating in a classless society in which ownership is abolished and peace and harmony prevail. Conflict, in other words, is inherent in the economic and class structures of all societies.

Democracy conceptualizes the world as consisting of rational and capable human beings who can live harmoniously without unnecessary coercion and force. Majority rule, representation, and constraints on government provide for peaceful resolution of conflicts and disagreements.

The cognitive dimension of feminism perceives a world in which men dominate all the political, economic, social, and cultural spheres and in which women are oppressed into a position of subordination. Human behavior, feminists believe, is a function of context or situation, not gender differences. Women demand full participation, legal equality, control over their reproductive functions, and freedom from any form of harassment.

The cognitive dimension of environmentalism concentrates on protecting the quality and continuity of human life through the rational conservation of natural resources. Environmentalism focuses on problems of overpopulation, pollution, hazardous and toxic substances, human waste, global warming, acid rain, and ozone depletion. Environmentalism imposes limits to unrestricted economic development; it sees human society as intertwined with the ecological web of life of past, present, and future generations.

The Affective Dimension

The affective dimension of nationalism stresses the feelings of belonging to a unique and superior group or nation. It follows, by definition, that every individual constituting the group is considered superior as well. These feelings of unity, distinctiveness, and superiority are captured in the concepts of civilizing mission, white man's burden, and manifest destiny.

The affective and evaluative components of fascism and nazism overlap to such an extent that one cannot usefully separate them. Nationalism—the promised restoration of national pride and honor—is as laden with values as it is with emotions. Racism has identical characteristics.

The overriding theme in Marxism/Leninism/guerrilla communism is outrage against the institutions and practices of capitalist societies. When combined with unceasing reminders of oppression, exploitation, and alienation, this dimension provides a most potent emotional appeal.

In its beginning as a revolutionary ideology, as we noted in chapters 1 and 7, democracy shared some of the same emotive constituents of nationalism: it began as a protest against tyranny and absolutism, glorifying peoples and nations instead. As Western democracy matured, the preoccupation with affect was overtaken by rationalism and pragmatism, except under conditions of national crisis or emergency. Even under normal conditions, however, the emotive ingredient is not altogether absent, as can be seen in the successive American invocations of such ideas as the New Deal, the New Frontier, the Great Society, human rights, and the like.

The affective dimension of feminism appeals to justice, fairness, and the necessity of reversing centuries of mistreatment at the hands of men. Women are capable of any masculine-type achievements, if only given the opportunity. The main impediment standing in the way of feminist progress is male chauvinism.

The affective dimension of environmentalism stresses the finite nature of the universe and calls upon human beings to appreciate that finiteness and to engage in acts of conservation rather than waste. Environmentalism appeals to people's public-regardingness rather than their self-regardingness and pursuit of personal interest. The global biosphere is deserving of everyone's respect and veneration.

The Evaluative Dimension

The evaluative component of nationalism is found in the glorification of peoples and nations, popular sovereignty, and individual rights and liberties. Other values include national dignity as well as collective welfare and security. In colonial contexts an additional value lies in getting even with the colonizers and righting historic grievances and injustices.

In addition to nationalism and racism, the evaluative dimension of fascism and nazism includes glorification of the state as the repository of all values. Similar attributes are associated with the party and, above all, with the heroic leader.

The evaluative component of Marxism/Leninism/guerrilla communism idealizes egalitarianism, communalism, and communal ownership and control of the national wealth. Eventually, historical development is to culminate in an idyllic society in which all conflict ends, peace and harmony prevail, and human creativity finds fulfillment on a grand scale.

The evaluative dimension of democracy is so familiar as to require only a bare mention: liberty, equality, fraternity, dignity, happiness, consent, legitimacy.

The evaluative dimension of feminism centers on the idea of equality, particularly equality of opportunity. Women believe that they are capable of any accomplishment, were it not for a repressive and male-dominated society. Beyond this, women are guided by the principles of justice and fairness to a greater extent than men.

The evaluative dimension of environmentalism includes an appreciation of all forms of life, a sense of humility regarding the human species in relation to the global ecosystem, a concern for quality of human life, a global rather than isolationist perspective, a long-term point of view of the global biosphere, a revulsion against all forms of waste, and an aesthetic appreciation of season, climate, and nature.

The Programmatic Dimension

Historically, the programmatic component of the nationalist ideology has found three expressions: formative nationalism, prestige nationalism, and expansive nationalism. Thus, having become a nation overnight, as it were, France set out to increase its power and prestige by violating the rights of other peoples and nations in a series of wars that dominated the nineteenth century. Similarly, having attained independence, the United States, under the presumably divine ordination of manifest destiny, set out to expand over the entire continent and to cross the seas to take over not only Cuba and Puerto Rico but also far-flung lands such as Hawaii and the Philippines.

The programmatic component of fascism and nazism has two aspects. Internally, the regime sets out to purify the society of the "undesirable" elements and improve the conditions of the "desirable" ones. Externally, it embarks upon a policy of expansionism in order to acquire fresh "living space."

The programmatic dimension of Marxism is weak, since it calls for spontaneous overthrow of the bourgeoisie by the proletariat. By contrast, Lenin developed a two-stage urban revolutionary strategy resting on leadership, organization, and planning. Mao masterminded a rural revolutionary strategy based on protracted conflict beginning with peasant guerrilla action in rural areas and culminating in an urban power seizure. Ho and Castro adapted the Maoist model to Vietnam and Cuba.

The programmatic component of democracy requires contending leaders and parties, election and representation, majority rule, popular participation, education, and information. It also demands popular control to assure responsible and responsive government. At times, the programmatic dimension of democracy has entailed an expansionist element as well, as in Woodrow Wilson's quest "to make the world safe for democracy."

The programmatic dimension of feminism stresses the necessity of rejecting sex role socialization and gender stereotyping. In the last three decades women have emerged upon the political, economic, social, and cultural scene, advocating their causes, lobbying the political system, and running for political office. On both the national and international levels, women have amply demonstrated a successful activist posture.

The programmatic dimension of environmentalism consists of a wide variety of groups and organizations—both lobbying and non-lobbying—that have appeared upon the American scene, going back to Sierra Club of 1892. These organizations engage in grassroots mobilization, education, research, litigation, and lobbying on behalf of the environment. Environmental organizations have succeeded in generating extensive legislation, and the twenty-first century is likely to see further developments along these lines.

The Social-base Dimension

The social base of nationalism incorporates the entire population except, perhaps, the internationalists and the indigents. In such multi-ethnic societies as the United States, national unity is more difficult to achieve than in homogeneous lands. Even in the United States, however, there is an umbrella ideology that brings together peoples of various regions, nationalities, and religions, and identifies them as "Americans."

The social base of fascism and nazism is necessarily limited to the loyalists: the disciplined and slavish followers of national supremacy and racial purity, drawn especially from frightened middle classes. Fascism and nazism make systematic efforts to identify friends to be cultivated and enemies to be fought.

The social base of Marxism is, strictly speaking, international: the proletariat, regardless of time or place. (In a classless society, of course, all distinctions will presumably vanish into one united human race.) In practice, however, as we have seen, Lenin, Mao, Ho, and Castro turned Marxism into national enterprises.

The social base of democracy incorporates the entire citizenry, except for the fringe groups on the far right and the far left. Seldom, however, do we expect the "entire citizenry" to agree on any major issue. As a result, as is commonly known, democracy is a political system in which conflicting issues and demands are resolved, as a rule, in peaceful ways.

Theoretically, the social base of feminism embraces all women. In reality, however, some women are perfectly satisfied with their traditional roles as lovers and mothers; other women have limited social, political, and economic objectives; and still others reject the status quo altogether. Until such time as a somewhat unified feminist movement emerges, women will face difficulty achieving their objectives.

The social base of environmentalism has significantly broadened in recent times. Because it is not an ideology of self-interest—and because self-interest is deeply ingrained in our capitalist society—environmentalism initially appealed to persons with a reasonable degree of economic security, that is, the middle class. As time progressed and as pressures of nuclear and other pollution became immediate, environmentalism crossed class lines. The activism of the 1960s focused in part on the environment and galvanized youth, women, and minorities to work on behalf of social issues. As problems of global warming, acid rain, and ozone depletion come into sharper focus, people from all social strata will take a fresh interest in environmental concerns.

Conclusion

This book has set forth a five-dimensional framework for the comparative study of political ideologies, examined some of the most enduring ideologies of our times, and shown how these ideologies can be broken down and understood in the light of the five dimensions.

I have stressed the importance of a comparative framework because it offers several advantages. First, a framework defines the parameters of a subject matter or a topic by specifying what is to be included and what is to be excluded. Second, and by the same token, it helps us analyze and understand a subject matter with a focus and clarity not otherwise possible: it sharpens issues and problems that may have been previously ambiguous or blurred. Third, it removes the necessity for routine memorization and the attendant boredom; once a framework is fully understood, its application becomes "fun," even exciting. Thus, if nothing else, the student of ideologies can now easily remember that, to a lesser or greater extent, all ideologies can be analyzed in the light of a set of common categories or properties dealing with cognition, affect, valuation, program, and social base. Finally, if the framework has any validity, its application extends not only to the topics or cases actually considered but to all similar topics or cases.

Accordingly, this book should be considered only a "starter" for the study of political ideologies. Having mastered the framework, and having seen some instances of its actual application, the reader, it is hoped, is equipped with the necessary intellectual apparatus for a more elaborate study of political ideologies.

Appendixes

APPENDIX A

Political Theory, Political Philosophy, Political Ideology

The foregoing pages have been devoted to discussions of political ideology as a concept (chapter 1), as ideologies (chapters 2 through 9), or as both (chapter 10). But as an abstraction or intellectualization, political ideology is only one part of a triad in the history of political thought; the other two parts are political theory and political philosophy.

For stylistic convenience, we have occasionally used "philosophy," "ideology," and "theory" interchangeably throughout the text. It is now time to replace stylistic liberty with scholarly precision. Accordingly, this section will briefly distinguish theory and philosophy from ideology, indicate where they converge and diverge, and point out the significance of each. Although somewhat abstract, this section is included for those who have an interest in the subject. Uninterested readers can skip the section altogether.

Political Theory

Were we able (1) to clarify the meaning of "political," (2) to specify the meaning of "theory," and (3) to successfully combine the two operations, we would presumably have an understanding of "political theory." The initial obstacle to any such attempt is the conspicuous absence of any generally agreed upon definition of "politics."

The word "politics" derives from the Greek *polis:* the small, intimate city-community. For the ancient Greeks, politics meant the science (that is, systematic knowledge) of the polis and its affairs. When Aristotle called man a political animal, what he had in mind was that man is a polis animal; that he cannot do without the polis.

Politics as knowledge of the polis meant virtually complete knowledge, for classical thought did not admit of any of the contemporary distinctions between "society," "state," "church," "community," and so on. Confusion became inevitable when "polis" began to be interpreted as city-state and, later, as just plain state. It is not happenstance that the earliest definition of "politics" was in terms of the state. The linkage with the state, however, narrows the field unnecessarily. It suggests, for example, that there is no "politics" in primitive societies or that there was none before the emergence of Western states in the fourteenth century and beyond.

More recent definitions of "politics" have been in terms of power, decision making, conflict and conflict resolution, influence and the influential, authoritative allocation of values, and the like. (I am here excluding such exotic notions of politics as Mao Tse-tung's "war without bloodshed.")

Underlying all these definitions is some conception of *order* in human affairs. What is power about—or decision making, or influence, or conflict resolution, or authoritative allocation—if not about order? This said, we confront a serious conceptual difficulty. "Order" as a criterion is not sufficiently precise to set politics apart from society, economy, religion, and so on. In other words, order is a characteristic of all human relationships, not just the political ones.

One way of resolving this difficulty is to look at politics as a system of human activities conducted on two levels. At the ordinary, or common, level, there is no distinction between political order on the one hand and social or economic or religious orders on the other, for those realms overlap to a considerable extent. At this level, politics and society, for instance, are one and the same. Both refer to systems of adjustment and compromise involving conflicting values and interests.

At the second, or less ordinary, level, what distinguishes political order from other types of order is the *effective physical control* of human behavior—by means of coercion and force, if necessary. Society, economy, and the church also exercise controls—social, economic, or spiritual, as the case may be—but not physical control. In short, politics differs from society, economy, and religion only to the extent that it provides for exercise of physical force.

A definition of "theory" is somewhat easier to come by. To begin with, we must take care not to confuse "theory" with "idea" or "opinion." When in ordinary usage we say that we have a theory about this or that, what we probably mean is that we have an idea or an opinion. "Theory" has a more precise meaning.

A theory, *any* theory, consists of a set of abstractions or generalizations about reality. It refers to a series of interrelated propositions derived from recurrent patterns of human or nonhuman (for example, physical or chemical) behavior. A theory is a mental image, a summary sketch of reality as perceived. As such, theory involves simplification; it makes no claim to completeness or totality.

A *political* theory consists of a set of abstractions or generalizations about that aspect of reality that is distinctly political: a system of human activities centering upon the adjustment of conflicting interests and values that may potentially involve coercion and physical force. A political theory is an overview of what the political order is about. It is a shorthand, symbolic representation of political reality. It is a formal, logical, and systematic analysis of the processes and consequences of political activity. It is analytical, expository, and explanatory. It seeks to give order, coherence, and meaning to reality.

During the heyday of "behavioral," or scientific, political science in the 1960s, a distinction was commonly made between two types of theories: empirical (those dealing with fact) and normative (those dealing with value). As understood nowadays, political theory deals with both fact and value, both description and prescription, both explanation and valuation. Political theory, in other words, is both empirical and normative: it can offer generalizations from which value judgments may ensue.

Political Philosophy

In its literal and broadest sense, "philosophy" refers to love of wisdom or knowledge. More specifically, the major components of the discipline of philosophy have included metaphysics (ontology and cosmology), epistemology, ethics, aesthetics, psychology, philosophy of history, history of philosophy, and, indeed, even politics itself. It follows, from this strikingly broad scope, that the hallmark of philosophy is final and complete explanation of man and the universe. *Political* philosophy, to use the late English scholar Michael Oakshott's apt definition, is "the link between politics and eternity." In a word, political philosophy deals not with what is attainable but with the most lofty ideals.

Stated differently, political philosophy attempts to identify final truths. It asks final questions, and it seeks final answers. It wants to know the *highest* good, the *best* sociopolitical arrangements, the *ultimate* criterion of justice. As such, it is characterized by timelessness, finality, and universality.

This discussion gives rise to the question of the relationship between political philosophy and the normative dimension of political theory. A distinction does exist, and it hinges on a matter of relativism, a question of degree. Political philosophy deals with value judgments that are absolute, ultimate, and eternal; normative political theory addresses value propositions that are relative, contingent, and conditional. Political philosophy asks: "What is the best political arrangement for all time and place?" Political theory inquires: "What is an appropriate political arrangement for this time and place?"

Political Ideology

Given the subject matter of this book, the discussion of political ideology need not be elaborate. I will simply remind the reader that political ideology is an emotion-laden, myth-saturated, action-related system of beliefs and values about man and society, legitimacy and authority, acquired largely (if not primarily) as a matter of faith and habit. The myths and values of ideology are communicated through symbols in a simplified and efficient manner. Ideological beliefs are more or less coherent, more or less articulate, more or less open or closed. Ideologies have a high potential for mass mobilization, manipulation, and control; as such, they can be called mobilized belief systems.

Convergences and Divergences

What do political theory, political philosophy, and political ideology have in common, and how do they differ? The three concepts converge on the following points: (1) all involve intellectualizations, though, of course, of varying kinds and at varying levels; (2) all involve abstractions of varying degrees; and (3) all involve simplification of the universe of discourse with which they deal. The divergences are far more significant.

Political theory in its empirical dimension refers to dispassionate, disinterested analysis of political reality; its aim is description, analysis, and explanation. The normative component deals with values, but in a relative and conditional manner, and as such it may serve as a basis for the making of public policy. Political philosophy begins with certain fundamental assumptions about the nature of the ultimate good. It is marked, as we have said, by finality, universality, and timelessness. Political ideology is distinguished by its emotional belief content, its mass character, and its utility in social movements.

It should be made explicit that political theory, political philosophy, and political ideology as discussed in the foregoing pages represent pure forms or ideal types. In practice, one usually encounters combinations or permutations of the three. Karl Marx is the supreme example of the theorist-philosopher-ideologue. Similarly, many political theories have a foundation in philosophy, particularly ontology (nature of reality), epistemology (nature and sources of knowledge), and ethics (nature of value).

Significance

What is the importance of the various distinctions drawn in the foregoing pages? What significance does one attach to political philosophy in contrast to political ideology and political theory?

Political philosophy serves to delineate the broad goals for a society. It establishes a set of ideals against which reality may be measured. And it provides dynamism in the collective striving toward the attainment of these goals and ideals.

The importance of political ideology is at least twofold. For one thing, no political system can long endure without an accepted body of supporting beliefs among its people. For another, ideology binds a society together; it promotes individual identity and social solidarity.

Political theory provides the analyst with an abstract statement of the parameters of his or her intellectual activity. It provides the scholar with the necessary analytical apparatus for approaching his or her task. Thus, for instance, a major difference between a political theorist and a political reporter is the conceptual apparatus that underscores the former's work.

Selected Bibliography

Ashcraft, Richard. "Political Theory and the Problem of Ideology." *Journal of Politics* 42 (August 1980): 687–705. [See also the exchange with Dante Germino and John S. Nelson in the same issue, pp. 706–21, and a subsequent exchange with R. Bruce Douglas and Gary C. Marfin in ibid., 44 (May 1982): 570–85.]

Brecht, Arnold. *Political Theory*. Princeton, N.J.: Princeton University Press, 1959.

Cox, Richard H., ed. *Ideology, Politics, and Political Theory*. Belmont, Calif.: Wadsworth, 1969.

Hacker, Andrew. *Political Theory: Philosophy, Ideology, Science*. New York: Macmillan, 1961.

Jenkin, Thomas P. *The Study of Political Theory*. New York: Random House, 1955.

Keohane, Nannerl O. "Philosophy, Theory, Ideology: An Attempt at Clarification." *Political Theory* 4 (February 1976): 80–100.

Lasswell, Harold D., and Abraham Kaplan. *Power and Society*. New Haven, Conn.: Yale University Press, 1950.

McDonald, Neil A., and James N. Rosenau. "Political Theory as an Academic Field and Intellectual Activity." *Journal of Politics* 30 (May 1968): 311–44.

Partridge, P. H. "Politics, Philosophy, Ideology." *Political Studies* 9 (October 1961): 217–35.

Rejai, Mostafa. "On Keohane, 'Philosophy, Theory, Ideology.' " *Political Theory* 4 (November 1976): 509–11.

Shklar, Judith N. *Political Theory and Ideology*. New York: Macmillan, 1966.

APPENDIX B

Ideology: Emergence, Decline, Resurgence

The Emergence of Ideology

The rise of ideologies, it will be recalled, dates back, generally speaking, to the nineteenth century, coinciding as it did with the French Revolution, intensification of urbanization and industrialization, advances in transportation and communication, depersonalization and anonymity of human life, and the resultant creation of a spiritual and emotional gap. Political ideologies did not appear in preindustrial, agrarian societies for a variety of reasons. To begin with—and to state the obvious—the foregoing developments had not yet taken place (for instance, the mass base of ideology simply did not exist). Moreover, preindustrial, agrarian societies were governed by the "iron hand of tradition": near-absolute control from the top did not allow (or immediately crushed) any expression of views from the bottom. Finally, in these societies, religion was for the most part the functional equivalent of ideology.

Ideologies of one form or another have now dominated, with ebbs and flows and with varying degrees of intensity, the countries of Europe and North America for some two hundred years. In Africa, Asia, and Latin America, on the other hand, ideologies began to appear just after World War I and the Russian Revolution. Not until after World War II, however, did ideologies flourish in such a way as to hypnotize and mesmerize the peoples of colonial and underdeveloped lands and to become the explosive forces of national and revolutionary movements.

More specifically, the Second World War and its attendant consequences breathed new life into militant ideologies in colonial and underdeveloped countries. The disintegration of the great empires shattered the myth of white invincibility, demonstrating conclusively that in principle the white man was vulnerable. Initial Japanese military successes further showed (as had the Japanese victory over Russia in the Russo-Japanese War of 1905) that the nonwhite could even *prevail* over the white.

Anti-Western nationalist and revolutionary movements mushroomed throughout Africa, Asia, and Latin America, and they were led, ironically enough, by men who had been educated in Western countries. Indeed, the genesis of many postwar independence and revolutionary movements can be traced to student and émigré groups from various colonies who met, planned, and organized in London, Paris, and other European cities and then transported the movements, as it were, to their native lands.

A related consideration in this regard is that once a colonial or revolutionary movement succeeded—once a colony attained independence—a contagion effect set in: other countries' expectations were heightened and the process of consciousness accelerated. Thus, for instance, the success of the Chinese Revolution set a formidable example for Asia, and that of the Cuban Revolution for Latin America. Similarly, the attainment of independence by Ghana in 1957 and the success of the Algerian Revolution in 1962 served as inspiration for independence and revolutionary movements throughout much of Africa.

Given the foregoing developments, it is not surprising that two ideologies, singly or in combination, have dominated the political movements of colonial and underdeveloped lands: (1) nationalism (of various forms), because it promises integrity, sovereignty, and independence; and (2) Marxism (of various shades), because it promises deliverance from poverty, disease, oppression, and exploitation. In fact, when combined, nationalism and Marxism have proved to be the most explosive political ideologies of the postwar era.

The Decline of Ideology

Some recent and contemporary developments in the advanced industrial societies of Europe and North America now warrant elaboration. To begin with, the unprecedented economic growth that occurred in these countries in the two decades immediately following World War II created an "age of affluence" (as it came to be called), accompanied by a "decline of ideology." Scholars and intellectuals undertook a series of studies subjecting the hypothesis of ideological decline to testing and verification in advanced, industrial societies. In general, the hypothesis held up quite well across the board.

The decline-of-ideology hypothesis referred to either one of two propositions: (1) a relative modulation of the ultimacy with which ideological goals were stated, or (2) a relative attenuation of the emotional intensity with which ideological goals were pursued. The hypothesis had relevance for both international and domestic politics.

Considered at the international level, the decline proposition suggested that extremist ideologies—Marxist governments, for example—had modified both their global objectives and the intensity with which these objectives were sought. When applied to domestic politics, the decline hypothesis suggested that the formerly intense competition between political parties over national policies had been moderated, that the ideologies of the left and right had to some extent coalesced into a united assault upon certain common social problems, and that there had been a relative attenuation of political cleavage and dissension.

It is necessary to be explicit as to what the hypothesis of decline did *not* mean. The hypothesis did not suggest the total disappearance of ideologies. The notion of an "end" of ideology was simply a misnomer or a misapplication. What the hypothesis did convey was an ending of "apocalyptic," "total," or "extremist" ideologies—that is to say, a decline of ideology. This is one of the key sources of confusion in the literature on the decline of ideology, and it must be attributed in large measure to the writers themselves, who stated their hypothesis in two different ways: (1) a "decline of ideology," and (2) an "end of [extremist] ideology."

The hypothesis of ideological decline was stated within certain explicit limits: specifically, it was both time-bound and space-bound. The hypothesis was time-bound in that it embraced ideological politics in the postwar period only. It was space-bound in that it applied primarily to advanced, industrial, Western societies. The second proposition requires elaboration.

The decline hypothesis stipulated certain conditions under which it would be fully operative. These conditions had largely materialized in the industrial West, were in the process of materialization in certain countries of the East, and were largely absent in most of the developing areas of the world.

What were some of these conditions? Internationally, two developments were especially relevant: (1) a relative discreditation of the ideologies of fascism, nazism, racism, and communism; and (2) the end of the cold war and the disintegration of many Communist regimes.

The most important internal changes revolved around economic development and its attendant consequences: an increasing general affluence; an increasing exposure to education and the media of communication; an increasing reliance on science and expertise to solve social problems; a gradual attenuation of class and party conflict; a gradual attainment of economic and political citizenship by the lower classes; a gradual emergence of a vast, homogeneous, professional-managerial middle class; a gradual transformation of laissez-faire capitalism into the welfare state; and a gradual institutionalization of stable political processes for resolving political issues.

The decline-of-ideology hypothesis characterized not only the established parties of Western Europe and North America (whether liberal, conservative, or socialist) but their Communist counterparts as well. The Communist parties of France, Spain, Italy, and elsewhere firmly established themselves as legal and "normal" constituents of the parliamentary systems. As such, occasional revolutionary rhetoric notwithstanding, their intention was not to overthrow the system but to capture a larger share of the political pie (as in parliamentary elections, for instance).

Indeed, during the abortive French upheaval of May 1968, the student revolutionaries denounced the Communist party as a reformist organization and a defender of the status quo. They branded the party as reactionary, counterrevolutionary, and "obsolete," calling for a more radical alternative. The students' charges, by the way, were not without foundation: the party supported the student moderates and urged cooperation with university and government authorities.

The Resurgence of Ideology

The age of ideological decline was punctuated—and punctured—by a series of developments over the last couple of decades. For purposes of illustration, I will focus on the United States. The country witnessed the civil rights movement, the student movement, the peace (anti-Vietnam and antinuclear) movements, the feminist movement, "stagflation," and the ascendancy of the Reaganites and the Moral Majority. Insofar as they bear on ideologies, however, there is nothing surprising about these occurrences.

More specifically, the charged environment of the 1960s gave rise to a variety of "radical" ideologies associated with the Students for a Democratic Society, the Weathermen, the Black Panthers, and similar groups. By contrast, the flaccid environment of the 1980s produced a group of "neoconservatives" who sought to reestablish the old social, political, military, and religious values and traditions. The 1990s have witnessed a return to activist and moderate politics, although right-wing and religious backlash is also at work.

In short, as the economic, industrial, and technological conditions that gave rise to ideologies in the nineteenth and twentieth centuries underwent transformation, so did the ideologies to which they had given rise. As these conditions transformed and stabilized, the ideologies in question underwent corresponding modification and modulation. By the same token, new conditions set the stage for the emergence of new and appropriate ideologies.

As with many other aspects of human life, ideologies are always in a state of flux, never remaining constant for long periods of time. Insofar as they constitute "normal" societal phenomena, ideologies will always remain with us. Understandably, "good times" tend to coincide with moderate and flexible ideologies; "bad times," with more militant and rigid ones.

Selected Bibliography

Aron, Raymond. *The Opium of the Intellectuals*. New York: Norton, 1962.

Bell, Daniel. *The End of Ideology*. New York: Free Press, 1960.

Benda, Julien. *The Betrayal of the Intellectuals*. Boston: Beacon Press, 1955.

Cox, Richard H., ed. *Ideology, Politics, and Political Theory*. Belmont, Calif.: Wadsworth, 1969.

Lipset, Seymour M. *Political Man: The Social Bases of Politics*. New York: Doubleday, 1960.

Rejai, Mostafa, ed. *Decline of Ideology*. New York: Atherton Press, 1971. (This book contains an extensive bibliography on the subject.)

Shils, Edward. "The End of Ideology?" *Encounter* 5 (November 1955): 52–58.

Waxman, Chaim I., ed. *The End of Ideology Debate*. New York: Funk & Wagnalls, 1968.

Young, James P. *The Politics of Affluence*. San Francisco: Chandler, 1968.

Index

A

Absolutism, 154, 207

Acid rain, 196

Activism, 63–64, 67

Adams, Abigail, 174

Affective dimension, ideological, 6–7

Afghanistan, 116

Africa, 41–43, 49, 50
See also specific nations

Agnew, Spiro, 53

Air pollution, 192–93

Algeria, 42, 44, 45–47, 52, 111, 147

Alienation, Marxist theory, 87–89, 97

American Revolution (1776), 15, 35, 47, 157, 169, 180

Analysis of Classes in Chinese Society (Mao), 124

Ancient Rome, 151–52

Angola, 111

Anthony, Susan B., 174

Anticolonial nationalism. *See* Eastern nationalism

Anti-imperialism, 27, 43

Anti-Semitism, 62, 64–65, 65n, 75, 76

Aquino, Benigno, 182

Aquino, Corazon, 180, 182

Argentina, 183

Aryan supremacy myth, 24, 64–65, 66, 76

Asia, 41–43
See also specific nations

Audubon, James, 188

Authoritarianism, 48, 70, 74, 166

B

Baird, Jay, 68–69, 69–70

Batista, Fulgencio, 137, 138, 139, 140, 141, 142, 143, 180

Beauvoir, Simone de, 175

Belarus, 192

Belief, as ideological element, 4, 24

Bella, Ahmed Ben, 47

Bentham, Jeremy, 157, 160

Beveridge, Albert, 38–40

Bhutto, Benazir, 180, 182

Bhutto, Zulfikar Ali, 182

Blackshirts, 59, 59n, 61, 66

Bodin, Jean, 32, 154

Bolivia, 147

Bolshevik Revolution (1917). *See* Russian Revolution

Bolsheviks, 35, 102, 104–5, 110

Borodin, Mikhail, 128

Bourgeoisie, 93, 94, 95, 98, 110

Brazil, 196

Brinkmanship policy, 53

Brown, Jerry, 163n

Brownshirts (SA storm troopers), 61, 66, 69

Brundtland, Gro Harlem, 180, 181

Brussels Treaty, 51

Burke, Edmund, 157, 167, 174

Bush, George, 5, 180, 189, 195

Butler, Samuel, 79n

C

Calvin, John, 153

Cambodia, 49, 137, 147

Campbell, Kim, 180, 181

Leninism *(continued)*
  and peasant class, 110, 124
  Russian context, 100–103
Lesbianism, 177
Liberal feminism, 175–76
Liberalism, 167–68
Liberia, 50
Liberty/equality balance, 159, 161
Libya, 50
Lincoln, Abraham, 157
Linguistic symbols, 5–6
Lin Piao, 127
L'Internationale (song), 114
Lipset, Seymour Martin, 160
Li Ta-chao, 119
Literacy, 16
Locke, John, 35, 47, 92, 154–55, 157, 174
Long Live the Victory of People's War! (Lin), 127
Louis XVI, King of France, 15, 32
Luther, Martin, 153

M

Machiavelli, Niccolò, 154
Male chauvinism, 176, 184, 207
Manifest destiny, 36–37, 55, 207, 209
Manipulation, political, 10, 11, 18
Mannheim, Karl, 17–18
Maoism, 97, 98, 101, 121–28, 141, 143, 146, 147, 148, 168, 209, 210
  global dimension of revolution, 126–28
  peasant revolutionary force, 123–24
  protracted struggle, 124–26, 144
  revolution's rural base, 122–23
Mao Tse-tung
  background/rise to power, 118–19, 120–21
  Eight Points for Attention, 125, 132
  guerrilla warfare, 125, 126, 132, 133, 134, 146
  leadership role, 70, 71, 74
  and Soviet Union, 123
  theory. *See* Maoism
  works
    Analysis of Classes in Chinese Society, 124

Mao Tse-tung *(continued)*
    Report on an Investigation of the Peasant Movement in Hunan, 124
  See also China
Marcos, Ferdinand, 182
Marie Antoinette, Queen of France, 15
Marx, Jenny, 84
Marx, Karl
  background, 82–84
  Marxist theory, 84–96, 100, 101, 104, 141, 148, 176
  scientific socialism, 78–80
  theoretical impact, 96–97, 114
  works
    Communist Manifesto, 83, 94, 98
    Economic and Philosophical Manuscripts of 1844, The, 85
    German Ideology, The, 11, 87
    Grundrisse, The, 96
Marxism, 78–98
  alienation concept, 87–89, 97
  and capitalism, 88, 92, 94, 95, 97, 98, 105, 109, 207
  Chinese context, 121–22
  classless society, 8, 95, 98, 210
  and communism, 89–90, 110
  comparative framework analysis, 97–98, 206, 207, 208, 209, 210
  and democratic socialism, 168
  distinguished from socialism/communism, 78–82
  essential concepts
    dialectical materialism, 90–96
    theory propositions, 86–90
  evolutionary/revolutionary change, 94–95
  and feminism, 176–77
  and feudalism, 93, 94, 95
  in Germany, 62, 65*n*, 95, 100, 101
  ideology concept analysis, 11–13
    private property/ownership, 12, 81, 89, 91, 93, 94–95
    substructure, 12–13, 91, 96
    superstructure, 12–13, 91, 92, 96
  labor concept, 86, 87, 92
  Leninist interpretations, 101–31, 110–11, 113–14
  and nationalism, 41

About the Author

Mostafa Rejai received his Ph.D. from the University of California at Los Angeles and is now Distinguished Professor Emeritus at Miami University, Ohio, where he has also been the recipient of an Outstanding Teaching Award. He is author, coauthor, or editor of the following books: *World Military Leaders* (forthcoming), *Demythologizing an Elite: American Presidents in Empirical, Comparative, and Historical Perspective* (1993), *Loyalists and Revolutionaries: Political Leaders Compared* (1988), *World Revolutionary Leaders* (1983), *Leaders of Revolution* (1979), *The Comparative Study of Revolutionary Strategy* (1977), *Decline of Ideology* (1971), *Mao Tse-tung on Revolution and War* (1969, 1970), and *Democracy: The Contemporary Theories* (1967). His articles have appeared in social sciences and humanities journals in the United States and Europe.